GENIUS
and
LUST

GENIUS and LUST

The Creativity and Sexuality of
Cole Porter and Noel Coward

Joseph Morella and George Mazzei

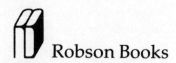
Robson Books

First published in the USA by Carroll & Graf Publishers Inc
First published in Great Britain in 1996 by Robson Books Ltd,
Bolsover House, 5-6 Clipstone Street, London W1P 8LE

British Library Cataloguing in Publication Data
A catalogue record for this title is available from the
British Library

ISBN 1 86105 014 3

Printed in Great Britain by WBC Book Manufacturers Ltd.,
Bridgend, Mid-Glamorgan

Acknowledgments

Grateful thanks to: Jim Bliss, John Madden, Austin Publicover, Jamie Specter, James Lossel, Steve Schemmel, Nancy Breyer, Ward Grant, Agnes Montaldo, Mrs. Stuart-Templeton and Donald Yonker.

Contents

Preface

Few would dispute that Cole Porter and Noel Coward were geniuses in their field. Their words, their melodies, and their timeless lyrics prove they were unique in musical theatre. In Coward's case, we can add comedy and even drama.

They were also lusty men—a strange adjective perhaps to apply to two fellows who looked so effete, who dangled cigarettes, drank cocktails instead of boilermakers, and had high-pitched voices and shrill laughs. Yet they were as lusty as John Wayne, Don Juan, Zorba the Greek, or any other macho hero, real or fictional, because they too, truly had a lust for life.

Their lusts were carnal, to be sure. They were both motivated by their sexual drives, which in turn fueled their creativity. But their lusts also included a lust for recognition. A lust for travel. A lust to experience and own the best of everything. A lust for fame. A lust for immortality. Their lives revolved around work and pleasure, success and sex.

GENIUS
and
LUST

Introduction

NOEL COWARD AND COLE PORTER were two of the most sophisticated men of the 1920s and '30s. Their creative genius was unparalleled. Their unorthodox lifestyles were envied by many. They led dazzling lives on both sides of the Atlantic—on the stages of New York and London; and in Hollywood as well as in the cafe society playgrounds of Venice and the French Riviera. They set fashion. Their faces adorned magazines. Their homes were photographed, their comings and goings reported to the entertainment world. And they did all his while hiding their homosexuality from the public.

In over a dozen books about Noel Coward and Cole Porter none deals specifically or directly with their sexual orientation. Coward wrote two and a half autobiographies in which he never mentioned it. He even forbade his official biographers from referring to it (although after his death one biographer who'd been his employee for decades admitted that Coward was homosexual). Neither did Coward's voluminous entries into his diaries mention his sexuality. Homosexuality was still a crime in England and Oscar Wilde had recently been vilified. Perhaps Coward feared that identifying himself as a homosexual would result in not being able to work or even ostracization. At the least, he may have felt that his audience would no longer take him seriously as a creative giant. Perhaps he felt no one would believe a gay man could (or should) write about male/female relationships.

How can our private lives, our choices on all levels fail to affect our creative output? Our sexual leanings pave the way for our future life experiences. If Coward were the same dowdy, rather chubby, little boy of thirteen, but heterosex-

3

ual, would he have been able to gain such easy entry to London's intellectual and artistic communities, just on the basis of a social contact? Would he have been invited into the upper class world of country estates and society, which he then observed and captured with such wit and incisiveness in his plays, stories, and even his song lyrics?

If Cole Porter were heterosexual would he have befriended the young and creative gay boys at Yale who remained his lifelong friends and encouraged his creativity? If he were straight he would not have had to overcompensate by writing his witty songs and club plays that made him the most popular Yalie of his time. He may not have needed the overkill of having to find ways to become the most all-around accepted person in an all-male school. He could have, if he were straight, assumed that he would automatically be accepted as a "regular guy—one of the boys." Since he was one of the boys all right, he could not just automatically start spouting about his sexual experiences or fantasies to a bunch of new classmates and roommates. He had something to hide, something that made him rejectable if discovered. Therefore he had to derail any possible suspicions and make a big splash in another area so the subject of his gayness would never come up. He would be "in" and no one would start looking for reasons to reject him.

The outcome was that Cole Porter became the most applauded, most sought after social personage at Yale during the time he spent there from 1908 to 1913. Even the snobbiest clubs tapped him for membership. So enormous was his prestige that he was asked back two subsequent years after graduation to continue writing his delightful musicals for his undergraduate collegians. The enormity of his impact at Yale is still extant; the songs he wrote for football games and about Eli Yale are still sung at that school's sports events.

He had a driving need to express himself through witty lyrics and tunes that verged on the risque. He already had money and social position. He'd been born a rich WASP. The strident urgency of his hidden sexual needs may have forced him to create songs that would make him accepted.

With Porter and Coward their genius and their astonishingly large creative output *must* be analyzed in relation to their sexuality and how it shaped their lives.

The greatest fear for homosexuals then as now was the thought that exposure would render them unable to earn a living and turn them into social pariahs. There was also the ongoing prejudice that if a homosexual created it, it couldn't be worth much. Even Somerset Maugham, himself a homosexual, bitterly derided the attempts of gay men to express something of value. Maugham, who wrote novels, plays and short stories, hid his sexuality and like many gay men of his class and time hated homosexuals who were openly gay.

The whole atmosphere of being gay and having to keep it well covered led to a deep inner loneliness and sadness. The driving need to overcompensate by gaiety, laughter, song, and fantasy, all in a whirl of brilliant social activity, contributed to Noel and Cole generating their large bodies of creative theatrical work.

Unlike most homosexual men of the time their money, fame, and mobility made it easier for Coward and Porter to live out their gay lifestyles covertly, but the mores of the time still made it necessary for them to maintain a facade of heterosexual correctness. As long as Coward and Porter maintained a constant outward pretense of being "for women" they could count on rave reviews and social acceptability among the show business crowd they needed for their professional continuity. Besides the immense social antagonism, homosexuality was illegal; in England, Coward's home, it was vigorously prosecuted.

Both of these creators of the lightest, happiest plays and songs to come out of English-speaking theatre lived under a daily cloud of possible blackmail, prosecution, and even financial ruin, if exposed. Yet each risked finding sexual partners to help them release their sexual and subsequently, creative energy.

Although Porter was so wealthy that stories of his lavishness are almost as abundant as his lyrics, he still needed the brittle and sophisticated world he helped create. He needed the adoration. Noel Coward needed that as well but he also needed the money from his work. If Noel's career was shattered by being exposed as a "queer," he would have no income.

Although quite alike in their artistic venues, the two men hid their sexuality very differently. Cole Porter chose "The Beard"; he married a woman for whom he had a genuine, deep affection. In those days if you were married you couldn't be queer; heterosexuals subscribed to the delusion that marriage somehow couldn't happen to a gay man. But Cole Porter, the husband, was so promiscuous with men of a certain low station that even many of his most liberal friends would have been left gaping.

Noel Coward, possibly because he was British and had the example of highly placed homosexual nobility as an example, got away with the facade of being a lifelong bachelor and womanizer. His public relationships with Gertrude Lawrence and Marlene Dietrich, among other famous and desirable women, gave him a cover for the general public. His shocking play, *Design for Living*, in which he costarred with Alfred Lunt and Lynn Fontanne, his famous married friends, perpetuated the myth of Coward as a free-living cad and bestowed at least bisexual status on him should suspicions arise.

In a sense Coward represented the British manner of ignoring the issue when one's fame made pretense mandatory. Cole Porter's choice is the quintessential American "easy out." While Noel carried on the eligible bachelor deception and Porter the happily married man deception, neither man denied his sexuality to his closest trusted friends.

Cole Porter compartmentalized sex: it was to be enjoyed on a one-time basis with anonymous men of a class lower than his own, the types referred to as "rough trade" among gay men—meaning heterosexual longshoremen, dock workers, sailors, military men, truck drivers, and laborers who let gay men service them for money.

Porter, while growing up, had a strong example of an aggressive virile man in his ultra-successful and forceful grandfather, James Omar Cole, who expended a good deal of energy on the young Cole trying to make him a newer version of himself. This early conditioning probably helped set Cole's erotic tastes later in life. Interestingly Cole Porter's wife had been married to exactly that kind of aggressive macho man in her first marriage, and had preferred Cole in the final run. In a sense if Cole could never become that kind of man, he could buy them whenever he wanted, or possess them sexually, even using the money made by his grandfather, as well as that bestowed on his wife at her divorce. Using money to dominate these men could have made Cole feel that he was getting the better of his grandfather in the end.

Noel Coward had a preference for the cleaner, handsome, urbane young man of higher station. The Arrow Shirt man was his physical ideal. He was attracted by the more accepted standard of male handsomeness. His sexual tastes were in keeping with the pastel world he lived in. His sexual partners would never clash with the decor in his carefully crafted and lovely world.

The fact that Noel sought romantic sexual liaisons with those of his own station—men of the upper classes—indicated that he personally did not look down on his own sexual bent, but enjoyed it as a romantic concept that was consistent with the rest of his life. Both of these sexual attitudes show themselves subtly and specifically in the lyrics of each man. Cole Porter was famous for torch songs about affairs that were lent a special magic because of their elusiveness, the lover who was always just out of reach.

Many of his songs are about nocturnal meetings, wrapped in the anonymity of night, backed by primal drumbeats.

> When dawn comes to waken me,
> you're never there at all,
> I know you've forsaken me,
> until the shadows fall.
> Then all through the night,
> I am lost in your love . . .

This lyric speaks of inhabiting two worlds—perhaps marriage by daylight and a lover by night.

Coward, on the other hand, wrote songs about public fantasies, such as "Mad About the Boy," a love paean to a movie screen idol. He describes in the song "tracing your nose and forehead," showing that he preferred the more refined, polished look, fully lighted for maximum glamour and beauty. No unwashed mysteries lurked in the night for him. His beauties were to be drunk in, a feast for the eyes, placed in an elegant high-level setting. His songs always refer to his "foolish heart," being unable to resist the classical physical charms of a handsome young male. He often wrote from a woman's point of view.

Noel wanted love; Cole wanted sex. Porter used his songs to interweave wicked, daring little digs about his gay deceptions; Coward coated his *double entendres* in sugary layers of social outrageousness. His lyrics broadly spoofed British society and his innuendoes about sexual preferences were slipped in.

"Maurice made a couple of passes—at Gus."

Homosexuality does not make people creative, any more than neuroses make people great writers or being Jewish makes people great musicians. However, there is a large percentage of Jews, neurotics, and homosexuals among the successful creative segment of our population. Why?

Perhaps an individual who was already considered different might go with the sterotype and allow himself the satisfaction of expressing creativity without worrying about social repercussions. Heterosexual men in our culture are expected to focus on noncreative areas or be labeled sissies, the worst epithet for a young male. Since gay boys already are sissies they have nothing to lose by pursuing these interests.

Perhaps seeing yourself as different means that your only chance of gaining approval from society is to excel in an area not easily succeeded in by the run-of-the-mill crowd.

The point of this book is not to analyze why Cole Porter and Noel Coward (or anyone) was homosexual. We leave that to the multitude of geneticists, psychologists, social scientists, and rigid moralists who come up with new theories periodically. We wish only to examine the correlation between the fact of their homosexuality and the fact of their creative genius, and how the social stigma of needing to hide the former led an overriding passion to achieve legendary status through such light entertaining works. The question will always remain. If they didn't have to hide it, would they have been the geniuses they were?

Until now very little has been written about the link between sexuality and creativity. A few light works have noted the connection between creativity and madness, creativity and depression, creativity and alcoholism. Many if not all homosexuals suffer from some degree of depression, if for no other reason than societal pressure to renounce their sexual preference or at least deny it or hide it. And this depression often leads people to the use of alcohol and other drugs to elevate the psychic pain.

Creative people, whether straight or gay, often use alcohol and drugs to escape boredom, depression, or creative angst and to release inhibitions in an attempt to tap the creative muses. In addition, in the early years of this century alcohol was a fixture among certain classes—certainty the classes to which Noel aspired. In fact alcohol was an essential feature of this lifestyle, as were cigarettes.

As both Coward and Porter were prone to depression and excessive use of alcohol and occasional, though deep depression in the case of Noel Coward and more severe depressions in the case of Cole Porter, we have many avenues in which to explore their creativity. We've chosen, however, to concentrate on their sexuality.

Cognitive psychologist and author Howard Gardener has explored the anatomy of genius. In his work *Creating Minds* he synthesizes creativity into four categories:

Bourgeois roots: The person is brought up in a typically middle-class surrounding and is imbued with the values of hard work and achievement.

Marginality: The person typically grows up in a place removed from scientific or cultural centers and has to struggle to stay at the margins of creativity by disdaining peer pressure or mainstream thought.

Social distancing: The person is absorbed in his work and chooses "the perfection of art over the perfection of life." This results in relationships being a secondary factor in his life. Creative people are often aloof, even cruel, and usually have strained personal relationships.

Childlike vision: Creative people draw inspiration from their childlike perception of the field in which they're involved. They retain a sort of innocence.

Gardener also feels that most typical "creators" have two bursts of creativity about ten years apart and he calls this the *10-year rule.* For scientific people, this usually means the first burst is a breakthrough, and the second a comprehensive synthesis.

Noel and Cole fit almost too neatly into Gardener's categories. Both certainly had bourgeois roots, and hard work and achievement were bred into each of them. Although Cole had been born a rich WASP, his valves were mid-American.

Both were on the margin, culturally speaking: Cole, geographically, in Indiana; Noel, socially and financially in London. Both certainly disdained and resisted any kind of peer pressure to conform. Both became absorbed in their work and kept their relationships secondary. And their friends and relatives allowed them to retain their childlike attitudes toward their writing all their lives.

Cole and Noel never really stopped writing, but Cole's successful spurts of creativity were about ten years apart, in college, 1913–15; during 1927–34; and again in 1948–55. He considered his best works to be *Anything Goes* (1934), and *Kiss Me, Kate,* (1948).

Noel's creativity came in shorter bursts, with critical success ebbing and flowing. His peak periods of real creativity were 1926–34 as a playwright and his renaissance was 1955–66 as a performer and celebrity.

M. A. Bronski in his 1984 book *Culture Clash: The Making of the Gay Sensibility,* outlines five attributes that characterize gay sensibility: camp, wit, beauty, male friendships, and dispossession (both psychic and physical).

Once again our subjects fit into these categories. Cole melded his campiness into the 1920s Parisian Cafe Society, Noel into the theatrical postwar London. Both were witty in their work as well as in their private lives. Though neither was handsome both praised and admired beauty and surrounded themselves with beautiful objects and occasionally beautiful people. Male friendships were extremely important to Cole, who had close friendships with gay men, straight men, and men who were presumed to be straight. Noel too had male friendships with lovers and servants, with producers, directors, and actors, with famous men both gay and straight.

These two were less dispossessed than most gay men, Cole, because of his wealth and marriage, Noel because of his early success. But like all gay men certain doors were still closed to them. They could not, for instance, publicly share the really important moments of their lives with their lovers (Noel took two women friends to his knighthood ceremonies); they could not express their truest feelings directly in song or story, or even private diaries or letters without fear or exposure and censure.

But being gay does have some advantages. For example, in the days of Cole Porter and Noel Coward, being homosexual meant belonging to a special private underground club, a secret fraternity. But the members of this fraternity were not restricted to one social level, such as the country club set, or one educational affiliation, such as the Harvard Club, nor to any other group. The secret club (fraternity is a misused word here since women were also included) was the gay community, and like the community of man itself, all people from all walks of life were included, rich or poor, regardless of ethnicity, race, religion, or sex. All you had to be was gay and you could enter on immediate intimate terms with everyone from royalty to the underclass often at the same place and at the same time.

Belonging to this fraternity greatly furthered both the careers and personal lives of Coward and Porter. Creative people who were also gay were exposed to many more people in power at an early stage, many more ideas and experiences, and had intimate interaction with these people more easily available than heterosexuals did.

Coward and Porter also were able to meet other classes of people, such as coal miners and common laborers, not as observers but as friends and often as lovers; this was not a situation available to heterosexual composers such as Oscar Hammerstein or Irving Berlin, or playwrights like Maxwell Anderson or Philip Barry. Coward and Porter had a common point of sudden intimacy and personal interaction with people of all social orders. Their life experience was broadened beyond the norm for creative people who were in positions of success and fame. Whereas heterosexual artists were either limited in scope by being confined to a marriage or family, Coward and Porter could continue to interact within this wide spectrum of people even while world famous. Thus Noel and Cole could write fine lyrics about high society types or street prostitutes or about common laborers based on personal experience.

In addition, both men saw love/sex as temporary. Compare the lyrics of Porter and Coward to their contemporaries.

A love song by Hammerstein: "Somehow you know, you know even then, that somewhere you'll see her again and again."

By Berlin: "I'll be loving you always, with a love that's true always."

By Porter: "It was just one of those things, just one of those crazy flings."

By Coward: "Though my world has gone awry, though the end is drawing nigh, I shall love you till I die, goodbye!"

Compare the battle between the sexes: Hammerstein ("Don't throw bouquets at me."—"If I loved you") and Berlin ("Anything you can do I can do better") stressed emotion; Porter ("Than ever marry one of them I'd rest a virgin rather) and Coward ("Six little foolish virgins, eager to be some good man's wife") stressed sex.

THERE IS A DEARTH of scientific research on the links between homosexuality and creativity. This can be explained by three factors: (1) There is a professional resistance to the study of homosexuality as a legitimate topic of anthropological research; (2) homophobia still exists and there is a cultural and social politics prejudicing the funding of such research; (3) there is still a great deal of secrecy among gay people reluctant to reveal themselves for fear of rejection and stigmatization.

As early as 1962, key American psychological journals argued that because the homosexual stands outside the mainstream he sees humanity differently and originally and hence stands closer to the wellsprings from which true creativity flows.

In 1964 a study by the Royal Air Force concluded derisively, "Most of the homosexuals were artists, extremely fond of their female parent and nonaggressive."

Noel and Cole stood outside the mainstream, were original thinkers, artists, and extremely fond of their mothers. They knew they were different at an early age and they weren't limited by notions of what men were supposed to be interested in. Both had been raised by their mothers to take up music and theater as a serious career choice.

Mothers and show business often go hand in hand it seems. Creativity needs nurturing that begins in childhood and is sustained throughout the artist's life. From the cradle both Noel and Cole had enormous support from their mothers. They were provided with an unusually wide latitude to develop their artistic and musical talents by mothers who fought and sacrificed for them.

This nurturing from their mothers was maintained for decades, well into each man's life. Having had this nurturing literally from infancy, both men were unable in later life to function on their own without some strong support.

The similarities in the childhoods of Noel and Cole are striking. Both Violet Coward and Kate Porter had been advised by fortune tellers that their sons (then still children) would grow up to be famous entertainers. Each woman was told she should work hard to keep her son on that track. Noel and Cole followed almost identical patterns in their relationships with their parents. Their fathers were vague, shadowy, rather unsuccessful men; Noel's was fascinated with popular music, whereas Cole's sought solace in poetry, although neither made active attempts to extend his knowledge to his son.

Each boy had a strong musical background emanating from his family, and particularly encouraged by his mother. Both women made pointed and continuing efforts to make sure their darling sons would some day establish musical careers. Both women focused on the lighter and lyrical aspects of songs to induce their sons' interests. Kate Porter satirized the words of the songs she sang to keep young Cole laughing so his short attention span would not wander from his lesson. This early example took hold; throughout his career witty satirical lyrics characterized his work.

Noel needed no such tricks; the attention and applause he received from singing—to anyone who would listen— was inducement enough. Noel had a deep craving for applause and attention, whether he was on a stage, in a parlor, at a party, or in church.

During their developmental years both boys loved the kind of pulp fiction that most boys have to hide. Cole liked smutty stories, but Noel, always the elegant romantic, liked the less lurid tales of "super" boys, who had heroic fictional adventures. These fascinations set the patterns for their later homosexual tastes, as well as some of their work. The rugged, muscular boys in the stories were the type Cole fancied; Noel preferred the clever ones.

Young Noel and young Cole also were spoiled, willful brats, who did exactly what they wanted when they wanted. Whatever they could get away with, they did. This trait followed them into later life, and many stories abound in their biographies and elsewhere of their selfishness and overbearing behavior that often overstepped into rudeness. The famed drama critic, Alexander Woolcott, complained that Coward "talked me to death." Elsa Maxwell hated Porter on sight at their initial meeting, although she revised her opinion of him and became one of his closest friends.

Both boys spent a good part of their childhoods entertaining in local situations (pushed by their mothers); and both gained extremely early semiprofessional acclaim in their teens and professional acceptance in their early twenties.

From the time they were children, living away from home, both Noel and Cole kept a strict and willing correspondence with their mothers, detailing all their minute activities, sharing every nuance and experience, and both kept this habit until their mothers died at very advanced ages. Both mothers became the keeper of her son's flame, saving every scrap and letter and clipping for future historians.

"Two Little Babes in the Wood"

COLE PORTER WAS BORN JUNE 9, 1891, eight years before Noel Coward, in Peru, Indiana, to Kate and Samuel Fenwick Porter. He was also born the grandson of J. O. Cole, who exerted much more of an influence on Cole's life than did his recessive father. Cole was the third child of this triangular parentage, the first two having died in infancy. As the first surviving male child his emotional worth was increased beyond the norm to his mother and grandfather.

The little boy, who was the spitting image of his mother, grew up with the assurance of lifelong wealth. His grandfather had inherited a fortune, then made another of his own. J. O. had gone west during the Gold Rush, but instead of breaking his back panning the riverbeds for nuggets, he went for the real money. When most people think of the millionaires from the middle of that century they remember Levi Strauss, who made the jeans that covered the haunches of the gold diggers. J. O. Cole also made his money selling provisions to the miners, and was one of the few forty-niners who died rich.

When J. O. returned home to Indiana he made even more money in farming and real estate, and through a brewery, and an ice plant. His many millions of dollars came from holdings in five states. This was long before income taxes and unions, and long before the idea that amassing enormous wealth was somehow indecent.

It was into this wealth and attitude about amassing wealth that Cole Porter was born. The only son and the favored grandson, he was expected to take over and increase the family fortune. At least that's what his grandfather expected; his mother had other ideas.

Kate was fully dependent on her father for her money.

J. O. was generous, but gave money to Kate only as she needed and requested it. He did not settle an income on her that would have made her independent.

J. O. Cole was not only rich and self-made, he also cast a long shadow. He had standards about what kind of man his daughter should marry—standards based on his own personality and achievements. Sam Porter was a druggist who was not in any way the larger-than-life overachiever his father-in-law was. At first he tried to be, with several entrepreneurial schemes that failed. It became easier for him to fade into the background.

Kate may have married Sam precisely because he was not like her father. She was strong-willed herself, and spent her life both loving and opposing her father. Much as Kate loved her father, she probably wanted some peace from his constant noise and demands and goading. A man like Sam Porter was a relief to a woman who'd coped with the loud, aggressive force of a man like J. O. Later in life, when her son married, it would be to a woman just like his mother, a woman who had plenty of money from another overaggressive manly type, but who wanted to enjoy life with a man who didn't ride roughshod over everything and everyone in his path.

Sam Porter may have been a fadeaway father to Cole, but he nonetheless exercised a subconscious effect on his son's career. Sam was deeply interested in poetry, and secretly wrote it himself. Although Sam never read poetry more than once or twice to Cole to try to establish a rapport with his son, Cole retained a positive attitude toward words and the versification of them.

Even if Kate had not spent most of his childhood spoon-feeding him on music and spoiling him rotten, Cole never could have become the rough-and-tumble supermale his grandfather was. Cole was in the first place a small fellow, almost a leprechaun in appearance. His frame was small boned and his appearance was more of a charming little elf than an imposing man, even when he was an adult. His appearance was part of what made him so appealing to almost everyone who knew him.

He was engaging, even as a child, with bright eyes, small features, and a droll, happy attitude. He was given everything he wanted, and maybe a lot of things he never thought of wanting.

Kate Porter was possibly the perfect mother from start to finish. She was a woman of unusual sensitivity and self-esteem. The particular kinds of sacrifice she made required a strength of character and unselfishness unusual in a rich girl and seldom found in stage mothers. She devoted all of her energies to making sure little Cole was given the musical background, the emotional protection and support he needed to establish his personality as a future songwriter.

Kate handled her father's demanding raids into her territory, refusing to allow him to gain influence over little Cole. It was a continuing battle, but she had decided that her son was going to have a musical career, which to her father meant she was training her son to become a professional sissy. She did not care. Kate was determined to push her son into the musical arena as early as possible. When he was five she began teaching him piano herself. She had wanted to be a professional musician and had decided that Cole would fulfill her own personal dream. He now had two strong people in the family determined for him to live the life they chose for him. His mother won out over his grandfather, which was a strong factor in Cole's life; he would always identify more strongly with the female role model and have little respect for the males in his life.

In addition to financial security there were two anchors in Cole's early life: his mother and music. At seven years of age he began professional music lessons and added violin to his piano skills. He traveled thirty miles each week to Marion, Indiana, for these lessons. When he was eight he gave his first recital on both instruments. More important than anything were the two hours a day of practice that Kate personally conducted with her son. Because his natural restlessness made concentration tiring for him, Kate would revive his interest by playing songs satirically, exaggerating the words and sounds to regain his attention. This ploy of

Kate's instilled in Cole the idea that his songs were primarily to amuse and delight. Even the more serious examples of his work contain elements of wit, and are designed to be appreciated by universal audiences.

When Cole was ten he composed "The Song of the Birds," and at eleven wrote a composition called "The Bobolink Waltz." Kate spent $100 to have it published, an act designed to instill in Cole the joy of seeing his work in print. This basic conditioning of rewarding his effort with solid visible validity must have gone far in making Cole want to write more. Unlike his father, Cole always had printed proof that he was a songwriter. This was further reinforced by the newspaper's favorable reviews of his recitals, also generated by Kate. The power of the press lies in the fact that a work is printed, not handwritten, not spoken about and forgotten after the congratulations. It is proof of one's talent that someone somewhere thought it worthy of printing.

Many biographers have used this publication as an example of Kate's pride in her son, perhaps unwarranted since Cole's early work isn't all that wonderful. Kate realized how important it was to show her son the thrill of achievement, especially because she knew how easily he would lose interest if he didn't have a strong reason to keep at his work. She saw clearly how unusually low his threshold for boredom was (a lifelong trait that caused him to walk away from people in the middle of a conversation, or leave a party without a word just because he was bored). Kate locked him into an interest in music by showing him the rewards he could reap if he stayed with it. Cole, after all, loved attention and approval, and because of his grandfather's constant bellowing about him being a sissy, he needed to have his good qualities pointed up even more strongly. Without his mother's early wisdom in building a strong self-image in him—and even she didn't succeed completely—he might have ended up as a wasted drunk or retreated into oblivion like his father.

His mother became his role model, not his father; he was

ashamed of his father, disliked him actively, and tried to be unlike him. In later years he even denied his father was a druggist, rewriting that part of his life.

Cole was conditioned to see the life of husband and father as dull and uninteresting. He saw his mother's life, however, as filled with color and song, fun and laughter. More significantly Cole couldn't help but notice that as a woman of that time Kate did not work, as her husband did (and at a dull job) but got money by asking for it. All in all the life of a woman was presented to him as much more attractive and interesting than a man's.

At that early age Cole was steeped in the conviction that he could play and sing and indulge his every whim without having to justify it. Kate also taught him to make up stories about himself. She used to take two years off his age so he would seem to be even more of a child prodigy than he was. This habit was retained by Cole all his life, and he began exaggerating and making up fanciful stories about himself at an early age, glorifying himself as he went along. Much of this would have to do with his intense fear of becoming bored; much had to do with the theatrical personality— what great star hasn't rewritten his or her history?

And much of that has to do with being different; creating stories that exaggerate one's outrageous or unusual experiences to overcompensate for not being one of the crowd.

As a mother Kate's ultimate unselfishness came when Cole was fourteen years of age. He was ready for high school and J. O. was snorting and pawing at the ground demanding he be sent to a military academy to make a man out of him. Kate refused. J. O. told her Cole would attend a business school or no school at all, and if no school was Kate's choice J. O. planned to put Cole to work learning the family business. Kate, knowing what would happen if Cole grew up at home, decided to send him east to a fine prep school, Worcester Academy, in Massachusetts. This removed Cole from what was turning into the emasculating attitude of his powerful grandfather, and placed him into a protected, genteel environment where he could learn more about the arts and obtain a liberal education. Kate probably also sent Cole away because of his relationship with his father. As the boy was entering puberty the resentment of Sam and the mutual dislike between them could have developed into conflicts that would have set the whole family against each other as Cole grew up. Sending him away was best for everyone all around.

It must have been a wrenching experience for Kate to implement this decision, in effect sending away the focal point of her life. In removing Cole from her father, she was also giving him up herself. Because her decision caused a deep rift between Kate and her father they stopped speaking for two years, so she did not even have the drama of fighting with J. O. She cut herself off from the most stimulating people in her life to spend all her time in her big house with her husband. She gave up everything that was meaningful to her so her son's future career would be assured. His future successes would be shared with her secondhand and could never again be enjoyed except as an honored spectator.

NOEL COWARD WAS A PRECOCIOUS CHILD. If Cole Porter's mother developed her son's talents through intense effort in leading him, Noel's mother followed her little boy's lead. Noel seemed to know what he wanted as soon as his baby eyes saw the world. He had been born December 16, 1899, near enough to Christmas to obtain his unusual name. Like Cole he was welcomed after his parents had lost a child. According to legend he kicked and screamed to be allowed to entertain. His mother said that when company came to call she would leave baby Noel in his nursery until—and only if—a guest would ask to see him. If they didn't she had to face Noel's explosions after they'd gone. Once in church when he wasn't allowed to get out in the aisle and dance, he threw himself onto the floor in a full-blown tantrum. He was a natural entertainer. He needed no special coaxing from Violet to fulfill her fantasy of him being a specially talented little boy. He performed because he loved performing almost as much as he loved the attention and applause. He said later in life that he quickly lost enthusiasm for singing in church because of the lack of applause. He also said later in life that he was his own creation.

In the 1920s the press called Noel Destiny's Tot, and surely he was. Whereas Cole Porter's mother had to coax and stretch to find ways to keep her little boy interested in the piano, Violet Coward had to hurry to keep up with little Noel. The Cowards were a musical family, whereas Cole's mother had to fight her father's objections to leading Cole toward a musical career. Noel had a sense of one-minded purpose as well, something that Cole had to learn before he could begin his beguine.

Noel showed acting and performing talent early; more importantly he had drive and ambition, unusual in a boy of ten. It was as if an adult inside waited impatiently for the outer boy to grow up and shed his skin so he could get on with his greatness. Noel was a professional actor by age ten. He never was without the inner goading desire to *get there.* The tantrums of his youth now manifested themselves in his highly nervous personality. Part of his general nervousness was that he wanted to be a full-blown star right away and was achingly impatient to achieve this goal.

Violet Coward was both proud of Noel and dazzled by him. Unlike Kate Porter at the beginning she questioned whether her motherly pride made her believe her son was more talented than he was. He was just a small boy who was making adult decisions. What if he were wrong and this was the wrong course for him? Noel was even neglecting his education. Violet sensibly asked herself at an early date while there was still time for her son to follow a more normal route, if he really did have talent or if she was just wishing he had, and perhaps helping Noel to ruin his life. Then she received a mystical sign from stage psychic Anna Eva Fay.

It may seem strange that a mother would base her son's future on the word of a psychic, but in England in those days psychics were considered to be reliable channels from heaven.

Psychics would appear in theatres and members of the audience would submit questions. When the famous psychic picked Violet's question out of the hundreds and loudly and emphatically proclaimed her judgment, the whole matter was settled in Violet's mind. She rushed home to tell the family that Miss Fay has spoken: Her son had a great talent and would have a wonderful career. From that point on Violet Coward was devoted to the goal of fulfilling her son's wish to be in the theatre. This determination took some odd turns, and many times it seemed that there was indeed a mystical guiding force protecting Noel from anything that might have stood in his way.

Violet had already answered an ad for a play called *The Goldfish*, which needed children to play roles. It was Noel's first professional exposure, at ten years of age, and he played Prince Mussel. It was a great success for him, he recounts, and his song was encored, "sometimes twice." Unfortunately the producer, Lila Field, was less than forthcoming with the money and he received only one week's pay for the several weeks he played the part. But it led to a one-liner in Charles Hawtry's company in *The Great Name*, which led then to nearly ten years of apprenticeship in the excellent company.

Charles Hawtry was England's leading comic actor; Noel attached himself to him like an adoring fan. Noel was a high-strung chattery boy. Once Noel was babbling so much backstage—and he was always within arm's length of Hawtry—that the star missed an entrance. Such a mistake must have rankled a professional like Hawtry, but instead of packing Noel off to tour with the gypsies, he swallowed his ire and used it as a point of instruction. Luckily for Noel Hawtry recognized real talent and was willing to nurture it.

By the time Noel was twelve Violet was accommodating his career in every way. She allowed Noel to take two days off from school a week to look for acting jobs. Her family objected strenuously, but she held to her decision nonetheless.

It is not clear whether Violet would have remained so

adamant in her decision if she knew little Noel was going with his new friends to steal candy, cigarettes, and sundries from stores while he was supposed to be looking for work. But the Cowards needed the extra money Noel could earn. His father, Arthur Coward, could not be relied on to provide a dependable income. Arthur had been a traveling salesman for Payne's Pianos. His disappointment at being unable to function at a job made the sweetness of life at home, singing around the piano in the warm glow of his brothers and sisters and being applauded for his sweet singing voice, a haven. He seems to have been crushed by the cruelties of life and when finally the sales job dried up completely he spent most of his time with his younger son, Erik, sailing model sailboats on a nearby pond.

Although Violet had more determination, in those days there wasn't much a woman could do to earn a living. She rented a large building at 111 Ebury Street and opened a boardinghouse. This solved several problems—such as where the family was to live and how they were to eat. Noel had a tiny room at the top that he occupied when not on the road. His mother did the lion's share of the work, pretending it was fun, and her husband, younger son, Erik, and unmarried sister, Vida, also pitched in. But it was really hard menial work, cooking and cleaning and laundering, and even with the hard work there were many times when they weren't sure how they would pay the rent.

Through all this travail Violet Coward was sustained by the prophecy, and was determined to make sure Noel had whatever opportunity he needed to fulfill it.

III

"Different from the Others"

DIFFERENT FROM THE OTHERS was the title of the earliest (silent) film about homosexuality. The German film made a star of Conrad Veidt. Being different from the others in 1920 meant being blackmailed and eventually committing suicide. Noel and Cole were different from the others but were intelligent, loved and accepted, and in no danger of suicide. Being different actually had its advantages. You could allow yourself to be more creative. The risk of appearing odd dried up if you were already considered odd anyway.

People who are different because they're gay, taller, shorter, fatter, have a facial birthmark, or whatever usually leave their home, and painful memories of taunting, to move to a more tolerant location. Usually this means the impersonality of a larger city where the general public is less focused on individuals, and there are other people with similar differences. The new locale positions the person to be exposed to more cultural and creative experiences, and better able to exercise the ability to move ahead into more successful modes. Whether or not the person partakes of the new opportunities is another matter, but the cultural effect is enhanced due to the new locale.

Cole Porter was "different" in Peru. His grandfather, and to an extent his father, formed the rejecting group, but he soon left for more accepting climes.

AT WORCESTER ACADEMY, Cole discovered Dr. Daniel Webster Abercrombie and the study of Greek culture. At the turn of the century it was attractive for a boy, especially one with homosexual tendencies, to study the Greek myths and the Greek ideal, which glorified the nude male form over the female and idealized the intimate relationship between males as more desirable than marriage. Also, the only way to look at pictures of idealized nude athletes at that time was Greek statues. The glamour of classical Greek civilization, with Socrates touting the male form and Plato affirming male/male relationships, and its homosexual heroes (Achilles and Alexander as well as its chief god Zeus) has an immediate attraction for developing gay males. In Cole's time, however, Greek classical studies were the basis for a liberal education, and it wasn't necessary to be gay to idealize it.

Daniel Webster Abercrombie, who was heterosexual, was a snob, a model of a gentleman, and an idealist whose aim was to inspire his charges with an appreciation of beauty and the ancient Greek ideal of perfect form as the highest achievement of the human spirit. Cole idolized him. Here at last was a man who could be emulated. Abercrombie combined masculinity and a sensitivity to literature, with art and elegance. He was a compelling teacher and his presentation of Greek myths and poetry and art, plus the Greek ideal of humanism, enchanted Cole.

After his grandfather's aggressive insistence on Cole giving up his sissy pursuits and his father's reticence interspersed with denigration, it must have been refreshing to find an outgoing, energetic male in a position of authority and respect whose main goal was to inspire boys to grow into sensitive men with an appreciation of beauty and manners. Because of Abercrombie, Cole applied himself diligently to his studies—the only time he ever did—and was an excellent student.

Cole's gym teacher, Donald Baxter MacMillan, also made a special effort to interest Cole in activities that would take him out of doors and away from his piano for brief periods. Cole made an effort to respond, but with minimal results. He went to summer camp under MacMillan's aegis, probably because he wanted to cooperate, possibly because every kid harbors some desire to take part in sports activities, and almost assuredly because the physical presence of the athletic teacher would have appealed to Cole. MacMillan reported that the results were basically disappointing as Cole had no real interest once the exposure to athletics was made and he would retreat indoors to the nearest piano. Because of his diminutive size and sophisticated temperament Cole wasn't gong to find much satisfaction or success in sports activities and he returned to an area where he was more assured of finding acclaim.

Once Cole left Peru, Indiana, for Worcester Academy, his days of living at home came to an end. He returned briefly for a summer vacation but his time with Kate was limited to short visits. He was voted valedictorian of his graduating class, and because of his one-time devotion to scholarship was able to attend Yale, where he abandoned forever serious studying. Studies no longer mattered, because the life Cole was to lead, and the career he was to succeed in, required exactly the foundation that Abercrombie laid down for him.

Cole's graduation present for being voted valedictorian was a summer trip to Paris, which established his lifelong love affair with France.

In the fall of 1909 he entered Yale as a freshman. In the next four years he gave up any efforts to become a scholar, but because of his wit, his piano, and his ability to write clever college reviews and pep songs, he gained a large and loyal coterie of friends and admirers. During these years he wrote ("Bingo Eli Yale," "I Want to Be a Prom Girl," "I Want to Be a Yale Boy"). His appeal to a wide cross section of classmates and upperclassmen made him popular with athletes, party-oriented college boys, and scholars alike. It was here that he made friends with Monty Woolley and Cleveland department store heir Leonard Hanna, both gay. Monty, in particular, became his bosom buddy, possibly because they shared similar family backgrounds.

Monty later said, "It would be an understatement to say that other Yalesmen distrusted us." Monty also recalled, "I introduced Cole to the theatre. From his very first days at Yale we developed a friendship and my instincts told me, here is a future genius who only needs the proper direction to sharpen his already budding talent. We often stayed at my father's hotel, the Marie Antoinette, on Broadway.''

One of their classmates was John (Jack) Bouvier—later known as "Black Jack." Many contend that Bouvier and Cole were sex mates. Although Bouvier married and fathered two daughters, the elder being Jacqueline Bouvier Kennedy Onassis, the future First Lady, there is ample evidence that he was bisexual. Some say he frequented gay bars (how was he to know his daughter would occupy the White House?); others note he had trouble keeping his fly buttoned (this was in the days before the zipper fly came into vogue). Almost all agree he was promiscuous. To his credit Bouvier never denied his college friendship with Cole.

But Cole also had many straight friends at Yale. It is even likely that Cole did not view himself as a homosexual at that time. He certainly dated girls and played at romance at least once with a girl from another college who was interested in him. Such an admission to himself, even if he were having postadolescent sex (not unusual in an all-boys school), would be too heavy for a boy that age to handle. The constant pressure to be a man would have made him sensitive to the fact that he wasn't overly masculine.

His adulation of big muscular men was not even considered a "queer" thing at that time. Male physical strength was an ideal in those days and Sandow the strong man, who posed nude, was as acceptable an icon then as Marilyn Monroe became during the 1950s. It wasn't considered odd to idealize the male body back then; it was considered obscene to display women's nudity, but male bodies and musculature were acceptable as signs of healthful achievement or athletic prowess. So it was not considered wrong for Cole to adulate football heroes; it was considered appropriate. It wasn't until Hollywood began to exploit feminine sexuality that women replaced men on the glamour pedestal. Even early Douglas Fairbanks (Senior) silent movies showed him totally nude (*The Half-Breed*) from behind; and the famous nude photo of Ramon Navarro as Ben-Hur caused a sensation and made him a matinee idol. In that film too the use of a naked slave chained to a wall was used as a background decoration. So Cole's adulation of athletes was normal behavior at that time.

Grandfather Cole spent a great amount of time, money, and energy trying to make little Cole grow up to be like him. Instead the youngster developed a different response. The men that he sought sexually in his adult life were exactly the kind of big, muscular, rough-cut types that J. O. wanted him to be. Subconsciously Cole, who had no desire to be like these men, still saw them as an ideal to be possessed. He paid them to be with him, but didn't want to have relationships with them. In a sense his grandfather's conditioning did bear fruit, but not the kind he could have hoped for.

To keep his grandfather's money coming after he finished at Yale, Cole was forced to enroll in Harvard Law School, instead of embarking on his career on the wicked stage. J. O. did not consider music a real career and insisted that Cole either come home and join the family business or attend law school. Cole chose the lesser of two evils. How he managed to be accepted into any law school at all, much less Harvard, is a mystery since he was not a student of worth. Perhaps in 1913 there was less law to read and law was more of a gentleman's profession. In any event, Cole soon switched over to the Graduate School of Arts and Sciences, to pursue his interest in music. Neither he nor Kate told J. O. about the switch.

Even at this early stage Cole admitted that only two things kept him from falling prey to that most fearsome of conditions—what he called the "old ennui." They were songwriting and sex. He did a lot of both, and his proficiency with songs was only matched by his profligate self-indulgence in casual sexual encounters.

Cole continued over the next few years to return to Yale to write the college smokers and reviews that had made his reputation. This odd hanging on to his undergraduate activities after moving on to Harvard had a real purpose. Despite the roaring appreciation of the college audiences, his work was still second rate, not professional. But he was making necessary contacts in New York. He and his pal, Monty Woolley, who had had early experience in the New York social underground, would stay for free in suites at Woolley's family hotel. Cole could use his allowance from J. O. for more important things. He indulged his passions for champagne, clothes, jewelry, and lurid books.

The magical influence of Manhattan worked its spell on the youthful hopeful from the "boonies." Cole soon had a burning desire to see his work produced on Broadway.

Among the gay people of influence he met during this period were Elizabeth "Bessie" Marbury and her lovers, Elsie deWolfe and Anne Morgan. (Elsie deWolfe is considered one of the most influential women of the twentieth century.) Although Marbury had first been lovers with Elsie, she added the younger woman, the daughter of millionaire J. P. Morgan, to the ménage. It was said by wags, including Cole, who wrote one of his "private parties only" lyrics, that Bessie was using Anne Morgan's organ.

Elsie was an actress, and later an interior decorator. Bessie Marbury was a very successful theatrical agent and producer. After Anne teamed up with Bessie, and Elsie accepted this, the three became friends and together helped launch the Colony Club, the first private women's club in New York. Along with another wealthy socialite, Mrs. W. K. Vanderbilt, the three women undertook a tremendous project. They bought and demolished two tenement areas along Manhattan's East River and rebuilt them to create the fashionable Sutton Place and Beekman Place. Earlier they'd gone to France, where they refurbished an old villa in Versailles. The Villa Trianon, their salon, was world famous in the international social and artistic set.

He was embraced by these women, who became champions of his talents. Cole seemed to have a special affinity for lesbian women, which is unusual among gay men. He was, in fact, quite at ease with women who were different from the norm. Women with quirks, or special talents, held

a strong attraction for him. It's safe to say that Cole's association with them would not have come about had he been
a heterosexual from Peru, Indiana, because he would not
have had entry into their world. His family had some
money, but by Yale standards he was not in the upper eche-
lons of finance. And he was not in their social set. But he
was soon adopted by Bessie and her gay friends, as one of
their own, as "family."

Elizabeth Marbury was a dynamic woman, both socially
and professionally. Cole was at Harvard, collaborating with
pal T. Lawrence Riggs on a musical, *See America First.*
Meanwhile, Bessie used one of Cole's songs in a Sigmund
Romberg revue she was producing, and another of his songs
in a Jerome Kern musical. (It was standard practice then to
interpolate songs from other composers into musicals.)

Bessie had her sights on a pretty, young debutante, Dorothy Bigelow, who yearned to sing on Broadway. Bessie liked
to cultivate people with influence, lots of money, and powerful connections. Miss Bigelow had those qualities in direct
opposition to her musical and dramatic abilities. As a producer Bessie was riding high. The Kern/Bolton show *Very
Good, Eddie* was a hit. So was *Oh Boy,* starring William
Randolph Hearst's mistress, Marion Davies.

Marbury knew she couldn't risk putting Bigelow into a
Kern show. She also knew Dorothy had no serious long-
range aspirations as an actress. Still she needed a vehicle
for her. Why not give Cole his first stab at Broadway?

See America First would have been a bomb even if the
weak-voiced Miss Bigelow (Cole said her voice didn't reach
the third row) weren't the star. Reviewers suggested that
people *See America First* last. After the show flopped, Riggs
entered the priesthood, Cole went off to lick his wounds,
Clifton Webb, the show's other star, went on to much better
things, and Bessie Marbury went into politics, eventually
becoming a power in the Democratic Party and a friend of
Eleanor Roosevelt.

The failure of *See America First* devastated Cole. Up
until this point he'd never suffered artistic rejection. Back

in Indiana his acceptance had been assured because his mother bought it for him. Who wouldn't rave over the small scion of the state's prominent family? At Yale he'd been the only game in town. His clever verses, not really all that sophisticated, but quite a bit more talented than the usual college try, had strong appeal to his captive audiences. But to the hard bitten audiences of Broadway Cole was just another rich kid dabbling in theatre until he came to his senses and returned home. It was obvious that the real world expected much more from him.

Kate's nurturing was no longer enough. Cole needed inspiration but more importantly, he needed a stronger influence, guidance on how to focus, refine, and discipline his talent.

WHILE COLE PORTER WAS EXPERIENCING his first professional failure, Noel Coward was still a boy actor in London. Because Noel often worked in touring shows he was living away from home and functioning as an adult. Although he had a chaperone of sorts in the person of a woman who conducted the troupe, nowhere do we see much evidence of her control as a duenna. Noel and the other children in the show lived very much the way an adult trouper would have lived, making his own friends and enemies, going where he pleased, freed from the strictures of school and rules. This sort of situation of leaving children of such a tender age to raise themselves would be inconceivable today.

We know too that if this chaperone had had any inclination to place restrictions on young Noel she probably would have met with the same fate as the early schoolteacher who was bitten by him. Since Noel never registered any complaint against the upstanding Victorian woman, we can assume that she let him go his merry way with the rest of the troupe.

Part of the way he went was to experiment with sex. These days it is assumed that any kind of childhood erotic experimentation leaves deep scars on the adult psyche, but

Noel seems to have been left remarkably unscathed. In fact his appetite for sex seems to have been as satisfying and nourishing as his appetite for fame. He never seems to have been a child in any way.

As far as we can determine the first in his line of partners was Esme Wynn, a girl who was part of the cast of *Where The Rainbow Ends*, and whom he met when both were at the start of puberty. Noel says in *Present Indicative* that during the first two seasons he had no idea she could ever mean anything to him.

"I always found her pompous, podgy, and slightly superior . . . and her majestic deportment at parties filled me with awe and a certain indefinite dislike."

Then one day Esme appeared wearing a white knitted jumper and skirt and wheeling a brand-new bicycle, which she was afraid to ride. The magic *eclat* occurred, and Noel became hand-in-glove with her, meeting her family, who, wrapped in an aura of glamour, also brought the pubescent Noel under their spell. Esme's mother had been a chorus girl and this fascinated Noel, who recounts, "I rode home that evening . . . ecstatic in the thrill of a new friendship." His "romantic visions were realized quickly. Esme and I became inseparable." They gave each other nicknames; she was Poj, for podgy, he was Stoj, for stodgy.

"We alternated between childishness and a strange maturity. The theater had led us far in precocity and we discussed life and death and sex and religion with sublime sophistication. We also dressed in each other's clothes. . . ."

Esme became a lifelong friend and confidante of Noel's, but this early affair shows that even he was ambivalent about admitting himself to be homosexual at that early age. Her spiritual interests later in life came to bore him and made their adult friendship perfunctory, but the early days brought great intimacy between them. Besides the innocent and admirable side, which was as sentimental as paintings of the time showing gleaming nude children frolicking through brook-riven glades, there was also a physical sharing and intimacy between them.

First Noel was attracted to Esme's special spirit and character. She was an unusually intelligent and creative girl,
who had deep insights and entertained dreams of being a
poet and writer. In fact her writings were so good that they
sparked a competitive jealousy in Noel, who couldn't stand
it if someone he knew could do something he couldn't. He
began to write as well, and hit back even further by making
fun of her more sentimental efforts.

She had too much self-confidence to be rocked by his
criticisms, and instead calmly challenged him to do better.
They developed a relationship that was remarkable both for
its maturity and its longevity. They had a special bond, and
if two people that young can be said to have had an ongoing
affair they did. Noel hinted at their intimacy when he said
that they would get so involved with each other that they
did not like to separate for such mundane tasks as bathing
or grooming. They simply carried their discussion into the
bathroom, where they'd strip down and bathe together . . .
intellectually yacking away *en flagrante.*

"It seemed affected to stop short in the middle of some
vital discussion for such a paltry reason as conventional
modesty," said Noel.

Knowing of his active curiosity about all things and his
need to be a pioneer and an adult early on, it is not a big jump
to assume that he and the pretty little Esme also explored
their differences physically as well as intellectually. Noel
himself intimated later in life that their love affair was consummated at least once during this long-term involvement.
When Esme deserted the theatre and found a man who loved
her there was a fine Victorian scene of outrage when the hus-
band-to-be learned (from Noel's remarks) that there may have
been more than innocent activities going on in the bathroom.
He raised a holy fuss and it was only through some skillful
and loud persuading by Noel and Esme that his fears were al-
layed and Poj went on to marry him, have children, embrace
Christian Science, and write tracts on spiritual realization
that annoyed Noel beyond endurance.

Esme was probably not the first to join Noel in the pleasures of the flesh. As a young boy actor he was a target for stage door Johnnies. He wrote or told with blasé abandon of the vicars who would come a-calling after a performance of a show, and allowing them to take small liberties with his inner thighs for a taxi ride and some candy or even high tea. His precocious promiscuity is like a story out of the old Victorian magazine *The Pearl*.

Just prior to meeting Esme, Noel tells in his first autobiography about meeting an artist named Philip Streatfield, who was fifteen years his senior. Noel doesn't say how or where he met Streatfield—a common deletion among gay men when explaining to straight people how they came to be suddenly close with someone who doesn't quite fit in with their public lifestyle. It is easy to make some educated guesses, any of which could be true. For all the antihomosexual laws and strictures in London at that time, sexual relationships between children and adult men were perhaps the easiest to conduct and camouflage publicly. People just did not think it could happen, any more than people are willing to believe the extent of sexual abuse of children today. It was such an inconceivable act, yet so common in England at that time, that it was easy for a man to be friends with a young boy without anyone suspecting the truth.

How did they meet? Possibly Streatfield, having an attraction for boys, would have gone to see a play that had a cast of attractive youngsters on stage to view, knowing it was easy enough to meet them, since adult supervision was nonexistent. In Noel of course there was no question of unwillingness. His adult mentality made the idea of sexual interaction easy for him to grasp. At the time theatre people in England were equated vaguely with prostitutes. Because the boys were underpaid and unsupervised and usually had half-empty bellies, it wasn't hard to persuade them to be accommodating. Noel always needed something he couldn't afford. If a boy actor was to become a success in this worldwise environment of the theatre, he had to be shrewd and willing to do things that later Hollywood starlets found necessary as well.

Noel was a willing partner in his relationship with Streat-field, probably even in love with him somewhat, and suffered no traumas. If nothing else Streatfield was an artist, and the romantic achievement of an artist making his living as such had enormous appeal to Noel.

Streatfield did a pencil portrait of Noel at the time. We see a cherubic, chubby face that only a mother and a peder-ast could love. Yet personal attractiveness is different now than it was then. An overlay of baby fat on a youngster or a woman, and portliness in a man, was considered pleasing. (Noel's later obsession with slimness, possibly because being onstage or on a film adds a good fifty pounds to one's appearance, did not come from the standards of his time. It was his own invention to equate a slim, lithe form with elegance and manly beauty.)

Noel tells of spending long afternoons in Streatfield's studio watching him paint a nude female model. The boy went on long trips with the artists, as if they were companions of the same age and no one saw anything wrong with it. The fact that Violet allowed her fifteen-year-old son to travel with the thirty-one-year-old Streatfield seems incredible today. But the idea that a sexual agenda lay behind the man's interest in her son probably never entered Violet's head. The material benefits and the opportunity to travel at the expense of a kind man were all that would be remarked on. Because there were such rigorous laws against homosexual activity, and the English had such a strong belief in the law as a deterrent, it would not be thinkable that this was something to fear—the law would take care of that.

The fact that Noel recalled Streatfield with real caring and was affected by his death early in World War I shows that there was no negative aspect to the relationship. Noel really was a little adult at that time. Noel's upbringing in the theatre, changing costumes without privacy, and having been unschooled in the regular channels of morality, would have given him a freer attitude toward matters sexual than he might have had otherwise.

However, the real benefit he obtained from Streatfield

was an introduction to a Mrs. Astley-Cooper, who invited the youthful actor to her home in the country to recover from his bout with a tubercular gland. It is an indication of his maturity that Noel was being invited on his own to socialize with sophisticated adults when he was still only fourteen. Mrs. Astley-Cooper was a rare bird—wealthy, socially placed, and a character. All the mirrors in her house were blinded with scarves so she did not have to look at her own face. He describes her lying on a chintz-covered mattress in front of her fireplace, "firing off witticisms." Her language and her rich lifestyle taught him all he knew about upper-class sophistication, and how among the idle rich a clever remark is worth a thousand college degrees.

He learned to admire wealth, and yearn for servants, parties, and beautiful surroundings. He also learned how to integrate upper-class sophistication into his plays and songs. This time spent in the country was his real formal education, giving him a strong grounding in brittle wit, satire, and poise—all of which came to bear in his wittiest and best writings.

Noel's mother, always a source of strong emotional support, was also quick thinking and resourceful. When he was off to visit Mrs. Astley-Cooper the first time, Violet had lost her purse with his tickets and money. She ran to a pawn shop and hocked her diamond ring to buy another ticket. She was with him every step of the way, using whatever resources she had to help him. Her strength of character, contrasting with his father's lack of spine and ambition, was the model set for him.

Almost entirely due to Streatfield and Mrs. Astley-Cooper, Noel became part of a society that became the basis of the image of his works. He wrote about it better and with greater sophistication than anyone ever had. Noel himself credits Streatfield with this kindness and when the artist died shortly after going to war, Noel mourned for him.

He describes how Streatfield, worried about Noel's health, had extended himself to ask Mrs. Astley-Cooper to help.

"He seemed to think that she would like me and that I

would not only derive much material benefit from her country air and excellent living, but also profit from the astringent wisdom of her friendship. He died the following year without ever realizing to the full the great kindness he had done me."

This simple tribute is touching beyond any expression of grief from Noel, protecting the privacy of their friendship and honoring the memory of a friend who had unselfishly reached out to make sure someone was protecting the young man. This kind of active understated expression of love is characteristic of the British, who must keep so much under a demeanor of decorum and hide so many facts of life that are deemed unacceptable. For Noel this elegance of form is uncharacteristic; he was used to giving full vent to his spleen over the simplest slights; yet this small tribute to his first lover shows that he really did know how to outclass the best of them.

The fact that Mrs. Astley-Cooper invited the pubescent Noel to spend time at her estate and meet her upper-class friends showed how absolutely acceptable it was for an adult male to have as a close friend a teenage boy.

It's difficult for people who aren't attracted to children to understand why they are targets for sexual attraction; but Noel was never really a child and we have his own affirmation that at an early age he had that "thing" that Cole Porter wrote about. We also have his clear inference that he was never an unwilling partner in any sexual situation he found himself. Possibly his deep need for approval was so intense that being attractive to anyone at any age was part of what he craved. We know that the only time he was known to turn his back on an audience was when they booed him.

Before going to recuperate with Mrs. Astley-Cooper Noel was in Pinewood Sanatorium for convalescent tubercular patients. He was the youngest patient there, and being witness to so many soldiers dying around him, while putting a brave face on it, Noel received special attention. The doctor there, Dr. Etlinger, had Noel staying at his own house on the sanatorium grounds so he need not have overclose exposure to the dying patients.

Noel describes him as a small weatherbeaten man with twinkling blue eyes and a passion for Russian tea, "which we used to brew at all hours of the day and night." There is probably no basis for a suspicion of sexual activity here, but what is interesting again is the fact that he could spend weeks at a time in close interaction with adults—educated adults of special talents—and not bore them. This is a remarkable testament to his precociousness and charm; so many adults who had interesting friends and lives were quite at ease having this fourteen-year-old school dropout sharing their lives even when there was no hidden meaning to their invitations to tea.

For Noel Dr. Etlinger was probably an attractive father figure, as was Streatfield. This attachment of his to older men is common among young gay men who feel an emotional void which their fathers should have filled. Unable to resolve it or overcome the dislike he felt for his real father, Noel went out to find some part of the relationship with other men.

It is absolutely certain that he had no kind of personal relationship with Charles Hawtry, yet there was a professional bond—and strictly that—between them. Although Hawtry understood Noel's talent as a performer and was professional enough to nourish it, he was himself a homophobe of the first magnitude. One might wonder if he would have been so helpful and long suffering with Noel's childish lack of discipline and arrogance backstage if he knew he was nurturing a pansy in his own breast. It was in fact Hawtry's testimony that had sent Oscar Wilde to "Reading Gaol" not many years earlier. Yet Noel in his autobiography made a stronger honorific memorial to Hawtry than he did to anyone else. Perhaps the basic lack of self-respect and the need to overcompensate to heterosexuals who help, even unwittingly, made him more grateful to the man than he might have been.

Through all these childhood peccadilloes it becomes obvious that if Noel had been heterosexual himself he might not have gained such easy entry to say Mrs. Astley-Cooper's house. It is not likely that someone like Streatfield would have used a social favor for someone he was not emotionally attached to, or who had rejected his advances. It isn't likely that many other pudgy, stodgy adolescents would have been entertaining to her; it would have taken someone of Noel's stripe to respond so flatteringly to her bizarre behavior. One can imagine an adolescent heterosexual wanting to escape from the queer old broad who got drunk and lay in front of the fire and the covered mirrors spouting witticisms. It took someone of an offbeat bent himself at that age to appreciate rather than scorn such a character. Most boys want to be with other boys who share their interests. It took someone of Noel's special makeup to appreciate the kind of funny offbeat personalities that form the society that people want to see on stage or to read about in print.

Throughout the early years of touring in the provinces pretty Esme Wynn remained Noel's dearest friend and *bête noire.* He might not have developed the need to write if she hadn't been doing it already. Although her deepening interest in spirituality, and her books on the subject took them in radically different directions, she gave him his first early sense of himself as a male, not just as a homosexual. Her willingness to be intimate with him, bathing nude together, showed him an acceptance of himself by women that must have widened his ability to write so convincingly of heterosexual relationships in his great plays. She rounded him, so to speak, and broadened his experience so he could write of heterosexual relationships with truth and authority, firsthand. His public image as a womanizer had at least some basis in fact.

Perhaps paramount among Noel's youthful promiscuities was his affair with Gertrude Lawrence, which blossomed into a close professional and personal friendship that spanned over fifty years. He met her when they were both young and starting out in theatre, although she was perhaps a touch more sophisticated than he was. He was thirteen and the play they were to be performing in was *Hannele*, which included a cast of ten children, again traveling under the careless vigilance of a Miss Itala Conti, whom Noel seems to have liked very much. Among the cast of *enfants* was Gertrude Lawrence, "a vivacious child with ringlets to whom (Noel) took an instant fancy. She was very *mondaine*, carried a handbag with a powder puff." She gave Noel an orange and told him a few mildly dirty stories and he loved her from then on. They stayed friends and their names are linked forever in theatre lore because of the play he later wrote for her, *Private Lives*. She was one of Noel's early crushes for a long time, partly because Gert, as she liked to be called, was a practitioner of free love, and Noel was not excluded from her parties.

At one party she took him into a private room and demonstrated the facts of life to him, he claimed far and wide. Gert's sharing of her own brand of sophistication with him helped shape Noel into the mature and worldly sophisticate he became offstage and on. Although he was later exclusively homosexual this early experimentation, plus the glamour of her early attitudes to free love (it was she who used to bring her lovers from the Coldstream Guards in job lots to his tea parties after his success as a playwright), helped him shape the unconventional designs for living he created in his plays. Gertrude Lawrence was a free spirit, and committed to sexual liberality; her early influence on Noel is visible throughout his work.

Despite this early indulgence at the heterosexual banquet Noel's emotional and erotic involvement had asserted itself already in his strong emotional attachment to another boy actor of his own age, John Elkins, who for a short time formed a trio with Noel and Esme. Elkins was a stagestruck lad, probably himself interested in Esme as a romantic partner and Noel as a friend. Noel describes how at the start he and Esme went around the shops, stealing chocolates to arrange a boxed gift for him.

Elkins was handsome and kind, the son of a minister. He

died suddenly at a young age and Noel never really got over
the sweet sadness of youth cut off in its first flower. He
was deeply impressed at that early age to have someone he
was romantically attached to and idealized, snatched away.
Elkins became his lost love. Coward romanticized him in
his play spectacle, *Cavalcade,* and again in *This Happy
Breed,* both works having young lovers who die early but
in Noel's plays both lovers die.

Violet must surely have sensed Noel's leanings, but what
mother does not blind herself to certain aspects of her son's
behavior, especially when the son is obviously gay and there
is no other explanation for certain situations? If any gay
man can be absolutely sure of anyone's unflagging love and
devotion, it is that of his mother. This classic case of intense mother-son devotion coupled with intense father-son
dislike or an absent or distant father, go to make for that
unresolved Oedipus complex that often accompanies the de-
velopment of gay males. To find it so clearly pronounced
in both Noel and Cole, both of whom became the models
for male style, wit, and sophistication in the most expres-
sive decades of the century, is remarkable.

Looking at the lives of Cole Porter and Noel Coward from
a sexual standpoint, it appears that Noel's early training as
a trouper in the theatre gave him a wider range of sexual
sophistication, firsthand. Cole, raised in the sheltered, controlled atmosphere of his home, then in a prep school, then
at all-male Yale and Harvard, was lucky to have had even
an inkling of what a woman might look like close up. It is
not likely that he ever saw a naked woman in person, as
Noel did. Any early homosexual tendencies Porter may
have started out with they would have been well guided in
that direction by the comfortable and attractive situations
of his all-male environments. Sexual experimentation
among boys is an unspoken given during puberty; being in
an all-boys' school it is inconceivable that it wasn't a regular part of life there. At Yale of course at a time when
heterosexuality asserts itself more definitely, and homosexual tendencies are rejected, Cole was still socializing with

classmates who became his gay adult friends. So it is likely that his pattern of sexuality could have continued uninterrupted. The fact that he had a strong libido, that eroticism itself was a constant throbbing in his soul, is indicated by the fact that he used to doodle naked girls in the margins of his notebooks. Cole was always fascinated by heterosexual desire, possibly because it involved the kinds of men he was attracted to, although he abstained from the female nude himself in practice.

Noel never found sexual activity of any kind barred to him, so he was able to view it in all its nakedness and varieties at all ages. To him sex was achievable—it was finding true love that eluded him. Cole, growing up in the American Midwest, where they made such a vociferous crusade against sex in any unmarried form, had reason to think that he could never really be sexually satisfied, that there would always be a wall between him and his sexual object. He must have learned early that he never really *connected* emotionally with his sexual partners.

From this point of view it is no wonder that Noel Coward's plays and writings focus on the social ramifications of unconventional romantic activity, whereas Cole Porter's songs always exhibit a delicious foreboding, a tortured longing and a wretched suffering over the thing that must always be just out of reach.

Porter's "By Candlelight" notes,

> Life seems such perfect bliss
> And so sweet every kiss
> I know that love like this
> Couldn't be true.

IV

"Oh, What a Lovely War"

COLE AND NOEL HAD BEEN BORN into a world that valued the decorative arts. First the Victorian, and then the Edwardian Era were given over to visual beauty. Houses, public buildings, parks, men's and women's clothing were all made as gorgeous as possible. It was a world where extreme ornateness and rich color were valued as a necessary part of life. The quality of living was of the utmost importance. Business matters, political matters, even war would be set aside as secondary to dinner and the cultured enjoyment of life. This was the classical Greek ideal, held dear to the civilized people of Europe.

This world of elegance and beauty, which formed Noel and Cole, was dealt its first severe blow when the military powers entered into the supreme folly, World War I. Although the war devastated Europe, to Coward and Porter it brought only some distressing inconveniences. Despite the fact that Noel was too young to be inducted into the service until almost the end of the fray, he still went through tremors the few months he was in uniform. It wasn't that he was unpatriotic, he just had other things he'd rather be doing.

Cole had no desire to march off to war either. Except for their predilection for men in uniform, army life held no allure for either man. Both had been raised to see themselves as superior creatures, and neither could abide the idea of being regimented into barracks and performing tasks with other lads their age who were of lower station, and with whom they had nothing in common. So hideous was the prospect, that they both went to enormous efforts to avoid the draft. They were among the first and cleverest of the "hell, no, we won't go" school.

Noel had reached the point when he was poised at the

brink of his career when he was drafted into English military service. It is not really clear how he managed to use his social contacts to get released the day after he was drafted, but he called someone who knew someone who got him released. The whole incident has overtones of a gay interlude that led this nineteen-year-old nobody to call an officer and suddenly get the kind of treatment usually reserved for sons of munitions manufacturers or politicians. Basically what happened was his country asked him to take a chance on getting killed and he declined the offer. In the next war he tried to make up for his reticence, but this war he was saving himself for the stage.

He describes this time in depressing detail in *Present Indicative.* His determination even as a youth to demand and get what he wanted and never take no for an answer was remarkable.

In January 1917 Coward was examined by the medical board, and learned that his prior bout with tuberculosis had made him unfit for combat or officer's training. Nonetheless they could still find something disgusting for him to do in the Labor Corps. A short time later he was cast in a "meaty dramatic part," in the West End when he was called up for active service. He described the first day this way:

"At the end of several hours of beastliness during which I stood about naked on cold floors and was pinched and prodded by brusque doctors, I was told to dress . . . and line up with a group of about fifty men in various stages of physical and mental decay."

This was a youth who had spent the last decade being applauded onstage, admired, cast in roles of sophistication and comedy and youth; one indeed who had hobnobbed already with famous people and artists, visited Mrs. Astley-Cooper's estate, where he dressed for dinner. There is a portrait of him at fourteen years of age in high silk hat and white tie, looking the picture of happy elegance. Now he's plodding along Waterloo Bridge, hiding his face so his theatre friends might not recognize him, like a condemned prisoner trudging off in disgrace to some work camp.

"All fifty of us" were billeted in one hut and given slices of bread and margarine and cups of greasy cocoa and three blankets to avert the cold in the unheated room. The man next to him was found to be covered with sores. When they removed the man Noel was offered his blankets. One can see his elegant disdain as he refused, "although shivering with cold." The next day, after a drill and learning how to wind his puttees properly, Noel was determined to get out of it. And he did.

We are never given the whole story in his breezy autobiography, but we learn that Noel had friends in high military places. He went to the sergeant and bribed him with ten shillings and demanded to see the commanding officer. He told the CO that he'd not had time to arrange his affairs and needed to do so. He was given leave. (Again we see the remarkable luck of the fair-haired child of Destiny.) He went home, where Violet greeted him as if he'd been away at the front for four years. He formulated a list of people he knew who could help him.

The list included two generals, two colonels, and a captain. It is amazing that this teenager should know such people in England. How did he meet them? Again, there are unanswered questions in this tale. Each officer actually talked to him on demand, which further makes one wonder why he had such clout with these men in uniform.

"The last on my list was a captain in the Air Force whom I had met casually at one or two parties." At last, some answers. Still one wonders how Noel could command an audience with these officers for the asking in the last darkest days of the war. This captain was as "affable as the others," and gave him a note to a Lieutenant Boughey at the War Office. The lieutenant saw that Noel was exhausted and "offered me a drink at once."

On hearing Noel's tale of horror he called his commanding officer and in sharp official tones said there was a disgraceful muddle and that Noel's possessions were to be sent home immediately.

"After this we had another drink and discussed Lord Kitchner [Britain's great nineteenth-century war hero], the war, the theatre and my immediate future in the Army."

Was there a secret gay code signal from captain to lieutenant that cued him onto Noel? Was the often touted radar-like ability of one homosexual to recognize another at work here?

Boughey offered to get him into the special unit and arrange for a couple of weeks leave before joining up. After one day of service, he had a two-week leave.

At this point it should be mentioned that unlike modern military attitudes, homosexuality and the military went hand in hand in Europe from the time of the ancient Greeks and Romans, through World War I. It was an open secret that military comrades, if they chose, often were lovers while they were young. In fact it had little to do with sexual preference; it was more a factor of immediacy and convenience, as well as a bonding that occurs sometimes between comrades. They still courted women and after a certain point the erotic part of the affair would dissolve when it was no longer needed. It was a military expediency when women were unavailable, and it cast no slur on either of the participants. It was not widespread, but it was far from uncommon.

No military unit in even the most uptight societies—and all of England was uptight—prior to World War I ever expected a group of young vital men in the full heat of their prime years to be celibate and function efficiently in the military. Until recently a young man's sexual needs were recognized and accommodated.

Without trying to depict the whole British Army as a chorus line from a Mel Brooks movie the real reason Noel was probably able to command such clout was because of his social networking. He had maintained an active relationship with Mrs. Astley-Cooper and she was his first entree into social partygoing, where he would naturally meet officers who were in positions of authority in the army. She was the kind of person who liked to meet and know all kinds of people, so Noel as her friend would have access to everyone who was anyone in London. He had a strong sense of net-

working, before its time, and was pushy and probably entertaining. And he never forgot to keep track of those he met.
His youth and profession as an actor, especially with Hawtry's company, would make him seem charming and unusual
to people at parties. He also had an early sense of style.

Noel was a name-dropper par excellence and had no scru-
ples about mentioning an influential name if he could borrow their influence. He had met these officers at parties
and if they didn't remember the chatty young man himself,
they would certainly respect a name like Mrs. Astley-Cooper enough to give him entrée into their offices. That was
also a part of the social class rules of politeness in those
days, like professional courtesy now. If Noel mentioned a
name they respected it would be an insult to Mrs. Astley-
Cooper to rebuff him.

It does seem, however, that when he sat around with the
lieutenant after the matter was solved drinking and chatting
about General Kitchener and theatre that there was another
point of contract that was personal. Noel gives this away
when he mentions that the lieutenant was killed in action
a short time later. He felt a great pang of regret, more than
just that of an acquaintance. It was through these mentions
in his memoirs that Noel tells us who his lovers were, without actually coming out and saying so.

Although Noel was reassigned to a less grunt-like unit,
and being in the Artist's Rifles had stronger appeal than
digging trenches with scrofulous comrades, this unit still
had to train for war. If Noel thought he'd be putting on
shows for the troops, he was wrong. Soon he was marching
and learning to stab Germans in the guts with a bayonet,
with his puttees coming undone every time he moved
quickly. Noel was in despair.

"I never learned to accept it all," he wrote. "I was tortured with the thought I was wasting my time. The needs
of my King and country seemed unimportant compared
with the vital necessity of forging ahead with my career. It
was a matter of pressing urgency that I should become rich
and successful as soon as possible."

Destiny stepped in again; while drilling, Noel tripped and hit his head on a plank, knocking himself unconscious for three days and nights. What followed were a series of hospitalizations and serious headaches. Although Noel was swift enough to see his opportunity and admitted much later that he had played up the headaches, he had suffered a bad head injury and despite his later breeziness had been in serious trouble medically.

During his convalescence he helped carry meals to bedridden patients, which is how he met a young New Zealander named Geoffrey Holdsworth. They became close friends and when Geoffrey was released he introduced Noel to a friend who was one of the cooks, and Noel got better food. He and Geoffrey became very close, and they used to escape through the wall at night to play in town. Noel showed Geoffrey his London. After several months of painful headaches and blackouts interspersed with escapes to tea parties and the theatre, Noel spent time in an epileptic ward, as the nearest treatment for his ailment; instead of recuperating, he learned how to help the nurses with their patients. Finally after one more snag with a military type who wanted to put him on active full duty, Noel was discharged with a six-month stipend of seven shillings and change.

"I reflected then, without a shadow of embarrassment, upon my unworthy performance as a soldier. There was no room in my heart for anything but thankfulness that I was free again to shape my life as I wanted."

Noel was the best example of the saying, "They also serve who sit and wait." His later service to his country in the form of artistic contribution was greater than any small thing he might have done as a soldier. On Armistice Day, however, he celebrated with as much patriotic fervor as if he'd led the fray.

"In the evening I dined with Tony and Juanita Ganderillas [wealthy Chileans], whom I had met at one of General Ashmore's musical parties. After dinner we drove in a dark-red Rolls-Royce through the Park and into Trafalgar Square, where we stuck, while hordes of screaming people clambered [over the car]. We screamed with them, and shook hands with as many as we could." He was candid about his real happiness: "I felt ignobly delighted in this moment of national rejoicing to be in a tail coat, a Rolls-Royce, and obviously aristocratic company.

"It was a thrilling night and I regret to say that the tragic significance of it was almost entirely lost upon me. I could only perceive that life would be a good deal more enjoyable without it."

V

"Pilot Me, Pilot Me, Be the Pilot I Need"

COLE PORTER SAW THE WAR as a diversion from the boring norm, a chance to drink Dom Perignon in the country where it was invented, surrounded by intrigue and stalwart young men in uniform. His experience in World War I is by now a classic account engineered by a creative genius who loved nothing better than to play tricks on people. His various tales about his military service were better than any of the shows he'd written to date, and a lot more convincing, despite their tallness.

There is no way now of knowing the truth about what he did in Paris during the First World War. It is certain that he was there, but he made up many stories, most of which he sent home to his mother. Kate saw each word as authentic, and she had them printed in the local paper. They could only have had the ring of truth in Peru, Indiana, where it's clear the Porters could make anything appear believable and where the Midwesterners had no real idea of what was going on in France at the time. The other thing that's certain is that Cole Porter was having the time of his life avoiding military service of any kind.

He had gone to France supposedly as a member of the Duryea Relief Fund, a private organization to distribute food and clothing. In France, Cole was seen by friends wearing different uniforms of different armies. There was even a fanciful tale of him joining the French Foreign Legion, a common romantic fantasy of men those days. In later life he continued telling this story, and in his biopic *Night and Day*, (part studio fiction, part Cole's fantasy), Cary Grant played Cole in the French Army, where he meets Alexis Smith playing Linda Thomas as a Red Cross nurse. This followed Cole's claims to have met Linda when he was a doughboy and she was a canteen girl in World War I. The only element of truth in this silly story was that both were in Paris at the time. The idea that this millionaire divorcée, who was setting the fashion for her time, should be a canteen girl must have set Cole into gales of laughter over his champagne when he thought of it. He was playing and singing his songs and Linda was as taken by them as she was obviously fascinated by the urbane imp who wrote them. Linda's reputed unusually keen eye for quality must have been genuine because from all accounts Cole was a dreadful piano player and had an even worse singing voice. That didn't stop him, any more than his rampant pursuit of men stopped him from moving heaven and earth to marry this diamond of a woman.

Linda Lee had been born the daughter of a well-to-do Kentucky banker about eight years earlier than Cole (although some reports make her as much as twelve years his senior). Linda helped establish the tradition that a woman never reveals her age—she and Cole had that in common. She had first married a wildly aggressive and virile macho man named Edward R. Thomas, who was extremely wealthy and extremely annoying. He had the distinction of being the first man in America to have killed another man with a car. He was a reckless driver and reckless about every other aspect of his life. If he'd been poor he'd be considered white trash ... except he wasn't poor, so he was a playboy. His family had made their many millions through newspapers.

Completely alienated by his wild lifestyle and wanting a life of elegance and serenity, Linda left Thomas. She returned when he broke his legs in an accident, just as Cole would do years later when she left *him*; she nursed each of them back to health. She was an enormously kind person. It seemed all a husband had to do to get her back was break both his legs.

It is easy to read a certain sadness and a tremendous ability to accept fate in her personality. She had enormous poise that came from within herself, not an artificial pose affected for publicity. She was well known as a social star, something on the order of Jacqueline Kennedy Onassis in recent times. What she did, others adopted as the thing to do. When she wore a simple black dress with a single strand of pearls that look became a standard in women's elegance. What Cole would do for songs, she did for enduring styles.

Her divorce from Thomas could have been a messy affair so his family made sure she'd be a woman of honor by settling over a million dollars on her, plus securities, a vast sum in those days. She settled in Paris in 1912, had a love affair with the Duke of Alba, and ran with the smart set of the day; this included Elsie de Wolfe and Anne Morgan, giving rise to the speculation that she was also lesbian.

She was considered a great beauty in her day and was much photographed. The generally accepted story is that she met Cole at the society wedding of Henry Russell and Ethel Harriman in Paris but other tales have Linda seeing Cole at a party and inviting him to play at one of her soirees, thinking he was a working musician.

What made someone like Cole Porter decide that he needed a wife? It had to be some sort of love. His first and only love to that date had been his mother. It was not some sick Oedipal fixation, but based clearly on the fact that she was the only person in his life who knew him and cared about him. Because he'd grown up watching the struggle between Kate and his grandfather, Cole saw life as a game of cat and mouse. Of course he was bored; growing up with money and not really having to worry about developing his talent, except as an amusement, had allowed him to slip into confusion about his career. Having money to play instead of an impetus to create had led him into indolence. It is often difficult for people born of great wealth to accomplish much outside of the business world. When they enter fields where they must compete creatively they often flounder.

When Cole met Linda he was becoming trapped in a life of ease but still had a deep urging to become a successful songwriter. When he met her he instinctively responded to that same persona he'd known in his mother. At that time he was living the devil-may-care life in postwar Paris and people wondered about the social and financial status of the young man from the Midwest.

When Cole was making the rounds of Parisian social events Elsa Maxwell (who hated him on sight and later revised her opinion when she found he had money after all) asked him how he could afford to dress in the manner he did when he had no visible means of support.

"Grandfather pays the tick," he told her, moving off to a less boring part of the room.

His attitude was that money was always there; all he had to do was convince J. O. to shell it out. Even after he started selling his songs, he remained dependent on his grandfather's fortune. He had been raised to know that it would someday be his, in full or in part, and it never occurred to him to chance forgoing it.

AT THE TIME COLE WAS RECEIVING $500 a month from J. O. as an allowance. If he needed more he could ask for it (or have Kate do it). At this point, however, his grandfather's disenchantment with Cole's life choices made the free flow of money more difficult. He could no longer depend on an automatic affirmative every time he asked for an advance.

If Cole thought that by marrying the wealthy Linda his grandfather would be pleased, he was in for a shock. His grandfather had disapproved of his lifestyle for so long and had become so set in the idea that Cole must give in to his demands, that he actually cut his allowance down from $500 to $100 a month when Cole announced his engagement. J. O.'s reasoning was that Cole didn't have a real job so he had no business marrying unless he could support a wife. The clash between rock-solid Midwestern values and the high-class European attitude toward life as a pleasure spa came into play, much to Cole's chagrin.

If J. O. thought that this ploy would finally force his rebellious grandson to bring his bride home and settle down to mind the family business he was in for a shock of his own.

Linda didn't care if Cole was worth two dollars or two million. She wanted him to be her husband and assured him that she had more than enough for the two of them to live in luxury on their own terms.

Cole put up a small protest, but Linda furthered her case when she told him she wanted him to concentrate on writing songs. Cole was not able to give up the things that large amounts of money could buy. He was addicted to the life of international high society, the fun, the silliness, the beauty and elegance, the wit, the drugs, and the river of fine champagne and *haute cuisine*. In addition the sex he craved was not to be had in Peru, Indiana.

When Linda reached out her elegant hand and promised him even more of what he had without having to appease J. O. to get it, and insisted on aiding his songwriting success, what could he say? Cole's buddy from Yale Billy Crocker, of the famous California banking family, generously loaned Cole $400 a month (this would eventually accumulate to $10,000, which Cole paid back in full). With his $500 a month and the royalties from his first genuine hit song, "In an Old-Fashioned Garden," and the knowledge that as soon as J. O. kicked the bucket he would come into his own fortune, Cole was ready to go ahead with the marriage, without feeling that he wasn't paying his own way.

Cole was now twenty-eight years old, a touch long in the tooth for a Yalie to still be waiting for his career to start, but it shows how deeply ingrained in him was the habit of being supported in a life of luxury. Despite his supposed reticence about marrying for money, it was easier for him than it might have appeared.

Being kept in luxurious style was actually secretly thrilling to Cole. The idea of being a gigolo had enormous appeal to him. So many of his songs refer to it in the first person, that we can only assume that Cole secretly saw himself as being trammeled in those sweet bonds of security. The idea of receiving large amounts of money without having to do anything except enjoy oneself in surroundings of luxury sat very well with him, as it did with Noel when he was first

invited to Mrs. Astley-Cooper's country estate. It also reveals a touch of the masochism in his character. But more
it shows that he had a certain contempt for his grandfather
and liked the idea that the old guy was footing the bill
while Cole was living a life of rich dissipation on the money
that J. O. valued so much.

From Cole's song "I'm a Gigolo":

> When I see the way all those ladies
> Treat their husbands who put out the dough
> You cannot think me odd
> If then I thank God,
> I'm a gigolo.

It is useless to fault Cole for feeling this way. He'd been
raised to live off his grandfather's revenues; his mother did
it as a matter of course, and J. O. encouraged it because it
gave him the right to control and try to run their lives. He
was such an overbearing, egocentric person that most people can empathize with Cole's desire to get even with him.
If J. O. wanted to buy and sell people the price should be
high.

In *Kiss Me Kate*, there is the wonderful song that Petruchio sings, "I've Come To Wive It Wealthily in Padua."

> If wealthily then happily in Padua.
> If my wife has a bag of gold,
> Do I care if the bag be old?

This was definitely a dig at Linda, who was rich and significantly older than he; in fact toward the end of her life
illness made her look like an old woman while he retained
his youthful appearance. Again we find the autobiographical
slur in his lyrics, the delicious thrill of marrying for money
and living richly on someone else's wealth, which was exactly the tenor of most of his own life. He always equated
happiness with money, but complete contentment with
someone else's money. His writing of that song shows another well-known aspect of Cole's personality. He loved to

play tricks on Linda; he must have gotten a thrill from seeing Linda's reaction when she heard that little verse.

Linda's enormous wealth certainly was a lure, but the real reason he married her was because he saw in her the same qualities that his mother possessed. The two women were very much alike, women of strength and determination who though feminine and pristine still refused to take abuse from anyone. Neither one could be pushed, yet both were gentle and caring. Both shared a devoted interest to seeing that Cole would become a success as a songwriter; Linda took over where his mother had left off years ago in her gentle determination to force him to concentrate on his composing. She could be his inspiration. In addition she was somewhere near his own age and had entrée to his fantasy world of taste, style, and elegance. She also had a sense of appropriate behavior, not from a social point of view (she had that decidedly) but from a stance of always behaving civilly. She was not a callous snob. She deeply cared about people and loved honestly and completely. She also stood behind her commitments even when it went against her own best interests to do so. This was a good thing for both her husbands, as each man seemed to go out of his way to test her.

She was not a doormat, however. She demanded as much from those around her as she was willing to give. If they had not the self-respect and discipline to maintain a basic pattern of dependable and mature behavior consistently, they would find themselves without her. She had a long fuse, but she did have a definite exploding point. She expected people to observe basic aspects of polite behavior.

She was famous for her discipline, and Cole took to it like a duck to water. He loved being forced to maintain a schedule, to be forced to work hours on hours a day even though left to his own devices he might easily have sat in a bar ordering martinis. Linda accepted his talent at a time when he was down on himself and felt like a failure.

Linda was Cole's soul mate, someone who believed in him, who'd provide companionship and style to his life—

and social acceptability. If people wondered why Cole needed a woman and not a male lover, the answers were simple.

He had gay friends like Monty, Len, Hanna, and "Sturges," but these were "sisters," not men attracted to each other. It would be fairly impossible for the kind of gay man Cole was sexually interested in to provide him with the ego recharge he needed. He did not respect these men. The kind of man he was attracted to would not give him what Linda did. In fact another gay man would drain him.

Because of his psychological setup only a woman like Linda could have been his life mate. Another woman, one who would make demands on him, would have been unacceptable. Linda had no demands to make. It is less clear why she wanted to marry him than vice versa. He was shorter than she, so he couldn't have appealed to her sense of design as an escort. He wasn't handsome; he wasn't always socially correct, often drinking too much, or walking out of a room without saying a word. He was a showoff and she certainly was aware that he was gay and outrageously so at times.

After they were married his outrageousness escalated until Linda had to curtail it several times. A sexless marriage may have appealed to her after her experience with the wildly aggressive and insensitive Thomas.

The fact that neither Cole nor Linda would be knocking on each other's bedroom door removed a serious source of possible friction from the marriage. As most of Cole's life was lived on the fantasy level, this drawing room marriage fit right in. Cole was not looking for someone to love and link up with and have a sexual/romantic relationship with; neither was Linda. Each wanted to share a life of brilliant social experiences, to travel to the best places, to be each other's glittering consort.

And that's what they were.

At first Cole took to marriage not because he needed the front, which he did, but because he liked Linda. If he didn't he could have let her go any time. Instead he made as great an effort to keep her happy with him as if he had been a devoted straight man.

Cole Porter needed a second mother and Linda was that. He also needed a strong support group. He had had it in college, comfortably ensconced in the admiration of his classmates. When that ended he was adrift and confused about how to handle the pressures of making it in show business. Professionally he was floundering. Linda was like a lifeboat that appeared when he was drowning. It is very possible that Cole would never have become the legend he did without her support. She revived his self-esteem, and made him realize that failures are part of overall success. Even though Elsa Maxwell later claimed the credit for restoring Cole's songwriting career, it is Linda who really did it.

Between Linda and friends, Cole had the happy splendid garden of intelligent moral support he had left at Yale, the kind of environment he needed to create songs. She insisted that he follow strict guidelines for working each day, for appearing at dinner, for dressing well and putting on a respectable public appearance. He took to the regimen as a relief from his maddening boredom and began turning out songs that were good. He loved being forced into a mold that enabled him to delve deeply into his talent and see it bring forth results.

Linda provided Cole with elegant and sumptuous surroundings.

The Great War was over. And Paris regained and increased its stature as the glittering mecca for artistic types from all over the world.

LINDA HAD A PASSION FOR HOUSES. She bought a place on Rue Monsieur for the *coleporteurs* to live in, a magnificent palace that they maintained until the Second World War. The house displayed all of Linda's antiques and furniture, art and objects.

The French called them the *coleporteurs*, amusing because the French word *colporteur* means "peddler." The two terms were so similar in sound and spelling and so divergent in connotation.

The Porters had a roommate, Howard Sturges, another rich gay man who was Linda's friend. Sturges (who had also gone to Yale) was an alcoholic. Linda was devoted to him. He had no profession; the most consistent task he performed was adopting stray animals who had been abandoned. When he was sober, which was usually, he was a delightful addition to their *ménage à trois,* and when he would go on his drinking binges, he would be found lying in the gutter (not a manner of speaking) and Linda would come from wherever she was and nurse him until the time passed. He traveled extensively with Cole as well, and remained his friend until he died. He was one of those people who help an artist sustain, rather than having any direct influence on a person's work. Sturge wasn't a sex buddy, as Monty Woolley was, and never bored Cole.

Among the most entertaining denizens of the group headed up by the Porters was Elsie de Wolfe. She had made a late marriage to Lord Charles Mendl, a sleepy old fellow with a title. Elsie had the money he needed; he had the title she aspired to. The discussion about whether or not they had sex, comic as it was, nonetheless was a constant one. For years the group speculated about whether this aging lesbian was sleeping with this drowsy old nobleman. Elsie was beloved by both Cole and Noel, who honored her in some of their funniest songs. She was a legendary character, being agile well into her eighties and purveying fitness for all ages.

Because of her friendships with lesbians and with gay men and the fact that she had no erotic encounters after her marriage to Cole, many have considered Linda to have been a lesbian. It is not at all likely that this was the case. People who knew Linda say the whole idea of sex repelled her, which was not unusual in those days. Many women were raised to be asexual, even frigid, especially southern aristocratic ladies. Her early female education could easily have conditioned her to feel that sex was no pastime for a woman. This did not make her a lesbian, just a normal American woman of the time. And after her marriage to Thomas Linda may have been happy to forgo sex entirely. Her whole focus was on living well and making Cole into a successful songwriter. Linda was friends with so many gay people because both the cafe society she was part of and Cole's theatrical world were populated so heavily by them.

Despite the extreme sophistication and style and sexual indulgence of the era, most people's moral attitudes had been shaped by Victorian standards and no sexual activity would ever be revealed to people outside their tight social circles.

Linda Porter liked people of a certain energy and a certain creative bent; she was as devoted to avoiding boredom as Cole was and the people she cultivated usually were highly entertaining, charming, and doing new and fascinating things. She was a partaker of their lives, and appreciator and a benefactor at times. Her letters show her close friendships with people such as fashion designers Mainbocher and Molyneux. Her focus was on style, not on sex.

COLE HAD A DEEP PREFERENCE for the social company of women and he seemed most satisfied with their social interaction. There was no doubt that he was deeply satisfied in his relationship with Linda, and that his early conditioning of having his mother as his only friend set this pace for his life. He had strong friendships with men as well, but these did not endure as did his friendships with women.

The divisions Cole Porter made in his social choices were varied indeed. Elsa Maxwell was a close, lifelong friend. He may have disapproved of her at times, but strangely—strangely because as a gay man it seems he would have had stringent limits for his female friends—Elsa was always held close to him. He had great fun with women, especially lesbian women, another oddity for a gay man, since usually gay men and gay women don't often really enjoy each other's activities.

No. 13 Rue Monsieur had become a Parisian landmark. Bricktop, the black singer, dancer, and nightclub owner recalled, "It didn't look like much from the outside—in fact it looked like it might come tumbling down any minute—but inside it was spectacular." Cole's wife was the decorator. There were zebra skins on the floors and on some of the walls. The chairs were painted red and upholstered in white kid. There was even a room with platinum wallpaper.

"The whole place was like a palace, and it took my breath away," Bricktop remembered. "There was one small room, close to the front door, that didn't look at all as if it belonged in a palace. It looked more like a monk's cell. That's where Cole did most of his composing."

Cole may have written with the diligence of a monk, but his songs from this era weren't attaining any lasting success. He had a minor hit here, a favorable review there, but nothing substantial. (The Dolly Sisters, Rosie and Jennie, introduced "I'm in Love Again" in the Greenwich Village Follies and the song was recorded by Paul Whiteman and his orchestra.) Nonetheless Linda insisted on keeping her husband's creating space special.

Money was not a problem for Cole Porter during these post-World War I years, but it certainly was for Noel Coward, then a struggling actor/writer on London's West End. He'd met such luminaries (and fellow travelers) as matinee idol Ivor Novello and envied their success. He thought himself destined for stardom too and was very impatient. Between jobs Noel liked to entertain in his room at his mother's boardinghouse at 111 Ebury Street.

He describes the tea parties as having "social elements tactfully mixed." In England, where one would never invite a servant to a party except to serve, and where the classes mixed only on the understanding that there were sharp differences between them, this could only mean that Noel was not adverse to inviting people who appealed to his sexual interests as long as they were discreet.

Gertie Lawrence would visit with her various haughty

young Guards—officers who sat about wrapped in regimental poise. Noel's old friend, the witticism-spouting Mrs. Astley-Cooper, would come too, adding spice to the conversation.

At one of the parties a young man named Stewart Forster appeared, a lieutenant in the Coldstream Guards (the elite group who protected the palaces). Stewart asked Noel to dine with him on guard at St. James Palace. Noel would be dining at the mess sitting there amid all of the staunch masculinity of the Palace Guards in uniform.

According to the nineteen-year-old Noel, "the traditional pomp of the atmosphere felt chilly at first, but there was an underlying glamour in it which thawed me presently." Soon some sherry and his natural theatricality warmed him further and Noel was making jokes about his strangely fitting rented tailcoat, which made him look like a cross between Pagliacci and Groucho Marx. At about 11 P.M. Stewart threw on an enormous bearskin hat and buckled on his sword and clanked out into the courtyard where he conducted the changing of the guard drill, barking shrilly and thrilling the hell out of his civilian guest.

"When he came back I had one more glass of port, said my good-byes and left, no longer oppressed by military tradition [Noel's reference to his depressing stint in the Army during the war] but definitely a part of it."

Whether or not sex had occurred between the guard and the playwright becomes irrelevant. The brilliant colors of the uniforms, the sight of all those superb young officers sitting around a table, maintaining the tight discipline of their special regiment, all that serving of extravagant masculinity, would be an erotic vision in itself to Noel.

"I walked home . . . past Buckingham Palace, much elated . . . and reflecting that a uniform was undoubtedly very becoming to Englishmen. . . ." One must always read between the lines here, especially since the youthful officer remained in close touch with Noel even more than twenty years later when Coward wrote *Present Indicative*. Noel was very taken with Forster's persona; he was a sexual trophy of the sort that gay men like to hold on to for no reason other than the egotism, one of those totally masculine men who nonetheless are amenable to being intimate with other men. In gay terms he's what would be called a prize, something like owning a small Rembrandt, cherished, protected, and always treated with the utmost kindness and respect so as not to mar its awesome perfection.

Noel described Forster's mustache as "a timid butter-colored moustache which, with the passing of time, I regret to say, has become large and quite red." This description, so innocuous, reveals the enormous sexual impact that the young guard had on Noel, and his attraction to the playwright in return was quite flattering enough to establish a physical friendship unsullied by falling in love or ending up gay "sisters."

Noel also became friends with Jeffrey Holmsdale (later Lord Amherst), another captain in the Coldstream Guards. Coward remembered meeting Jeffrey during the run of *Polly with a Past*. He described Amherst as small and fair and noted that his gallant military record seemed slightly incongruous, until you had known him a little. In Noel's words, Jeffrey was "gay and a trifle strained, and there was a certain quality of secrecy in him." Noel thought him "over wary," but eventually broke down the young officer's reserve and they became great friends for life. Noel recalled: "I dined with him several times, 'on guard' and at home with his family. I watched him twinkling and giggling through several noisy theatrical parties, but it took a long while for even me to begin to know him."

Besides liking each other tremendously Noel was not unaware that this friendship opened doors to people of influence. Meeting officers, future lords, and matinee idols appealed to his tastes. Noel was enormously starstruck in his youth. He hungered to be part of that elegant wealthy world of comfort, silk dressing gowns, and stardom that he had so far viewed only as a guest.

And he had chutzpah. It enabled him to go up to perfect strangers and make conversation, then make friendships and professional arrangements with them. He also used sex as a tool to get ahead. In the gay world sexual contacts usually preceded lasting friendships. After the initial attraction of the one-night stand came the social connection if the participants so chose.

After you've been pleasantly intimate with a person it is easy to be familiar with them and talk without restraint, make invitations and introduce them into your social circle. Since Noel's contacts usually were made within the social circle of the theatre, his subsequent social introductions were formidable. Homosexual sex can differ from casual heterosexual affairs in that there is usually an immediate "old boy" network available immediately after sex. Unlike Cole Porter, whose sexual contacts were based on a series of paid one-nighters with people he seldom wanted to see again, Noel made his contacts within his own social set, and was able to build on them. Of course Cole did not need to build on sexual connections. He had college and social connections. But Noel had to take whatever steps he could to establish a foundation for networking.

It should also be mentioned that Noel Coward would not be considered particularly handsome today, but in his time he made an attractive appearance, and did exude a strong masculine presence when performing. He never does seem to have had a problem with getting into bed those he wanted to be intimate with. Stardom and enormous success has never been considered a strike against a person in the sexual arena of course but in neither case does it appear to be the main reason Noel attracted his lovers, male or female. He must have had a strong libido and exuded a certain sexuality; people of intense energy and high achievement almost always have such a strong sex drive that it ignites passion where there normally wouldn't be any.

Soon Noel's London social life was burgeoning. His charm and energy enabled him to engage and befriend a wide variety of people as he built his theatrical career. He was very young and very vital; he had no sense of shyness and went after everything he could as long as it had the trappings of the star's life he was determined to lead.

His old friend Mrs. Astley-Cooper took him to Alassio with her. Like all the upper-class English they found winter in Italy preferable to winter in Britain. But more important than the sunshine Noel encountered a woman who would become an enormous influence on his life and career, a divorcée, Gladys Calthrop. Gladys was an artist and she and Noel found immediate rapport talking of theatre sets and costumes. They became inseparable friends and Gladys designed most of Noel's productions from then on.

Noel returned to London and wrote and starred in a show, *I'll Leave It to You*, which flopped. He decided to visit New York, even though he had little money. Jeffrey Amherst was sailing for America to make a dedication at Amherst College, which had been founded by one of his ancestors. Realizing that Jeffrey's connections would be useful his first time in New York, Noel invited himself along.

This was a chance to cement his friendship with Jeffrey, being in forced closeness on the ship, and a chance to meet other influential people on the crossing as well. It was a good opportunity for a very young and aspiring actor, and Noel did well to scrimp together enough money to sail.

He arrived in New York in June, just in time to meet producers such as the legendary actor/playwright/director David Belasco (from whom he got the idea to wear a silk dressing gown for social occasions at home), who were just leaving town for the summer. When the stifling heat of July and August hit Manhattan, sensible people, or at least anyone who could afford it, got out of town. Soon Noel found himself broke, with no contacts, and in limbo. He moved out of his room at the Brevoort Hotel and accepted an invitation from two kind lesbians, Gabrielle Enthoven and Cecile Satoris, to live for free in their studio apartment while they also found refuge from the heat.

Noel spent many penniless days in Washington Square sharing bread with kindly strangers he'd meet on park benches. He saw New York, used every opportunity to make headway in his career, and wrote incessantly. He brought his manuscripts wherever they'd accept them.

Eventually it began to pay off. The providence that guided him through all his life showed its hand several times and he managed to sell some short stories to *Metropolitan* magazine for an incredible $500 apiece.

When autumn returned, so did the people of the theatre and Noel made up for lost time. He was on the make. He was the ultimate theatre self-promoter, except he actually had the talent and manuscripts to back him up. He had something to show as soon as he found someone who would say "yes." Eventually, however, he had to return to England.

In New York, using his friendship with Jeffrey, he went to parties, saw plays, and established friendships with, among others, Lynn Fontanne and Alfred Lunt, who were not yet man and wife. However, Noel had another interesting vignette to report. One wonders why he reported it in his autobiography. On the surface it seems a "kindness from strangers" story; to those who know the gay erotic mind it strikes the reader as a tale of one-upmanship designed to give the impression of yet another erotic fantasy realized.

Noel was still living in the studio apartment of Gabrielle Enthoven and Cecile Satoris. He had no money left and was living exclusively on bacon and cheap wine bought on credit from the butcher—a New York coup in itself, getting credit from a butcher. Noel's charm was an asset, and probably his clipped English accent didn't hurt either, giving him an aura of trustworthiness. Because the bacon cooking in the tiny studio would fill the room with smoke and impregnate his clothes with its smell, Noel adopted the habit of stripping down and cooking and eating naked until the smoke cleared. Noel's penchant for taking off all his clothes and running about naked was a lifetime habit.

The practice resulted in a meeting with a New York policeman, who, viewing the nude without violin through the window, came over for an explanation. The cop came banging on the door, Noel writes, and hearing the knock, the nude with bacon threw on a dressing gown, ran downstairs still holding the bacon fork, and received the full force of the cop's red-faced rage. This evaporated when Noel invited him, again in his accent, which had the effect of changing the picture in the cop's mind immediately, to come up for a glass of wine. The policeman accepted, went up to the studio and polished off three glasses in the sweltering heat. Instead of carting Noel off to the station house for indecency, he loaned him his revolver "because," he said, "it's a dangerous neighborhood."

"When he had gone," Noel wrote, "I lay awake for most of the night restraining the impulse to shoot at every shadow."

The story ends there in the book, but the unanswered questions twirl around in one's head like blithe spirits. Did the policeman ever come back for his revolver? Why did he leave it with Noel? Didn't he need it himself? Why would he be so concerned for Noel's safety that he would give him his gun? All in all Noel's life is a series of these unexplained serendipitous chance meetings that lead him to success in large and small ways. Even his trip back home was a matter of chance. Rumors say that one of his New York society friends had given him free passage back home on one of her husband's ships.

Returning to London from his first trip to America, Noel found he had almost exactly as much money as he'd left with, around seventeen pounds. He once again took up the struggle to earn a living. His attitude toward money was actually quite breezy. He never hesitated to do whatever was expedient to get immediate funds, usually by borrowing from friends. He spent it as soon as he had it, although that was due to the fact that being poor he always had something that had to be purchased immediately. But he had the charm and ability to continue to widen his circle of friends. He met Elsa Maxwell. She and her lover Dorothy (Dickie) Fellows-Gordon took Noel on an all-expenses-paid trip to Venice.

Noel had also become friendly with a young singer/comedienne, Beatrice Lillie, who was in Andre Charlot's *Revue*. He'd wangled an intro to the producer/director through Bea and had sung several songs "with incredible vivacity." Charlot was unimpressed. He took Bea Lillie aside and said,

"Bea, never do that to me again. That boy has no talent whatever!" But the boy had plenty of drive and ambition. He knew one of Charlot's main backers was a young peer of the realm, Lord Ned Lathom, who also was gay.

Lathom was a playwright himself and liked to be around show folk. Lathom had even formed his own company, The Ventures, producing plays that the official censor, Britain's Lord Chamberlain, deemed inappropriate. It was sort of the off-off Broadway of its day. When his own plays or productions weren't hits, he spent considerable funds investing in other West End productions. A few years after Noel's disastrous meeting with Charlot, he met him again through Ned Lathom. Noel invited himself to Lathom's retreat in Switzerland at Davos and knowing that Ned put up money for Charlot, impressed Lathom with songs and sketches. Lathom wired Andrew Charlot to join them and naturally he did. Charlot, always a smart showman, knew Noel's material wasn't good enough to carry a new revue. But he also knew his prime backer wanted Noel's material in the next show.

"Good God!" Charlot said, "he can't even write music. He just sings the songs *a capella*!"

"So hire someone to write down the notes," Lathom suggested.

They would introduce Noel to Elsie April, who would serve this function. Though he certainly didn't think he needed any help Coward agreed to collaborate on the composing of the music with Philip Braham and collaborate on the writing of the sketches with Ronald Jeans.

And so since he couldn't get the producer to produce his work on its own merits, Noel, clever from the start, went to the right source. Follow the money.

The revue *London Calling* was a success. Noel performed in it with his pals Gertie and Beatie. He was not only collecting a salary but extra money from the royalties. It was more money than he had ever earned before but he donated a good deal of it to his mother to help defray expenses for the boardinghouse on Ebury Street, where he still lived. And his high style of living necessitated that he still borrow from friends. He went to Ned Lathom and asked to borrow money to help Ebury Street from going over to creditors. Lathom refused to loan money to Noel, but insisted on giving the money as a gift instead, which saved the day and made Noel loyal to him forever.

In 1923 during the run of *London Calling* Noel also had a brief fling with Prince George, the Duke of Kent, the fourth son of King George V (who thought men like that shot themselves). They were to remain lifelong friends. The Duke's brother Edward, Prince of Wales, did not like Noel and didn't like the idea of his younger brother running around with the theatre set. The prince proved to be a trial for King George V and Queen Mary. In addition to theatre and drugs, he liked sleeping with black people, both men and women, and his choices of sexual partners were indiscreet, since he was often blackmailed.

His addiction to drugs was finally obliterated (with the help of his brother Edward) and he eventually married. Noel then became great friends with George's wife, Marina, Duchess of Kent, and was often a guest at Coppins, their home in the country. But Edward and Noel remained distant and cold to each other through most of their lives.

When the revue, which included his song "Parisian Pierrot," written for Gertrude Lawrence, went to New York, Noel was not going to be in the cast. But he decided he wanted to be there for the production anyway. Again, on his own, he embarked for the city that he loved so much. Beatrice Lillie, Gertie Lawrence, and Jack Buchanan were afforded star treatment in New York. Buchanan played the part Noel had had in England, singing a song called "Sentiment," a song that had failed every night in London, but Buchanan made it work brilliantly every performance.

Coward had grandly checked into the Ritz. When he got the first week's bill, however, he checked out and moved in with a pal, Lester Donahue (but kept the Ritz as his address).

Being the writer of a successful play gave Noel his own

entrée into social and theatrical circles in New York and he made the most of it. He himself admitted that he went to great lengths to take advantage of every situation that could lead him to stardom. He found his friends the Lunts were now married, but still not powerful enough to perform only plays they could do together. Each was playing in successful shows. His friends Eva Le Gallienne, Ethel Barrymore, George S. Kaufman, and his wife were now almost uniformly famous.

Noel made friends during this autumn with Laurette Taylor, her husband, Hartley Manners, and their unusual family. They were an odd crew and Noel wrote the play *Hay Fever* about them.

Laurette's husband, Hartley Manners, was an extremely conservative man in such broad issues as religion, politics, and sexuality. He was talkative but quickly offended, which made for abrupt conversations with Coward. Laurette, very theatrical, never hesitated to unsheath her scathing wit and uninhibited humor.

The family liked to play parlor games and Dwight and Maguerite, children by Laurette's first husband, would frequently argue about game rules with their mother and stepfather. These regular battles would result in all family members stalemating and retreating upstairs to their separate quarters. From a guest's point of view, this made for a very bizarre situation, but for a budding playwright, what better fodder? Noel later said he churned out *Hay Fever* in three days.

As the theatrical season heated up Noel met more and more people, including the acerbic Alexander Woolcott, who was the most famous critic perhaps ever to write about theater in America. Woolcott was as much a star collector as Noel, despite his own fame, and they became in a way, strange bedfellows, but not in the sexual sense. Noel often used "Smart Aleck's" apartment as a base for his future trips to New York and both delighted and drove the irascible critic nuts with his talking and intensity. They remained loyal and bitchy to each other. Noel also met

George Jean Nathan, another highly respected drama critic and writer, whose reputation is less commercial than Woolcott's, but was nonetheless formidable during his lifetime.

Reports differ as to when Noel Coward met Douglas Fairbanks and Mary Pickford. Douglas Junior says it was at his studio, but another story says it was at a party in 1924 at Laurette Taylor's. One thing is certain; when Noel learned that the famous couple were sailing for England on the *Olympic,* he booked passage home on the same ship. He was an expert at publicity. He stood next to Doug and Mary at the ship's railing. There was a huge crowd on hand to see the celebrated couple and scores of reporters and photographers. And naturally the same hullabaloo greeted them (and Noel) when the ship arrived at Southampton.

Back in London Noel was having a difficult time getting anyone interested in producing his plays. Many of these early works were not good, as he found out bitterly in later years. But he did have two plays that seemed producible, *Fallen Angels,* with two star parts for women, and a daring new play about drug addiction, *The Vortex.* He finally found a rather undependable producer named Norman Macdermott to take on *The Vortex.* It was not the subject matter that concerned producers; it was Noel. Gladys designed the sets and costumes for *The Vortex,* and once revealed,

"As a matter of fact the reason no management would touch the script of *The Vortex* was because of Noel. They were all mad about the play, and said it was one of the best they had ever read, but would have nothing to do with it if Noel played the lead. You see, they didn't consider him good enough. But as he'd written it for himself, he wasn't having any of that and wouldn't give way."

During production of *The Vortex,* Macdermott told Coward that the production would have to be canceled because he had run out of money. Noel spent a black twenty-four hours in a panic listing everyone he knew who might be good for the 300 pounds he needed to float the production into opening night. He combed his list, coming up with blanks. This one had loaned to him too often recently, that one was rich, and rich folks were "only good for a fiver." One of the main characteristics about Noel was that he had no qualms about asking for loans from whomever happened to be nearby. It was one of his many talents.

At last he thought of one person he'd never touched on, a young man named Michael Arlen, who had been through the poverty and stress of trying to make it recently and therefore might say yes. Michael Arlen's novel, *The Green Hat*, had been a recent success. Arlen agreed readily and gave Noel the money; Coward suddenly was not only the playwright and star of the show, but the major backer as well. He used that clout in the weeks to come to force his wishes on Macdermott.

In the next few months he and Arlen palled around together. Since Arlen was thirty and unmarried it gave rise to rumors that they delighted in encouraging.

Noel needed these loans, material representations of loyalty and support, not only from friends but from acquaintances as sort of a litmus test. Noel never hesitated to ask anyone for money when he needed it, even after he was famous and supposedly rich. Actually Noel was often on "empty." If someone refused him money when he determined they had no reason to, he would drop them. But if they gave him money he never forgot their kindness.

Arlen's loan saved *The Vortex*, which became Noel's first commercial success. It is different from the works that followed. This is a play as dark and tortured and strange as anything by Tennessee Williams or Eugene O'Neill. It is usually described as a play about drug addiction, inasmuch as the "Nicky" character (Noel's role) takes drugs and gets testy about it in the play. In reality it's a play about an aging beauty (Nicky's mother, Florence) who is involved with a young smooth-brained jock (Tom Veryan) and is desperately trying to hang on to her famous beauty and youth at the expense of her husband and son.

Being a theme play it has no real plot. But even reading it is so compelling that no one wonders why it was such a sensation. A play having the same theme and written as well would probably take the theatre by storm even today. The same theme was used in the late 1930s in the Bette Davis film *Mr. Skeffington,* and recycled several times by Tennessee Williams in his own plays. The idea of an older woman having an affair with a young, virile man was a mature theme for the twenty-three-year-old Coward to devise and execute so successfully. But it was the sophistication of the idle rich people he depicted that caused him to become the icon of the gay young theatre goers of Jazz Age London.

Noel's play had some innovations. He wore the famous silk dressing gown over pajamas that became his trademark. All the characters did things with cigarettes that were intriguing; cigarettes were just becoming the prop of the jaded sophisticate, and in one scene Florence applies her favorite perfume to a cigarette before lighting it, saying to her friend, "Do you ever do this? It's divine." At the start of Act II Noel's stage directions for the party scene state, ". . . the air must be black with cigarette smoke." But this scene is startling for another reason. Coward insisted that there must be sense of a whirling gay party with everyone talking at once, but actual lines spoken while dancing timed perfectly to reach the audience as the speakers pass near the footlights. (We must remember that this was written in 1923 and movies were still simple and without much visual spectacle.)

"This scene will probably be exceedingly difficult to produce, but it is absolutely indispensable," said Noel. Indeed, this kind of picking out key characters at certain times during an ongoing dance scene, with pan-ins and -outs, and a sense of getting closeups during a crowd scene was extremely advanced for the time. It wasn't until movies began using the technique that it was actually perfected. To attempt it on a stage at a time of limited, almost nonexistent technology shows the early Coward genius that created such a storm in London.

Noel did not invent the kind of bitchy sophistication dialogue that characterizes this play, but he voiced it better than anyone else in the '20s and '30s and so it has become known as "Cowardesque."

Lines such as these (which were of course modeled after the work of Oscar Wilde and George Bernard Shaw) are imbedded throughout the first act:

"He's divinely selfish; all amusing people are."

"I've got a frightful headache."

"Why don't you take off your hat?"

"Oh, my God, look at that lamp shade!"

"I gave it to her last Christmas."

"Wasn't that naughty of you?"

"Now I must lie down *flat*—Get out of the way, Helen."

"Perhaps you'd like *both* of us to go *right* out of the room and sit in the *hall*?"

"No, Pawnie, I should never expect the least consideration from you. Thank you, Helen darling—I shall always come to you when I'm ill."

"That *will* be nice."

Or, most bitchy:

"Poor Clara—she eternally labors under the delusion that she really matters."

There are several gay insinuations in the play, with varying flushes of overt and covert innuendo. The character of Pawnie is an aging queen fully immersed in interior decoration, with a sharp interest in straight athletic young men. He is dryly caustic about those he considers gay as well. Pawnie is described in Noel's directions as "an elderly maiden gentleman," whose real name is Pauncefort Quentin, hardly the kind of name you'd give to a rugby player. Coward uses his rapier on his own character as well; he has Tom Veryan (a good jock name) describe Nicky as "up in the air—effeminate." A rather daring description to make about a character one has written for oneself.

It is subtly insinuated throughout the play that the Nicky character has a secret other than simple drug abuse. There is something dysfunctional about the Lancaster household. Nicky has a strained reserved relationship with his father, who feigns interest. His mother automatically rejects his girl before meeting her, obviously reflecting her fear of having a child old enough to marry but also worried about having a pretty young woman around to compete with. When Bunty is not as pretty in person the mother accepts her, then gets really angry when the girl steals Tom Veryan from her.

It is made clear that Nicky does not really love Bunty and is only superficially angry when the short engagement is broken off. His more immediate concern is resolving his thwarted relationship with his mother, and he uses his minor drug problem as a tool to get her to focus on becoming more a mother and less a social butterfly. The Lancaster family relationships are similar to those of the Coward family in some ways. But if the play is autobiographical at all the characters are from Noel's early exposure to the high-society sophisticates he met at Mrs. Astley-Cooper's house. What is important here is that he presents his own character as a closeted homosexual dilettante. Ironically, for a time, the character of Noel/Nicky become the epitome of what every young man of society, straight or gay in London, wanted to be.

Besides becoming an innovative playwright Noel also made a name for himself with his particular brand of acting. Actress Sybil Thorndike gives great insight:

"Oh, my goodness, what an actor! As an actor he was absolutely in the front. He could play these nervous strange people, hysterical people, which is very rare. I think that if he hadn't been such a wonderful playwright he could have been right in the forefront as a really hysterical actor. And it's only people who are hysterical who can play hysterical parts. He was absolutely wonderful. You see, he could scream! He was nervous, you know. He had awful nerves. But he couldn't have been the hysterical actor he was if he hadn't."

Noel, the hysterical, nervous actor was also often the nervous person. He needed, like all creative people, to surround himself with people who understood him, encouraged him, because he'd react hysterically whenever he ran into the slightest hint from his company that he wasn't wonderful and right all the time.

Like Cole Porter in Paris, Noel Coward too had assembled his family of nurturers. His own real family had become somewhat of a drain.

With Noel's spectacular success in the mid-1920s Violet's wish to vindicate her long suffering began. Unlike Kate Porter, Violet became demanding, determined to get some of her own back. She had supported Noel's struggle, sacrificed for his career, and now she felt that it was her career too. She probably didn't understand the magnitude of her son's new fame. He was not just a successful playwright and actor, he soon became a superstar. In those days the term hadn't been coined yet, but the status existed and had the same social benefits and privileges that it carries today.

It also meant that the star was suddenly removed from his one plane of society and transported to a higher echelon where almost none of his past associations could go with him. Because Noel never interrupted his special brand of affection and interaction with her, sharing in letters and conversation all that he did, Violet could not understand why she was left behind more and more as his fame grew. Not for her this business of struggling selflessly to help her son, then stepping aside so the world could have him. She still wanted him too. But Noel now had others who could give him the support Violet had once provided: Jeffrey, Gladys, and Lorn Lorraine.

Lorn began doing secretarial duties part-time for Noel. After *The Vortex* caused an avalanche of mail and phone calls Lorn immediately was "raised" to Gal Friday, and remained in that position all her life. Noel and she were as one; they agreed on everything. She can be likened to the character Della in *Perry Mason*. Noel's life was her life; his friends were her friends. At one time she developed a close friendship with Tallulah (Bankhead, in case there's another one out there), and because Tallulah was rumored to be girl crazy, Lorn asked her about it. Tallulah told her, with her usual frankness, that when she played with herself she thought about men.

After *The Vortex* Noel's *Fallen Angels*, starring Tallulah, took London by storm. Noel could not take Tallulah's obnoxious behavior for long. Her drunken foibles and undisciplined girlish behavior made her company basically too much to handle even for theatre people. But she and Lorn became friends and remained so.

Noel trusted Lorn with his privacy. He was completely at home with her, even more perhaps than with his own family and even with Cole Lesley, who would become his secretary/companion/valet in the 1930s. Noel regarded Cole as a servant, despite his real love and attachment for him. Lorn was considered an equal, a person who could make decisions for him if need be because she thought exactly as he did, reacted as he did, and was openly and lovingly working toward his goals as purposefully as Noel was.

Lorn also may have been the only "real" relationship he had with a woman. He had a strong commitment to his mother, and deep friendships with Marlene Dietrich and Gertrude Lawrence, but these all had some other aura to them. Lorn was simply a woman who was close to him and accepted him as he was. She was not a legend, nor a star, nor a servant, relative, or fellow actor. There was no fantasy involved with her, no sex, no adoration—just a solid and realistic relationship between two ordinary people. Lorn helped Noel to keep his bearings because she was always there, at home, on call for him. He considered her an equal. This kind of relationship was vital to his sanity. She could say things to him that no one else could and he would accept them. She knew when not to speak, when to make a point. This kind of presence is extremely necessary for a person who must make his life in the public eye, and especially make his living in a world of pretense, fantasy, and egotism.

Lorn Lorraine was her chosen name. She'd been Lorn MacNaughtan and had had actual theatrical experience as a girl, which surprised the little coterie because she was so retiring and hated being with large groups of people. She was a loner and as such was eminently suited to her job with Noel. She was no competition for his at-home performances, although she did have some wicked ribald stories to tell about her early theatre days, that delighted him. Lorn concentrated on details, which enabled her to comfortably handle the large amount of correspondence that flowed in. She preferred working in the background, preferred to fade after she'd done her job of preparing and arranging.

Although she was perhaps the closest person to Noel for forty-six years—she died shortly before he did—there is little in the way of stories to tell about her. She was like his heart; it was always there beating and keeping him going.

Gladys too was like an accepting, loving big sister. They were professional as well as personal friends. Throughout his career he insisted that producers hire Gladys. She did not work exclusively for him, of course, and he often used the designer Molyneux's dresses for his characters as well. After Noel and Gladys took *The Vortex* to New York Gladys at one point went to work for Eva Le Gallienne's company. Le Gallienne was one of Broadway's leading actresses of the '20s and she'd had the audacity to found her own repertory company.

Certainly "Miss Le G," as she insisted on being called ("Le G" by privileged close friends), was noted for her grand manner offstage. She was a lesbian of reknown. In fact her own girlish tendencies caused a scandal during the time of her repertory company's many rebirths and she was unfairly linked with actresses who were not inclined to homosexuality at all. Theatre was her first love, her temple, and she did not mix sex with professional relationships. One of her protégés was Farley Granger.

Noel had no use for Eva's attitude toward theatre; he thought it silly, pompous, and tiresome. To him theatre was supposed to entertain first and foremost. He disliked the artsy crowd. Still Gladys wanted to work in New York and this provided her with an excellent entrée, for despite Noel's razzberries, Miss Le G had a staunch battery of supporters and admirers who retained their devotion to her all her life.

The camaraderie and support he obtained from his gang also made it possible to keep the pose of womanizer required by his public image now that success had made its nosy way to his door. There is not a lot that needs to be detailed about these people except that they provided excellent support for him and devised the nickname "The Master," which became his title for life. Noel now socialized with famous people and made a lot of money. He soon bought a country home, Goldenhurst, and established a permanent home in London at Gerald Road. His little family adored him, helping him through both dark days and bright. They traveled with him, or kept the home fires burning. When he moved they helped him pull his houses together into sanctuaries of work and privacy. When he hosted the famous they helped with the meals and arrangements, the beds and the conversation.

All these people continued the nurturing of the creative Noel, which had begun with Violet. Creative people need feedback, even if it's from noncreative people. They need to be told how clever they are, how the world is waiting for their next contribution, their next bon mot.

VI

"Don't You Know, Little Fool, You Never Can Win"

NOTHING FUELS CREATIVITY LIKE PASSION. We all experience passion, either in spurts or—as in the cases of Noel and Cole—as a prime motivating focus of their lives. They were passionate people, headlong in love with life and all its emotional wonders. Even though both of them saw being in love as something foolish, that didn't stop them from falling when the arrow of love picked them off. Always it was doomed to fail because neither could afford the emotional or professional pretense of letting down the facade of brittle wit and urbane sophistication to dissolve into romantic jelly.

The phrases "fool for love" or "my foolish heart" appear again and again in the lyrics and writings of both men. Cole wrote:

A fool there was, goes the story,
A fool there was not long ago,
Who dreamed of love in all its glory,
He was mad, poor fool, he didn't know.

Noel wrote:

I know it's stupid to be mad about the boy. . . .
I know I'm potty, but I'm mad about the boy.

Noel particularly was nagged by the idea that he was no good at love. In a way it was a self-fulfilling prophecy that afflicts many gay people; they take it for granted that romantic love, as defined by heterosexuals, is not achievable, and must be denied them. Although Porter and Coward considered love a foolish thing even to attempt, both kept attempting it, and both got stung. (The self-fulfilling prophecy at work.)

John C. Wilson (known as Jack) was a very handsome WASP from Yale (there several years after Cole) who knew how to peddle his looks and personality on the romantic front for personal gain. This is a type that is well known among gay men, the handsome hustler, who is nonetheless talented and might have an education, a career, even a family fortune, but needs the kick of knowing he got there on his looks. He was exactly right for Noel, who was a pushover for a handsome man. Jack Wilson came into Noel's life at a time when everything had suddenly exploded for the playwright. *The Vortex* was the major hit in London; Noel was being idolized, analyzed, lionized, and adored; he was suddenly rich enough to buy all the silk dressing gowns he wanted and a place in the country, as well as a used Rolls-Royce to get him there.

Who could blame him for thinking that Jack Wilson was part of his dream come true as well?

Noel had sex with scores of men, and emotional involvements on a short-term basis with many people, including women, but had only two relationships that truly qualified as love affairs. Jack Wilson was the first and Graham Payn was the other. The two men were direct opposites of each other in temperament, personality, background, and approach, yet both evoked the same kind of responses in Noel.

Jack Wilson was aggressive, caustic, and manipulative. He had a difficult time with his own homosexuality and it was reflected in his relationship with Noel, whom he saw as not only a lover but a father figure (despite their closeness in age) and a source of wealth.

Both relationships caused Noel Coward frustration, but for different reasons. Both men illustrated Noel's bewilderment about how to conduct himself in a love relationship. If these relationships with men had been based purely on sex it would have been no problem; if they had been professional and social interactions they wouldn't have caused him confusion. He had a natural ability with people in all kinds of situations, except when it came to love. Then he was lost and the self-confident Noel Coward disappeared.

JACK WILSON IS ONE OF THE CURIOSITIES in the lives of both Noel Coward and Cole Porter. He would later produce and direct some of their best shows. Wilson would become, in fact, a brilliant theatrical showman, who came to the theater with no training except as a stockbroker and Noel Coward's first lover.

Wilson's theatrical career began with *The Vortex*. He was in the audience one night in London and soon he became one of the strongest and often most negative influences on the youthful Noel Coward. When Jack Wilson made his entrance Noel was giddy with his first rush of overwhelming fame. He was only twenty-five, and had just achieved everything he'd ever wanted. When he looked out across the footlights during the early part of the show one night he saw sitting in the front row a young and strikingly handsome man so deeply absorbed in the performance that both Noel and his costar Lillian Braithwaite began playing to him. It was a sudden case of the spectator having as much effect on a performer as the reverse. For that performance Noel was the enraptured spectator and the real star was sitting in the stalls.

When Jack came backstage two nights later to introduce himself, for Noel it must have been a situation akin to "all this and heaven too." No one can blame Coward for falling headlong and dizzy under the spell of the aggressive young American. Many others were to follow suit in the years to come, either because of Jack's personal charm and smooth beauty, or because Noel forced them to accept Wilson whether or not they liked him.

Noel was soon to go to New York for the show's opening there; Jack, who was a stockbroker on Wall Street, invited him to have lunch on his arrival. Gaga with lust, Noel said yes.

John Chapman Wilson was born in New Jersey in 1899 and attended Yale, where he actually studied theatre under Monty Woolley. He spent some years as a stockbroker, which he disliked. Once paired with Noel he used the opportunity to establish a fine reputation as a Broadway producer. Jack was a genuine talent, so his other behavior seems at odds with his ability. He was definitely a con man to an extent but his successes indicate that he didn't need to use sex to get ahead.

Meanwhile Noel's success continued. The press gave him the star treatment and naturally he encouraged them in all they wished to do. Interviews? Yes. Photographs of Noel sitting up in bed, smoking a cigarette, and wearing silk pajamas and robe? Yes.

Turtleneck sweaters, adopted by Noel, soon became the rage in London, as did anything he did or said. And he did and said plenty. He discoursed about everything from the length of women's skirts to the political situation.

Noel's nucleus of people now also included Joyce Carey, the daughter of Lillian Braithwaite and matinee idol Gerald Lawrence. The coterie moved as one in those days, the little hardy band, unaware of how soon it was to change when another large bird would settle into their nest, crowding them all.

Noel went to New York armed with the invitation to lunch with Jack during his first week there. He appeared at the appointed place and hour and Jack did not. Noel waited for "ages"; one can read hesitation, doubt rationalizations, excuses made for the lateness, until it became obvious no one was coming. Noel ate alone at a drug store and fumed, "Boy, let that be a lesson to ya!"

When the show opened Jack appeared at the age door in a rage, accusing Noel of not answering his invitation. It was all due to a postal mix-up, but the two of them had it out in the theatre alley. After two more false starts, Jack came to dinner at Noel's digs, and the sun shone once more. Within a few months Jack had deserted the bulls and bears of Wall Street.

It's perhaps too easy to be cynical about Wilson's motives. Did he share the emotional feeling that Noel had for him, or was he using Noel to establish a career in the theatre? The answer is probably that he was attracted to and fond of Noel but much of his feelings were based on the help Noel could give him. The handsome young Wilson would have sex with anyone who could advance his position. Perhaps only Lorn Lorraine knew for sure whether Jack had any genuine feelings for Noel. The fact that she backed off from her initial dislike of Wilson indicates that she might have decided that his feelings were genuine even if his actions were upsetting. In any case Noel was in love and was determined to believe in Jack no matter what the appearances.

When Jack hitched his wagon to Noel's star he hardly left his side. They were always together, dressing alike, being photographed with Noel's arm draped over Jack's shoulders, a happy smile illuminating his face.

At first there was a real resentment, even hostility toward Wilson from Lorn and the other members of Noel's "family." Why this parvenu from America should have suddenly been given czar-like control over Noel's whole life was incomprehensible. But Noel was adamant. He later even signed an agreement giving Jack a huge percentage of everything he made all his life. The arrows of love pierced that sophisticated exterior deeply.

Subsequently Noel wrote a song, "Mad About the Boy."

> I basked in his attraction for a couple of hours or so,
> His manners were a fraction too meticulous,
> If he was real or not I couldn't tell
> But like a fool, I fell.

It was madness that made Noel give over his life at the start of his career to this person. He said in the song,

> He has a gay appeal
> That makes me feel
> There's maybe something sad about the boy.

Jack had many qualities that appealed to Noel. He seemed to know all about money and Noel was fascinated by money, although more as a spectator than a speculator. Noel lacked the patience to sit down and learn how to build a secure financial base. He assumed that Jack would do it for him. That matter neatly settled he gave Jack carte blanche to do his worst—and Jack loyally did just that. Eventually Wilson almost ruined his lover financially.

But in the glory days of first love Noel basked in the fact that Jack was to be his manager and financial Svengali. The objections of his coterie were turned aside, as were the jealousies that were to arise through the years. Noel was in love.

It may be difficult for people to understand how important it was to Noel to have someone like Jack Wilson as his bona fide lover. Even though Noel had had his share of "trophies" on the sexual field of endeavor, Jack represented his ultimate ideal of the prize. This factor is of no small import to many gay men who continually seek the next sexual trophy. As soon as they obtain one the fantasy vanishes and the person becomes ordinary, not godlike. Jack's ploy of never really being possessed, of keeping just one step ahead, of keeping Noel insecure, is what enabled him to control the playright for so many years; he never lost his luster.

This factor was momentous to Noel, who needed to succeed with the best and not just succeed, but possess. It's why he became the kind of legendary star he did; why he needed to seduce a member of the royal family, to be friends with as many of the others as he could; why he needed to compete and succeed on so many levels of the theatre. He had to be the best and always have the best. In Jack Wilson he found a counterpart to himself, he believed. Just as Wilson wouldn't have allied himself romantically with a nobody, so Noel wouldn't have fallen in love with him had he not been such a catch in so many ways. The whole relationship boiled down to "look what I got."

Besides his wonderful appearance, which became renowned as he and Noel traveled to the Riviera, the Lido, Paris, and other haunts frequented by Cafe Society, Jack had a cutting, caustic wit. Only his looks and charm—the latter a product of his smooth WASP upbringing—enabled him to get away with the outrageous things he said and did.

Wilson continued to make his home in New York, so the love affair was usually a long-distance one. This was not unusual for the international denizens; even heterosexual married couples in that milieu spent little time together. Noel gave Jack power of attorney, a startling move and a dangerous one, considering he didn't know much about Jack; Jack had very little experience to warrant trusting him with so large a responsibility.

Noel wrote ruefully later in life that he was no good at love; Jack Wilson was very good at it from a career point of view. He assuredly was extremely uncomfortable with his own sexual predilections and needed to find some other justification for being in a homosexual relationship with this highly visible star. Many men like him, raised in traditional and conservative situations, find themselves at odds with themselves as their gay tendencies crash against what they have been taught is the correct way of conducting one's life. There was an inner battle raging, and Jack turned to alcohol to ease it.

Jack needed to rationalize, "Well, I am his manager, his personal manager, so there is a very valid and acceptable business reason for us to be hugging each other here on the beach at the Lido." In truth they both needed the respectability of the arrangement. Noel probably jumped into the idea so quickly because he was anxious to cement the relationship, and felt that love alone was not a strong enough adhesive.

If Jack needed the front, Noel needed the security. There is no doubt that sincere or not Jack would not have bothered with a long-term commitment if there was not something else in it for him.

From the start it became evident to Lorn and Noel that Jack was stealing. It was treated as a joke at first, a harmless trait, and there would be funny letters in verse back and forth about it. Jack accepted the fact that they knew and joked back. Why he needed to steal the silver when the house was being handed to him shows how twisted his psyche was. He may have done it as a way of proving that he was only in this for the money, that he wasn't really gay. It was a way of getting back at Noel for forcing Jack into a gay marriage that he basically had contempt for—a way of rejecting his own homosexuality, a statement to himself that he wasn't really queer. This hustler mentality has buzzed through homosexual life for decades; as long as the hustler is getting paid somehow he can say to himself and to society that he isn't really gay, he just does it for the money.

Yet Jack was tremendously jealous of his position as Noel's lover. They moved in international circles where perhaps half of the powerful people in their set were gay or lesbian. Cole Porter and Elsa Maxwell, Elsie de Wolfe, and Bessie Marbury all accepted the two lovers. Whatever emotional or financial motives he had Jack wanted the relationship and was willing to make great efforts to keep it going.

If Lorn and the rest of Noel's extended family wondered what made him go so overboard on Jack Wilson, some of the answer had to do with a sudden acceptance of his own homosexuality upon truly falling in love. Two things can happen when a gay man falls in love and agrees to be a partner to another man. He either wants to shout it from the housetops, or he has a lot of adjusting to do to walk down the street with his lover, feeling that every hostile eye is upon him. Noel was part of the first group; Jack might have been part of the latter.

Coward claims that during the long American tour of *The Vortex*, in 1925, "I had forced myself to write a play. It had been a tremendous strain and I felt that many months of creative impulse had been frustrated."

He called the play *Semi-monde* (an appropriate English translation would be "part-world" or "half-world"). The setting was the public rooms of the Ritz Hotel in Paris and the action took place over a three-year period.

"It was well constructed and, on the whole, well written . . ." but Coward knew "its production in London or New York seemed unlikely, as some of the characters, owing to lightly suggested abnormalities, would certainly be deleted by the censor . . ." He meant that they were gay.

The obvious question is why Noel chose to write about the plight of the homosexual during this period. Was it because after years of masquerading he'd finally come out himself in his relationship with Jack Wilson? Love motivates people to open up. The sudden acceptance of himself as a lover by someone who until then was a fantasy in his mind—one that he feared might never be realized—made him feel whole. He liked himself. He liked his gayness. He began to move around in himself as a different person, someone who was loved in a special exclusive way for himself. It had nothing to do with being a big star—it had everything to do with feeling loved. His self-doubt was erased. The simple act of having Jack say "I love you" made a new person out of him.

Semi-monde was never produced in Coward's lifetime. (It was finally done in 1977, in London after his death and during the heyday of gay liberation.)

According to Noel: ". . . Max Reinhardt, however, was enthusiastic about it, and it was translated into German by Rudolph Kommer, and taken in due course to Berlin, where for years it escaped production by a hair's breadth until eventually Vicky Baum wrote *Grand Hotel* and *Semi-monde* being too closely similar in theme, faded gently into oblivion."

One wonders what might have happened if this play had been produced back in the 1920s by a playwright of Noel's talent and stature. During the same period Mae West wrote the play *Sex* for Broadway, which included homosexual characters. She went to jail for one night for it, but the play broke new ground.

But Coward gave up the idea of serious drama and returned to writing the fluff comedies so popular in the era.

Throughout the decade Cole and Linda and Noel and Jack

attended the marvelous party that was the 1920s for those who had money. They met all types in their lives of fame and brilliance. In London, New York, in Paris, on the Continent—there were few places on earth they didn't go.

The Porters made places fashionable just by visiting. Their friends included everyone from "Elsa" to Gerald and Sara Murphy, who popularized the phrase "living well is the best revenge." The Porters lived very well.

Douglas Fairbanks, Jr., first met Cole Porter at the salon of two gay men in postwar Paris, Jerry Thayer and Noel Sullivan. Doug's mother was a great friend of Thayer's.

Fairbanks recalls, "Noel's salons attracted a marvelously mixed bag."

It was here that Fairbanks met Jean Cocteau, Gertrude Stein, Louis Bromfield, Sasha Guitry, Ernest Hemingway, and "I think it was also the place where I first met the friendly Cole Porter and Elsa Maxwell, who was bowling her jolly way through the Europe of the whirling early twenties."

Miss Maxwell was prominent among the large group of famous dragons who inhabited the arena of fame during the first half of the twentieth century. She was known primarily as a party giver. She described her first party when she was young and had no money as having some royalty and others to her humble studio where they sat on crates and ate her small fare and had a wonderful time. As her popularity grew and her famous friends continued their RSVP's this homely overweight lesbian became more and more famous for the tacky-sounding parties she threw. The difference was now that she threw parties for money, as a business. She became the power broker of the smart set and whatever she was doing became the thing to do. Among the people who loved her was Cole Porter. They were great friends and Cole confided in her often.

It would be fun to recount the first impressive meeting of these two sophisticates of the early twentieth century. Cole Porter and Noel Coward—one can imagine the bon mots—the dueling solo piano performances of witty lyrics.

Alas, their first meeting, sometime in the early '20s in Paris, was not momentous. Both were headed for success but neither had reached it. Both had published songs but neither had had a big hit. All they really had in common at their first meeting was that both were struggling songwriters who happened to be gay. They didn't become great friends immediately—it was only after Noel's success and his friendship with Jack Wilson that he and Cole Porter became serious friends.

Elsa Maxwell dubbed them Noely and Coley. In turn Noel referred to her as "a rose by any other name dropper." And she was. It is hard to locate a written tract by Miss Maxwell that does not refer to one of her famous friends within a few sentences. Her need for status came close to matching her physical bulk, and name dropping was her career. It was an extremely flattering necessity for anyone seeking fame to have Elsa consider them worthy of mention. And people wanted Elsa to drop their names. They wanted the fame and the sucking up she so willingly lavished on them. To have Elsa Maxwell approve of you meant you were worth something; otherwise she wouldn't bother. Cole was one of her obvious favorites, possibly because his affection for her was genuine.

Like her or not, and most did, she was not to be ignored any more than denizens of Hollywood could afford to ignore Louella Parsons. After Elsa and Cole became friends, she fell in love with his songs before most of the rest of the world did. Although Cole certainly gave bigger and better parties than Elsa could afford, their friendship deepened with the years. When he gave a famous party at his palazzo in Venice while Linda was away (which included drag queens running amok in Linda's designer originals), Elsa was there being as outrageous as the rest.

Cole and Elsa had many fallings out. It's interesting that he called her "Miss Liar" to her face because Cole invested much in his own fictions. Elsa's stories are as entertaining as her parties were. And that was the key to her popularity. She was immensely entertaining. For that Cole always had to patch up with her and they remained lifelong friends. Noel Coward did not seem to care much about her. But like Cole he worked her into his lyrics to capture the inanity of the society in which they traveled.

Elsa Maxwell was Cole's favorite real-life person to appear in his lyrics. One of his very best songs, written first as a parlor piece for her birthday, is "I'm Dining with Elsa." It was written over seventy years ago and is as fresh and relevant now as it was the night he first sang it to her in Paris. He refers to the guests secretly going to dine with Elsa and her ninety-nine most intimate friends. That phrase has been used again and again—it's one of his lines that people respond to so well, they want to say it themselves. In recent times it was used for Truman Capote and his 300 most intimate friends, and Malcolm Forbes and his 2,000 most intimate friends and for Michael Jackson, and for Elizabeth Taylor's most recent wedding.

Cole often wrote the names of his Cafe Society friends into his lyrics, knowing that their names would be immediately recognizable to the public. Elsie de Wolfe had become famous for her black-and-white designs. Cole immortalized her and the trend in interior design in 1919 with his song "Black and White Baby."

> Now since my sweetheart Sal met Miss Elsie de Wolfe,
> The leading decorator of the nation . . .

Of course he also plugged the scotch whisky:

> She even drinks Black and White . . .

On a personal level Cole needed socially acceptable friends who were homosexually oriented, and of course Elsie de Wolfe and Elsa were lesbians of the first magnitude. Elsa Maxwell's ingenuity and ability to sell her plain and ugly self to the world's elite impressed Cole. And she was probably more of a beard than Linda ever could be, allowing Cole to camp it up at the Lido with his necklaces and parasols and ogling of the beefy common men passing by. Elsa would be privy to all the gossip and know who was screwing whom, which was very high on Cole's list of interesting topics. She was his friend, and she was never boring, two things of inestimable value to Cole.

Elsa claimed to have saved Cole Porter from despair, from giving up his songwriting career. He was depressed, according to her tale, and she bucked him up. "You're too good," she told him, "it's just that the world hasn't caught up with you yet." Small wonder she and Cole became tight friends. She as just the kind of outrageous charlatan he loved, and she supported him wholeheartedly.

In reality she was a good musician and this contributed to her relationship with Porter, as well as with Coward and others who could give credence to her support and criticisms.

Her job, she said, was to entertain the rich. Despite her claim to detest this whole group of people on the one hand (and she claimed Cole detested it as well) she continued doing her job, pressing on through the money, the parties, the royalties engendered by her later books. When the Waldorf-Astoria opened its doors, they offered her a free apartment, with all services gratis as a means of establishing the hotel as *the* place. They gave Cole Porter his penthouse at a nominal charge for the same reason. It worked. Elsa's name and Porter's magic combined to make the Waldorf the most exclusive hotel in New York City. It has never lost its luster.

Elsa's life is an example of how people of that generation could become rich and successful just by being rich and successful. She was the focal point of the social structure that held these people together. She more than anyone personifies the generation of rich, spoiled, bored people from all countries who formed what has come to be known as the haute monde. Some people say this is a fictional world, but it existed and it met at Elsa's place, wherever Elsa was. People like Elsa and Cole created it because there was a need for it, and it shaped much of the world during those times.

Elsa was one of the most intriguing personalities of that

whole era of famous people. She was the only one who
didn't seem to have any reason to be there, yet she knew
everyone. She had no talent, no achievement, no money, no
social position. She was no beauty—decidedly not that! She
was a lesbian, so she couldn't or wouldn't marry a millionaire—nor would one marry her. She once wrote that she
had nothing to recommend her, yet she was popular. Her
honesty was refreshing in that group of self-deluded suckers,
and maybe that's why they needed her, even more than the
diversion she provided during those otherwise empty hours.

If she influenced Cole's work it was through her friendship, encouragement, and appreciation during those early
days before the world accepted him. And Elsa indirectly
introduced him to the one man of his dreams.

The city of Venice had hired Elsa to promote the Lido
and in 1923 she convinced Cole to join her there. Paris, like
any big city, was too hot in the summer (in the estimation
of the idle rich) so the Cole Porters went off to the beach.
For four consecutive summers Cole and Linda rented palaces in Venice—first the Barbaro, then the Papadopoli, and
finally the Rezzonico. They threw lavish parties. Cole
brought Bricktop down from Paris. Then he imported Leslie
"Hutch" Hutchinson, and his jazz group. Cole loved to brag
that the black musician had more talents than just *le jazz
hot*. Eventually the police asked Cole to leave Venice because of his outrageous behavior.

But it was in Venice, that romantic dream of his youth,
that Cole Porter fell in love—gushing, cliché-ridden love.
He hated it. Being in love with cobwebs in your eyes and
marshmallow in your shoes is inelegant.

When Cole hosted a spectacular production at his Palazzo
Rezzonico by the Ballet Russe of Serge Diaghilev, he came
in close contact with Boris Kochno. Boris, Diaghilev's personal secretary, was about as pretty as a man can get and
still look like a man. He was not Cole's usual type, being
intelligent, refined, and enormously well-mannered. Cole
tumbled backward, struck by something in the serious,
quiet Kochno that he'd never before encountered.

Kochno had been Diaghilev's secretary from the time he was sixteen. He and the ballet maestro were Russian refugees from the then-recent, now-defunct revolution. Boris was not Diaghilev's lover, as is usually assumed, but their relationship was deeply close and connected because it involved the ballet, and that was the maestro's life. Diaghilev could never bring himself to be intimate with intelligent men, preferring the homosexual equivalent of dumb blondes, so the association never became physical. Serge was involved with his lead dancer Serge Lifar at the time. Lifar, like Diaghilev's previous star and lover Nijinsky, was brilliant about ballet but basically stupid about worldly affairs. Kochno was *not* naive, and there was a deep mutual possessiveness and love between Kochno and Diaghilev.

Kochno was an extension of Diaghilev. He functioned as his alter ego, freeing the maestro to concentrate on the artistic side of the company while Kochno handled the details of his personal and professional life.

In Russia dance is considered a manly art, the ultimate expression of the Russian soul. Emotion is displayed through dance by these taciturn men. The fierce Cossacks danced their mazurkas when happy, angry, jealous over a lover. One Cossack story tells of a Russian father being enraged with his rebellious son, and dragging him outside and dancing a mazurka on his body to punish him.

Russians are also mystical; dancers must see their art as a religion and devote themselves to it completely. They must have no other life. Russians, at least at that time in history, had had a long nondemocratic tradition. It had not been so long since they'd been serfs and the idea of one person having total ownership over another was not unreasonable. This leads us to the kind of relationship Diaghilev had with Kochno.

At sixteen Boris was sent to meet the maestro. He was received by mistake into Diaghilev's apartment by the butler, who was expecting someone else. The butler opened the door, took a surprised and appreciative survey of the boy, and advised his employer to see him. Diaghilev was an older man then; he looked like a wall-eyed Billy Joel with a paunch. The maestro hired Boris on the spot and moved him in. He told him early that he expected Boris to anticipate all his wishes and fulfill them if he expected to be his secretary. Diaghilev needed someone who could instinctively anticipate his needs. Even though a psychic bond sprang up between them Boris was never Diaghilev's lover.

Boris was extremely intelligent and forbearing. Although not a dancer he had the same whole-minded devotion to theatre, to his master, and to the ballet company Diaghilev headed. Diaghilev was a genius, almost a deity among the haute monde of the times. He never paid Boris a salary of any kind, although the secretary's lodgings, clothing, and food were taken care of. If he wanted cigarettes, he had to ask for the money to buy them. He was like a Russian monk devoted to serving one person, an arrangement common to their ethnic tradition. Diaghilev owned Kochno as surely as if he'd bought him in old Russia, where they used to advertise serfs for sale in the newspaper classifieds.

When Cole Porter met Boris to discuss the mechanics of producing the ballet they spent hours together over extended periods of time. It is evident that an affair took place.

Cole Porter, with his kind and considerate nature toward people in general and handsome men in particular, was a welcome relief to Boris, who'd spent his whole life bowing to autocratic behavior from great people. Here was Cole, richer than a king, successful and talented as well, treating him with genuine warmth and respect.

Cole put the make on Kochno in short order. This was an area in which he was well versed too, and he'd had much practice. Soon Cole found himself in love. It was obviously the kind of thing that can be called an infatuation, although it is also obvious that Boris reciprocated some feeling. Cole sent him letters saying things like, "How you've complicated my life and how I welcome it." Cole would have gone the whole route and taken Boris as his mate if he could. But he could not.

How the affair ended is unclear. There were several factors at work. Serge Diaghilev had no use for Cole. He might envy the unearned wealth that Cole commanded but he was snooty about the kind of music that Porter wrote. Diaghilev always pretended not to remember what Cole did for a living. When this upstart from America tried to woo away his right-hand man Diaghilev must have viewed it as an act of war. Serge saw Boris as his possession. When Cole's letters began to arrive and the declarations of love, not to mention the flowers and candy and cigarettes, Serge forced Boris to reject the flood of attentions. It worked. Perhaps Boris, who was an intelligent man and had built his life squarely on reading the artistic temperament, knew where his best interests lay. Unpaid though it was he had a career and it was tied up with Diaghilev. Boris went back to the maestro, but he did not destroy the love letters that Cole Porter had sent him. He kept them until his death.

It is unclear whether Linda knew of the depths of Cole's infatuation for Boris. Cole may have harbored thoughts of including the Russian in their *ménage*. The precedence of group living with Howard Sturges already had been established. When it became obvious that Kochno was not going to make the break from Diaghilev, Cole put his feelings on ice, and decided not to fall in love again. Instead he threw himself full throttle into empty sexual encounters until the end of his life. We can speculate that even if Boris had come over to Cole, it wouldn't have worked. Cole had no inclination and no place in his life for a real lover. Boris was a fantasy, and probably Cole would not have fallen in love with him if he'd really believed he was available. For many people it is the game of love, not the fulfillment that is so thrilling. As soon as something becomes available it loses its allure.

ALTHOUGH COLE HAD MISSED his try at true love, Noel was basking in his newfound amour with Jack Wilson. In 1926 with several hits running in New York and London, Noel Coward and his lover toured the Continent. They visited

Somerset and Syrie Maugham in Nice, where they were witnesses to Maugham's caustic treatment of his wife. Writer Beverly Nichols was there that summer too, and remembered Jack Wilson as the handsomest of men and Noel as the wittiest. Then the couple joined the gay gang at the Lido.

Although Coward and Porter had met before, this vacation for Noel and Jack with Cole and Linda in Venice marks the beginning of a friendship that was to last their lifetimes. Coward and Porter instantly recognized the genius in each other and realized they were kindred spirits who shared a sense of outrageous fun. They also knew they'd never be close friends if they spent a lot of time together. Each was a "queen bee" who needed his own world of adoring working bees.

Jack Wilson would also know Cole Porter all his life and became an important person in Cole's future success. But in 1926 Cole regarded him as just another handsome Yalie from another wealthy family. On the Continent Noel could be more himself. He didn't have to be as discreet as he needed to be in London or New York.

Cole never really tried to be discreet about anything he did, whether it was a gay romp or a party trick. He threw lavish outdoor parties in Venice with a typical selfish disregard for his neighbors, and was deeply resented and criticized by the Italian press. He didn't care. He gave even louder and more lavish parties on the Grand Canal. When Linda was away, he simply recast the guest list and gave great parties for the local queens and gays, hosting them like some Mardi Gras King reigning over the mad festivities in his marble palazzo. One party gained public outcry when Cole hired an all-black jazz band to play outdoors. During these party years Cole's prankishness, drinking, and drug taking became legendary. If he were enormously bored, anything could have been licensed to keep the party going. Finally one wild fling was raided by the Venetian police (that must have delighted Cole seeing all those magnificently uniformed swarthy Italians pouring into his house). The scandal was hushed up when it was found that the police chief's own gay son was a guest. Still, Cole was asked to get out of town (the title of a later song). He did.

Throughout the 1920s the Porters alternated among Paris, Venice, and New York. Cole was already making his way up to Harlem, as did everyone seeking some sort of special entertainment in that decade.

Cole wrote two songs at this time, neither of which was presented or published. Neither could possibly be introduced in today's political climate, since it reflects black people in a way that could only be referred to as a cartoon stereotype. One is called "My Harlem Wench," which focuses on the macho discussion of which color of women is better. The other, "The Heaven of Harlem," although reflecting the dreamlike state Cole fell into when he went there, refers to "Lulu Belles," which was a common epithet then for young black women, and he rhymes "soon" with "coon." Enough said.

Harlem nights created an exciting diversion for Cafe Society types in the 1920s and '30s, and even during the '40s. Harlem was used as an after-hours entertainment center by wealthy white folks who went there for the jazz music, the speakeasies, and ultimately the sex that was available in the brothels there. Songs were written about it, some by Cole himself. Ethel Merman recorded a song in which the lead-in verse has a line that goes, "I went up to Harlem, but Harlem failed . . ." to end her depression.

Slavery had ended only about twenty-five years before the birth of Cole Porter but mention of "coon" notwithstanding, Cole does not appear to have shared the same prejudices toward black people as his society friends. He once went to Edward Molyneux, the Paris designer, for a formal gown to be worn by Bricktop, the famous American expatriate whom Cole had helped establish as a singer and nightclub owner in Paris. Molyneux demurred, saying that Princess Marina of Greece had chosen the design for herself and it would be scandalous if she discovered it was being worn by a . . . well, you know.

Cole's face went hard and cold. He reminded his designer friend that Linda Porter spent more at his salon in a month than the whole Greek family did in a year. He escorted Bricktop to an elegant opening wearing the magnificent gown, which he gave her. Cole delighted in puncturing the overblown self-aggrandizement of these society people, knowing full well where they all had come from. Although he was a snob himself, he decided what to be snobbish about. Porter was not stupid or cruel, nor was he interested in denying himself the company of brilliant people just because they were considered to be on a lower scale socially.

Bricktop was not only intelligent and talented, she made the best impression on the egotistical Mr. Porter anyone could: she sang his songs the way he wanted to hear them. Cole, who would get up and walk out of performances of his songs when they weren't being performed "right," stayed, applauded, and kept coming back for more. Bricktop confessed that after she learned about his habit of walking out she limited herself to doing the songs he'd already approved of for fear of sending him flying.

Cole liked Bricktop enormously and she idolized him. He introduced her to society during the 1920s when he arranged for her to teach the Charleston to his friends. He helped her build her Paris bistro into *the* place to go in that city.

In Harlem black people and white people were more segregated than in Paris except in one arena: sex. New York in the Roaring Twenties had brothels for men who wanted women and for men like Cole Porter. One of these houses in Harlem specialized in young black males. Both Cole and Monty Woolley shopped there. So did Jack Wilson.

The pimp Clint Moore "dealt" in mahogany merchandise. His house in Harlem was fully and richly furnished in this wood and with the mahogany male beauties who serviced the rich homosexuals who frequented the place. It was an exclusive and expensive club comparable to the fabled houses of female prostitution in old New Orleans. Nude black men mingled with the elegantly dressed famous and wealthy males who came to spend the evening. The only attire allowed the prostitutes were white terry cloth robes. Boys in training acted as servants, and guests could watch sexual training sessions through peepholes as older prostitutes taught newer ones the ropes.

Cole was one of the regular and favored customers, drinking and dining with Moore, along with Monty Woolley and Lorenz Hart. Cole became friends with Clint Moore. In later years Moore would sometimes send one of the prostitutes to deliver a fake package to Cole's penthouse at the Waldorf. (This was in the 1930's when his legs had been crippled and he had lost the ability to go out in public without help.) The location of Moore's house was a closely guarded secret. Cole would go there and spend the night steeped in fantasies. Never mind that many of the boys available were fifteen years old, or that the actual "employees" of the place led lives of virtual slavery and degradation. In those days the social consciousness was different; the idea that rich people could buy anything they wanted was a time-honored tradition.

Cole took few precautions to avoid scandal. He and his close buddy Monty Woolley used to cruise the streets of New York (or whatever city they were in together) for the kind of potentially dangerous sexual encounters they favored. Cole liked the tall, burly unwashed truck driver or longshoreman type, the kind of man who would as likely knock his teeth out with his fist as with his genitals. Cole naturally paid for this kind of sex, which was also a kick for him, because his attitude toward sex was tied up with his attitude toward money. He was deeply titillated by the idea of paying for sex.

Cole knew that the kind of men he favored could never fit in with the international high society in which he was a leading figure. He was not about to give up either sex or society. He also was not the kind of person who could be pigeonholed or categorized. Although he loved picking up or sending out for the kind of man that would have a teamster's union card, Cole also liked to surround himself with the more usual types of homosexual coteries that fit the stereotype: bright clothes, flamboyance, fun, and laughs.

His attitude toward his "tricks" was that they were purchases, not unlike his clothes, his champagne, and his houses, and he treated them as such.

By the late 1920s Cole's own disappointment with true love had found its way into lyrics for two of his most popular songs, used in the revue *Wake Up and Dream*. In both songs Cole seems fatalistic, accepting the fact that mere mortals have no control and no answers, when it comes to questions of amour. In "What Is This Thing Called Love?" he writes,

> Love flew in through my window,
> I was so happy then.
> But after love had stayed a little while,
> Love flew out again.

Then even more cruelly, in "I Loved Him but He Didn't Love Me," he muses,

> Then the gods saw you two,
> And indulged in another whim,
> Now he loves you,
> But you don't love him.

This last example expresses the feelings of many who are obsessed with someone until that someone returns the affection. Then the first person loses interest completely. During the turbulent 1920s Cole, highly sexed and having a great number of encounters, experienced this rather common phenomenon. It surely would have happened had he successfully won Kochno from the Ballet Russe.

Cole was finally to have some success. His shows were being produced and well received. Noel's career meanwhile was about to hit a snag.

AFTER THE SUCCESS of *The Vortex* and *Fallen Angels*, as well as *Hay Fever* and *The Queen Was in the Parlor*, Noel was riding high.

Cecil Beaton wrote, "I remember when I was at Cambridge, one night I was on top of a bus going to see a play of his called *The Queen Was in the Parlor,* and I thought really this is worth growing up for. I loved everything that he wrote and copied out sentences and thought he was the most remarkable pattern of the new playwright." Years later Coward and Beaton became friends and Noel advised Cecil: "Your sleeves are too tight, your voice is too high and precise. You mustn't do it. It closes so many doors. It limits you unnecessarily and young men with half your intelligence will laugh at you . . . It's hard, I know. One would like to indulge one's own taste . . . I take ruthless stock of myself in the mirror before going out. A polo jumper or unfortunate tie exposes one to danger."

Noel the "new" playwright, one of the leading "Bright Young Things" as they were called then, knew the media could be his enemy. The worst thing about being famous is seeing oneself misrepresented or criticized for all the world to see. Even constructive and fair criticism made Noel's blood boil. This vulnerability to criticism first surfaced when his play *Sirocco* opened three years after *The Vortex.* It was a dreadful evening as described by Noel himself in *Present Indicative,* and the caustic reviews in the London press led him into a vortex of his own.

By the time *Sirocco* opened Noel had already staged several flops; some were plays he'd written years before, those neophyte efforts that are training for a writer and should have remained hidden. The final curtain at *Sirocco* brought catcalls and hisses from the audiences, unnerving the stars Frances Doble and Ivor Novello. Noel made the mistake of going out for the usual author's ovation and was greeted by silence. "We expected better," someone called out.

"So did I," Noel answered, maintaining his posture. He meant of course that he expected better from the audience. Noel was blaming them for their reaction! Later at the stage door someone spat on him. English audiences didn't spend their theatre shillings carelessly in those days.

This disaster put Noel's ego on the line. He was filled

with self-doubt, depression, and a nagging worry that the press was right—maybe he was indeed a flash in the pan, maybe his genius had been a fiction and his early reception a false start. He describes how Lorn, Gladys, and Jack Wilson eyed him with almost "clinical watchfulness" to gauge his reaction to the slashing reviews. He recalled he was under tremendous pressure to strike just the right pose during this time, not too angry, not too jocular, when what he really wanted to do was throw himself on the floor and scream and rave. But now he was an adult, a paragon of style and poise, a public figure, and the eyes of the haute monde were on him. Now with no training to fall back on, he had to act the part that he had written for himself after this nightmare debacle of *Sirocco*.

Jack accompanied Noel to Edward Molyneux's villa in France, where he exhibited the same concern any other lover would have. Jack's emotional support was strong during these crises. Noel's nervous breakdowns brought out the best in Jack. He was devoted to making sure that Noel was going to survive whatever depressions he went through.

Years later when Noel was again suffering from nervous exhaustion after overextending himself, Jack escorted him from New York to San Francisco and put him on a ship to the Orient, where he was to get away from the pressures of his career. A more cynical person would have allowed him to go alone, as Noel wanted. But Jack insisted on making sure his friend was safely on his way to recuperation.

Jack Wilson and Edward Molyneux kept a constant watch on Noel, who was continuously prey to depression far out of context to the true state of his career. It's not unusual for any great star or writer to follow a dazzling success with a major flop.

But Noel was temperamentally unable to handle this setback from universal success to sudden rejection. He even offered the producers of the upcoming production of *The Second Man* the opportunity to release him from his contract. This was one of the few times Noel would star in a play he hadn't written. The producers gallantly refused.

Noel's name was still box office. Some maintain that this period was a ridiculous self-indulgence. It was often difficult to distinguish Noel's attention-getting acts from his real tendency toward debilitating stress.

With Jack's help Noel recovered and his spectacular career continued. Jack had not yet deserted him to go back to America, had not yet disappointed him in any way.

Noel bounced back with that old standby, the musical revue. It was called *This Year of Grace* and contained such hit songs as "Mad About You," "A Room with a View," "Dance Little Lady," and "World Weary."

The show was a smash and Noel followed it with *Bitter Sweet*, his sentimental operetta. It was planned for his old pal Gertie Lawrence, but it was soon clear that the part of Sarah Miller called for someone with a stronger voice. Peggy Wood, then one of Broadway's musical comedy stars, later a TV actress on "I Remember Mama," played the part in London, and the show was another big success.

Noel left on another of his trips. Though still very involved with Jack, Noel often traveled alone or with Jeffrey Amherst. On these trips he usually wrote something that would see the light of theatre. Since she hadn't gotten the role in *Bitter Sweet*, Gertie pressed Noel to write a play as a vehicle for her and for himself to star in as he'd promised years earlier.

He tells a wonderful story of how he was reminded—gently badgered really—to get "her" play written for her. He was about to embark on an extended cruise to the Orient, which would keep him on board a ship for weeks. Gertie's going-away gift was a small gold book from Cartier. When opened it contained a charming little clock, a calendar, and a thermometer on one side, and "an extremely pensive photograph of Gertie herself on the other." It was Gertie's way of delicately reminding Noel that he'd promised to write a play for them and the time was fleeting. Since she knew he'd be wandering around a barren and elegant cruise ship she figured he was a captive and could best utilize the time to write the damn play.

Nothing came to him. The pressure became a burden, and he found himself wanting to throw the farewell gift out the porthole into the China Sea. He vowed he'd never make a promise like that again. It caused too great a strain.

When he reached the Imperial Hotel in Japan he was supposed to meet his friend Jeffrey Amherst. Jeffrey was late, having been delayed in Shanghai. So Noel went to bed, but instead of sleep he encountered a vision of Gertie herself appearing "in a white Molyneux dress on a terrace in the south of France and she refused to leave until five A.M., by which time *Private Lives*, title and all, had constructed itself."

Noel himself often expressed amazement at how themes for his plays and musical compositions emerged full blown in his mind. He describes riding in a taxi and having the whole theme for one of his operettas suddenly born in its entirety in his mind. All he had to do was get home, get out of the taxi, and write it down.

Noel's work developed inside him on a subliminal level. He *had* his plays similar to the way a woman has a baby. If his baby was healthy and strong, it lived; if it was a bad play, it flopped. Noel's problem was that he thought every play was brilliant before it opened on stage. When it flopped, as his plays often did, he had no real idea why. He had no interest or ability to rewrite anything, which stemmed from his lack of formal education and lack of self-discipline, as well as his unusually nervous temperament. He was like a parent who didn't know what to do with a child when it went wrong.

Private Lives is delightful, a lovely pastiche of Elyot and Amanda, two ex-spouses who marry two other people, and find themselves on a terrace in adjoining honeymoon suites. The new marriages are never consummated and Elyot and Amanda elope back to Paris, deserting the new spouses (originally played by Laurence Olivier and Adrianne Allen), who get together themselves. It is a black-humored play masquerading as a light farce, designed primarily for acting fireworks. It has no real plot, and all the action is designed around rough-and-tumble fights between Coward and Gertie Lawrence. It was brilliant and still is good, but because it was written as a vehicle for the two stars, it requires real skill to make it plausible or even interesting today. It is still delightful to read, containing some of the best dialogue Noel had yet written.

The original production did not come easily. After writing it while recuperating in China, Noel held on to it for a while, possibly out of spite because of Gertie sending him that expensive little clock as a reminder. When he did send the play to Gertie she wasn't effusive in her thanks.

First she cabled to say that there was nothing wrong with it that couldn't be fixed. Noel wired back to say the only thing to be fixed would be her performance. Then Gertie wired back to say she had a "moral obligation" to do a revue first for Charlot. Then it became a legal contract, not a moral obligation, and could Noel get her out of it? Then it changed back into a moral obligation again when Noel became angry. Then it went back to being a legal issue and she sent him the information he needed to contact Charlot, which could have saved him 40 pounds ($200) in cable fees if she'd sent it at the start. Finally he told her he'd get another actress and all the cable anxiety stopped until he returned to England.

By that time Gertie blithely erased any knowledge of the cable drama and arrived fresh and eager and free of all legal, moral, or professional obligations to Charlot. She also was unaware that she'd been "fired" or that anything needed to be "fixed" in the script.

Noel wrote that Gertie had "an astonishing sense of the complete reality of the moment." Meaning she was an actress, yes, but could turn into a hardheaded practical businesswoman when it came to making sure she played in a surefire hit. This was business—show business.

Gertie was a real actress who blurred reality and fantasy as effectively as any other great star. Noel said that apart from eating, drinking, and sleeping it was hard to tell what was true about her at all. This kind of personality, though not necessary to be a great actress, does seem to exist most prominently in those who become legendary. It is not something that can be learned; it is definitely a personality trait much like having another sense not possessed by others. Laurette Taylor had it; Bette Davis, Joan Crawford, and Garbo certainly had it. Their private lives were a mess because they could never really come off stage or off the screen. They hate the mundanities of life, are bored by the realities, those things one must do that are usually handled on screen by cutting from one scene to another. Noel himself had this trait, and it messed up his finances (as it messed up Gertie's). He fortunately was able to grab hold of himself and correct it. Gertie never did.

Her financial situation was always in turmoil. But she could elevate a nothing role with a brilliant performance. She lived for her art; that fatuous cliché was absolutely true about her. She maddened the people who loved her, including Noel. But also incited deeply ingrained loyalty in them. Noel's own temperament made him less willing to endure her mannerisms. Still he knew that Miss Lawrence was an actress beyond compare when situated in a less than perfect role. Certainly the part of Amanda was one that required an artist of her sensitivity and powers.

It is difficult to understand why she balked about committing herself to play Amanda when Noel finally wrote a play for her. Perhaps it had to do with the fact that up until then she'd been stuck doing mindless revues, nothing that would require her to stretch her talent. Although she was capable of enormous feats of acting, she'd fallen into the ease of doing low-risk shows. No actor has so much self-confidence that he or she doesn't get hit in the stomach when they think of putting themselves on the line with a major innovative, ground-breaking role such as Amanda. It was, in short, a role that would demand her to turn in a hair-trigger performance every time or the play would fall apart. Unlike Noel, whose self-esteem made him fearless, she was probably worried about her ability to bring it off.

Private Lives was also risky because of the way it trashed the sacrament of marriage, treating it as a toy balloon to be inflated or burst as the mood of the spouses changed. In those days most people still disapproved of women who smoked or colored their hair, and here was a play that trivialized marital fidelity, that deemed it appropriate to walk out on a spouse without notice simply because he or she was dull. The niceties of legalities, divorces, or even a good-bye note were treated as fripperies.

But Gertie and Noel lived their own lives based on these premises. She had taught him initially about sexual freedom, sex without love, the physical act for immediate and temporary gratification. Boredom was the greatest sin to them and their social set. It was only natural that he should think of such a theme when putting together a play for the two of them.

In almost all biographies Noel and Gertie are depicted as having spent their whole lives in a sort of partnership. Other analysts feel that their closeness was overstated. It is true that they remained friends all their lives and there is no doubt that Gertie had an enormous influence on him in their developing years. They were soulmates. Nonetheless Gertrude Lawrence was a straight woman and an actress, and her world had herself staunchly at its own center. It is surprising that such an ego could abide long in close proximity to Noel's own blazing ego. They loved each other and were physically at ease with each other, which made their on stage histrionics so comfortable for them to play, and made their roles as man and wife so convincing.

The Lord Chamberlain wanted to censure the play at first, and even demanded that Noel rewrite the second act before allowing it to be presented in London. In those days the English censorship was worse than Boston or the Hays Office with their constant demands for script laundering. In the scene where Amanda and Elyot make love to each other the Lord Chamberlain objected on the moral grounds that they had each remarried other people. Noel's frantic resistance to rewriting anything meant that he instead had to perform the offensive scene before the Lord Chamberlain and demonstrate that what went on wasn't obscene but totally acceptable emotional expression.

Gertie herself in real life would never have passed the censors. Her erotic dalliances were as free and numerous as any of the characters in a Noel Coward play. When she died an untimely death during her triumph as Anna in *The King and I* on Broadway in the 1950s, it was learned she had cancer of the cervix, which is commonly associated with sexually transmitted diseases.

It was easy to understand her need for sexual gratification. She had a tremendous talent and energy, the sort of creative power that can incite the artist to voracious sexuality. She also was enchantingly attractive and had a marvelous sensual body and way of moving. Even in still photographs her ease with her own body is strikingly evident, as is the insinuative way she uses it. She was at home on the stage. Many actresses find it difficult, often impossible to move around a stage easily and convincingly while spouting lines. Gertie was a perfectionist about her movements on stage, often rehearsing well past when anyone else would be more than satisfied. This self-demand may be a clue as to why she hesitated about taking the role. It was going to be a lot of work, especially because Noel demanded as much of her as she did of herself.

Gertrude Lawrence was a star in her own right and of her own making, just as Noel Coward was. He respected that kind of success—that which is made on one's own and not handed over through birth.

Noel followed the success of *Private Lives* with *Cavalcade,* a smash hit of a spectacle, and then wrote another revue, *Words and Music.* It was during this period that Jack Wilson's influence caused Noel to become disenchanted with his longtime producer Sir Charles Blake Cochran, called "Cockie" by Noel and others. This wonderful man had stood by the youthful Noel through success and public rejection for the nine years of their association. After *The Vortex,* when Noel was riding high in his new used Rolls-Royce, Cochran was with him. After the terrible reception of *Sirocco*, Cockie closed ranks with him to keep him writing. Such a vote of confidence showed more than just loyalty; it showed an unusual perception and foresight in the producer, as well as a willingness to take financial risks.

Cochran had a formula for successful shows, although he himself said there were no rules. The most obvious flop in rehearsal could turn into a major hit in front of an audience. Sometimes the most promising tryout caused the loudest boos when they toppled on opening night. Still Cochran's formula, star names, lots of girls, lots of dance numbers and elegant costumes, was based on his innate sense of what made a show that people would likely sit through for an evening's entertainment. Like most good producers he was in it to make a buck. Like the greatest producers he was hopelessly in love with shows and theatre and the whole magical world created on stage. His was that classical mix of hardheaded businessman and soft-hearted theatre aficionado.

Whether Noel should ever have left the canopy of Cochran's production company has been bandied back and forth among his biographers, especially Cole Lesley, his closest and most objective confidant. Lesley, despite his position of general secretary and house man to The Master, had a cool eye and an amazingly perceptive intelligence about Noel's weaknesses and strengths.

It was Cochran's sharp assessment of what the public wanted that most assured the success of the shows he produced. Noel had a tendency, stated in many accounts, of being overbearing to the point of hurting himself. He insisted that if he liked it, everyone else had to as well. Cockie knew that no one was a big enough name to compel an audience to sit through something they didn't want to watch. Because Noel initially was not in a position to override the producer, Cochran's view prevailed. After the enormous success of *Cavalcade* the balance of power shifted. In *Words and Music* Noel insisted on giving up three of the main ingredients of a good show (according to Cockie): glamourous star names, exceptional dancing, and an assembly of brilliant designers.

Noel had Gladys Calthrop design the whole show, then he put in some downbeat songs for mood shifts and indulged himself in an overembellishment of satire that worried Cochran. The producer was right; although it received warm critical acclaim the show did not run.

By this time Jack Wilson was in full command of Noel's finances. He had given up his day job long ago to begin managing—mismanaging—the star's money. Noel purposely blinded himself to the fact that Jack wasn't trustworthy. He made jokes about it, sending him poems in his letters that referred to Jack's thefts and the shortages that showed up in Noel's accounts, but he continued to allow Jack to have his way. Lorn saw the truth, but was powerless to change things so she went along with the poems and jokes as well. However, Lorn's little verses lack Noel's lightness and pointedly dig at Jack's thievery.

The father/son alliance between the two lovers was evident in their nicknames for each other: "Baybay" and "Dab" were what Noel called Jack; in return Noel was referred to as "Poppa" or "Pop."

One of their verse exchanges began when Noel tried to reprove his lover's foibles. Jack replied with outrageous glee:

> Baybay's got Attorney's Power
> Growing richer every hour

Noel replied:

> Darling Baybay, darling Jack
> Just a kleptomaniac.
> Pinching gifts from Poppa's house
> Like a predatory louse.

Then fearing Jack would really get mad:

> Still although you snatch and grab
> Poppa loves his darling Dab.

Noel's fear of losing Jack's love was the motivation in allowing the overt thievery to continue for years. It was all accepted and treated as a wonderful joke. When the joke turned serious Noel ended up paying the bill and having to finally break with Jack. If he had not let his anxiety about losing Jack rule his sensibilities he could have saved himself much trouble. If he had only realized that Jack needed him more than he needed Jack he could have controlled the relationship just as he controlled the nonerotic ones in his life. Noel seemed to lose his way whenever he was in love. Being accepted as a lover meant so much more to him than anything else that he would do ruinous things.

Noel always did seem to pick his sexual partners for their exceptional physical beauty; some say he wrote his song "Mad About the Boy" as a paean to Douglas Fairbanks, Jr., who typified the classic refined handsomeness that Noel idolized. This attachment to beauty is in character for someone who pursued the ideal of form and style in other aspects of his life. What is out of character is that he was willing to throw away much of what he'd worked for to keep Jack Wilson his lover. In other aspects of his life he made demands on people; when it came to lovers he turned into a spineless, confused fool who let himself be used and duped. It made no sense. Noel's ego was supreme when it came to being a star. His judgment was clear and on target. He knew exactly how to talk to any member of the royal family, in situations that would turn most people into speechless robots.

When defending his work against critics or audiences he wouldn't bend an inch. He was so supremely confident that his brass alone had to be respected even if he'd written a flop. With his beloved mother he also could be cold and fair, demanding that she shape up when it was needed. For all his loyalty he never allowed her or any of his dog-loyal entourage to overstep the line and interfere with his career. He was able to prune away deadwood people who stood in his way; even when he made the decision to leave Cochran, he was firm and clear. But when it came to Jack Wilson, all of his strength faded. The man had control over Coward.

Nothing in Noel's life indicates why he was such a slave to love. He was idolized by thousands of people who wanted

to be just like him. He may have been the most famous
celebrity in the world until Elvis Presley came along. People
who've never read a word of his work still understand what
exactly is meant by "Noel Coward wit." He was so famous
that people in England grew up knowing his name just as
they knew who the King and Queen were, yet Noel had no
sense of self-worth when it came to love and lovers.

Perhaps in his case it was merely that he had no experience either by example or by experience that showed him
how to behave in a relationship. It was and still is true of
many gay people; they have no model for learning how to
act in love affairs unless they pattern them after heterosexual relationships.

Noel also had a tendency to glamourize beautiful people,
possibly because he knew he was not handsome himself.
To find a remarkably handsome man who was also willing
to commit himself to being his lover meant Noel would
automatically place this person on a pedestal. Whereas Noel
gave most people a very short line to test his patience in
other areas of his life, Jack Wilson was given a long bun-
gee cord.

Love was so important to Noel that he seemed to value
it beyond anything. At Jack Wilson's urging Noel decided
to leave Cochran and go into the business of producing his
own plays.

VII

"Has Anybody Seen Our Ship the HMS Peculiar?"

CENSORSHIP, WHICH WAS PREVALENT THEN, forced creative minds to be even more creative as proven by all those wonderful screwball comedies of the 1930s. Today authors just use four-letter words (as Cole Porter wrote) and truly anything goes. But in the '30s creative talent had the added task of masking what was truly being said in ingenious and entertaining ways.

Three of Porter's tunes from this period exemplify the homosexual lament. "Why Shouldn't I?" (take a chance when romance passes by) questions why someone in love shouldn't take the same opportunity afforded to all living creatures. "Weren't We Fools?" explores the love not taken, when for some unexplained reason the participants "choose another." The third song, "How Can We Be Wrong?," says, "the moment we touched I knew" and expresses the universal feeling "it feels so right it cannot be wrong."

Of course the beauty of these lyrics is that they're androgynous. Cole wrote another song about unrequited love—or lust—for the revue *The New Yorkers*. In it he says, "I've Got You on My Mind"/"You're not so hot you/Still I've got you on my mind." The next verse is even more direct. "You're not wild enough/You're not gay enough." And the song concludes, "Not until I get that famous thrill will I be resigned." In other words let's have sex so I can get over this obsession.

(The word gay, as used by Cole, Noel, and others in the 1920s and '30s, meant more than most people thought but not exactly homosexual. It referred to someone who was "with it," "fey," not exactly a straight arrow—someone

115

who, if not homosexual himself, was at least not anti-homosexual.)

The Wall Street Crash of 1929 had tumbled the rest of the world into economic depression but both Cole Porter and Noel Coward came into the first flush of their real success. Neither had participated in the worldly involvement of the Great War, and it seemed they had the same impatience about participating in the Great Depression. Cole was riding high on the success of two musicals, *Paris* and *Fifty Million Frenchmen*. In 1930 *The New Yorkers* opened and included the controversial song "Love for Sale," which was banned from the radio. The instrumental version became a hit anyway even without the provocative lyrics.

Although this play had a short run coinciding with the failure of the Bank of America, Cole's career continued to bring him the success he had been aching for all these years. He was not young anymore; he was hitting his forties, a time when most men then looked fifty. But Cole was enjoying his lifestyle and his success, as was Noel. They were able to express their real desires while writing for the masses.

Noel was fascinated by the potential of sexual relationships as a dramatic theme, as well as sex as the primary focus of a relationship. He addressed it many times in his best plays. Although he also wrote plays about more conventional relationships as well, perhaps bringing greater realism to the standard middle-class marriage/family situation, his greatest triumphs came when he used sex as a dramatic focus. When he attempted to use homosexuality directly as a theme (as in *Semi-monde*) he was not successful. So he continued to write plays about heterosexual relationships. In his writing he was able to transfer his obsessions of sex for men to the obsession about sex between men and women.

All of Coward's plays have a common theme of unusual marital status. In so many of them the main characters are on their second marriage and although constantly pledging their love for the second spouse, the previous spouse hangs above it all like Damocles' sword. It is the basis of *Private Lives, Blithe Spirit,* and *Design for Living.*

In *The Vortex* marriage is merely a state that enables people to have affairs without commitment. Spouses provide the money and respectability to enable one to whore around with impunity. Noel's frustration with the impossibility (in his mind) of the validity of marriage shows itself so frequently that it invites analysis. Although the playwright himself pooh-poohed such delvings, the repetitiveness of the theme is too pronounced not to wonder why Noel kept returning to it.

There are probably several reasons. Even if Noel were heterosexual the kind of marriage he had been exposed to, that of his parents, was limited in scope and hardly successful. His parents fought constantly, his mother ceaselessly denigrating his father, who receded always to another room, like Nicky Lancaster's father in *The Vortex.* Mrs. Astley-Cooper's husband also provided some of the basis for Nicky's father, a vague, shadowy appendage to the strong woman whose brilliance dominated the household. One marriage Noel admired was Laurette Taylor's, which he immortalized in *Hay Fever.*

In Coward's comedies, marriages are often based on bickering that erupts into violence, and yet the two combatants cannot keep away from each other. In *Private Lives,* Amanda and Elyot were divorced because of their violent quarrels and remarry two bland pudding types. When on their honeymoon they meet and desert their new spouses they pick up their quarreling again. They break things over each other's heads; they hit and throw things. They cause physical damage and ruin furniture. It is not until they manage to alert their new spouses to the art of domestic violence that they happily steal away at the end of the play. Today, of course, people would be calling 911 and going to cry on talk shows about such actions on the part of a husband or wife. Noel Coward wrote about it as a normal and healthy state of affairs.

His thwarted view of marriage, which replaced the need

for a plot in many of his plays, was seen as proof that he was heterosexual. In those days the "battle of the sexes" was viewed as normal and needful. It gave the tang to the whole idea of a man and woman living together for years and was presented as the spark that kept one sexually attracted to one's mate.

But Noel still wanted to write about his kind of "marriage." How could he? He came up with an idea—a new vehicle for himself and his old buddies Alfred Lunt and Lynn Fontanne.

In the early years when they were all sharing some deli potato salad and pickles in New York and looking to the future, they decided when all were famous they would firmly secure their stars to the firmament by having Noel write a play for the three of them.

The play that emerged years later was *Design for Living*, an awesome and shocking play that rocked the theater in New York and London and caused the names of the three stars to become inextricably interwoven. It also did what it was supposed to do. Although the Lunts did not exclusively perform Noel's plays by any means, the friendship of this trio became more than just an adjunct to their fame in the public perception.

Design for Living was Noel's most controversial play. It clearly shows his impatience with the conventions of marriage and his ongoing boredom with mundane relationships and situations. What is most interesting about this strange and dark humored play is the bitterness and disgust it reveals in Coward's view of fame and the empty socializing that goes with it. He rips apart the whole facade of conventional sociality that successful artists are drawn into at the moment of success. He rips into the false veneer that uses conventional morality as a coating to pretend that free spontaneous sexual behavior doesn't go on constantly.

This play marked the second time Noel had made a "pre-dawn" promise to write a play for a friend. The Lunts reminded him of his promise when he was off on another vacation, by cabling him that their Theatre Guild contract was coming up and did he have a show for them.

Alfred Lunt, Lynne Fontanne, and Noel Coward
gave life to Noel's "Design for Living." The play about a
ménage-à-trois was decades ahead of its time.

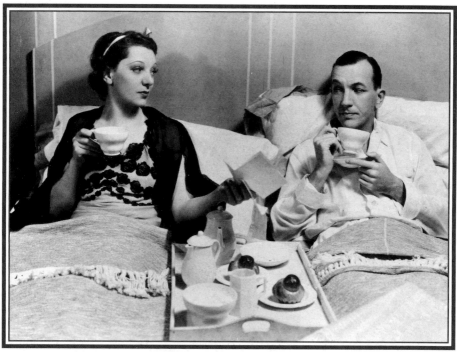

PHOTOFEST

above:
Gertrude Lawrence
and Noel in
"Tonight at Eight-Thirty."
The team of Gertie
and Noel helped aid
Coward's reputation as a
sophisticated bachelor.

PHOTOFEST

left:
Douglas Fairbanks, Jr.,
at about the time he
met Noel Coward.
Doug was then married
to Joan Crawford
and contends Noel
was charmed by his
vivacious wife.
Others say it
was Doug—
a Jack Wilson type—
who helped inspire
Noel's song
"Mad About the Boy."

above:
Jack Wilson and
Noel Coward
visit Cole Porter
in Venice.

right:
Noel relaxes
with his lover
Graham Payn.
They were
together from
1945 until
Noel's death.

Mary Martin
went to Noel's estate
in Bermuda to
rehearse their
television special.
Old feuds were
now forgotten.

Noel's great pal
Marlene Dietrich
visited him at
the opening of
"Nude with Violin."
Noel's eyes may
have been on Marlene
when the cameras
clicked but insiders
knew his thoughts
were elsewhere.

Noel, in one of his trademark
dressing gowns, welcomes a visitor backstage.

above:
Noel is flanked by
Gladys Calthrop and
Joyce Carey as he
attends ceremonies to
be knighted. Gladys did
most of his sets and
costumes. Joyce acted
in many of his plays.
They were his most
intimate female friends.

left:
Cole Porter
on the Lido in Venice
in the mid-twenties.
He had so much fun
in Venice he was
asked to
"get out of town. . .
before it's too late."

COURIER JOURNAL AND LOUISVILLE TIMES ARCHIVES

above:
Linda was
years older than
her husband and
many thought
she looked more
like Cole's mother
than his wife.

right:
Monty Wooley,
one of Porter's
best friends,
even portrayed
himself in Cole's
bio-pic. Of course
in the film
he chased women.

PHOTOFEST

Cole chats with
dancers Ann Miller
and Bob Fosse
on the set of MGM's
"Kiss Me Kate."
Porter was always
attracted to dancers—
he felt they knew how
to enjoy life.

Bob Bray,
an actor in
"B" films,
was Cole's
last "intimate
friend."

The play was written on a small freighter on which Noel was the only passenger with an all-male crew. He writes about going naked all day, putting on shorts only to dine with the crusty captain, and being free from any social pressures at all.

The play reflects how onerous and obnoxious society and success can become, while showing how addictive it is as well. The play also puts forth the idea that two men can have a love relationship with each other as easily as with a woman. When Leo and Otto are both betrayed (with each other) by Gilda, who was married to each of them, the two males go off together for two years and become one personality. At the end all three of the characters realize they are in love with each other and decide to form a permanent *ménage à trois*.

It is not a pleasant play and the humor is always black. None of the easy brittle wit of Noel Coward surfaces, but it is a strong if two-dimensional play. The characters, charming at first, at the end are brazen and unlikable, having reached a point of bitterness before they can accept the fact that they are in a totally unconventional situation from which they can never emerge.

It is an unedited first draft of a play, and its two-dimensional strength lies in its dialogue and relies on the virtuosity of the actors to make it work. It has some of his usual devices, the prim old successful faggot who acts as a ninepin to feed dull lines to the forceful stars, and to get knocked down by their cleverness. It has the mulish Cockney maid, who is portrayed as dull and moralistic. For American audiences of the time (it opened in New York, not in London) it has a Stepin Fetchit butler, who is described as "black but comely" in the stage directions. He spends his time staring wide-eyed and flabbergasted and is treated more like a slave than a servant.

Design for Living is not a subtle play. It's very explicit and hammers the theme hard and long about bisexual erotic freedom being the thing. It was very daring. Even though some claim that Otto and Leo are not lovers, the play's action makes no other interpretation acceptable. If they aren't lovers the major point of the play evaporates.

During the breakdown prior to writing this play Noel must have been thoroughly disgusted with having to maintain the pretense of being a womanizer. The play is a catharsis, even if Noel was not aware of it. He always maintained poise about his private life, but a reading of this angry play reveals how thoroughly he wanted to vomit away the maddening pretense he was required to keep up.

This play was a catharsis in other ways too. During the second act Leo (a playwright) gets back at the critics when his play is reviewed. Coward makes wonderful fun of them and the London newspapers that gave him such a hard time. Leo reads from one review:

"Here we go, dear! 'But the play, on the whole, is decidedly thin . . .'"

"Thin—thin! What do they mean 'thin'?"

"I shall write fat plays from now onwards. Fat plays filled with very fat people!"

The ongoing criticism of Coward's plays being tenuous and thin was a constant thorn in his side. His plays were often criticized adversely and as he said, he had to content himself with commercial success for a long time.

Design for Living was the first of Noel's plays to open in New York instead of London. It provided a very daring role for Alfred Lunt, an exceptional man. For him to agree easily to play the role that cast him, a heterosexual, in a part that made his character a cuckold and a latent homosexual and finally a member of a *ménage à trois*, showed enormous self-confidence. One should always remember how difficult it is for actors to divorce their egos and selves from the roles they play. It is easier to go on stage and play a hero. It is enormously difficult to go on and play a character that is viewed with scorn. Even in a comedy such as *Charley's Aunt* it is hard for the leading man to go on in drag. Plays with homosexual themes often go begging for actors of repute. Even the musical version of *La Cage Aux Folles*, forty-plus years after *Design for Living*, had a hard time casting a name actor to play the "masculine" partner in the gay relationship. Gene Barry, who finally agreed after much soul searching and family discussion, refused even to hold hands with the actor playing his lover—and this was after the movie version had become a beloved worldwide hit.

But Alfred Lunt was a pro, as were Lynn Fontanne and Noel. To them theatre was the prime directive; a role was their work and their art and such nonsense as a role "tainting" one's reputation was utterly disregarded. This attitude made it possible for Noel to have a completely open friendship with the Lunts. They were part of his theatre family and support group.

IN *Design for Living* the homosexual references were still rather oblique. But in *Bitter Sweet* Noel had inserted a song, "We All Wore a Green Carnation," sung by a quartet of fops, which has no other purpose in this tragic operetta except to acknowledge the fact that homosexuality existed and had to be camouflaged.

The singers are Vernon Craft, a poet; Cedric Ballantyne, a painter; Lord Henry Jade, a dilettante; and Bertram Sellick, of course a playwright. Each one has a line before leading into the song.

> BERTIE: It's entirely Vernon's fault that we are so entrancingly late.
> VERNON: My silk socks were two poems this evening and they refused to scan.
> HENRY: It's going to be inexpressibly dreary, I can feel it in my bones.
> CEDRIC: Don't be absurd, Henry, your whole charm lies in the fact that you have no bones.

They sing:

Blasé boys are we
Exquisitely free
From the dreary and quite absurd
Moral views of the common herd.
Later:

And as we are the reason for the Nineties being gay,
We all wear a green carnation.
Also:
  Haughty boys, naughty boys, dear, dear, dear!
  Swooning with affectation
  Our figures sleek and willowy
  Our lips incarnadine,
  May worry the majority a bit
  But matrons rich and billowy
  Invite us out to dine . . .
And:
  We like Beardsley and Green Chartreuse
  Women say we're too
  Bored to bill and coo
  We smile wearily
  It's so drearily true!
Finally:
  But when we rise reluctantly but gracefully
  From our graves
  We'll all wear a green carnation.

This song was put there for the jaded rich and bored homosexuals who abounded in the audience, just as Judy Garland pandered to them in her audiences several decades later, and just as Tallulah Bankhead during her heyday used to indulge in "camp" on stage to please her gay coterie of fans in the front rows. Coward did it out of a sense of private vindication for having to hide so much of his life in order to reap the benefits of stardom in England.

Noel was the William Gilbert (of Gilbert and Sullivan) of his day, making fun of people who were paying good money to see his musicals. In the American touring company of *Bitter Sweet* the song was dropped, but to his credit Noel insisted it be reinstated for the New York production.

Noel's homosexual references are more prevalent in his songs than in his plays or short stories. Perhaps this is because a quick reference can be sneaked into a long lyric.

One of his earliest is "Choir Boys" who "pinch their friends' behinds."

Cole Porter also dealt with homosexuality in his lyrics. In his 1929 song from *Fifty Million Frenchmen*, "I'm Unlucky at Gambling," a girl laments her love for a handsome young man who won't give her a tumble. She takes him to the movies to see John Gilbert and still he won't, even in the dark of the theatre, give her a kiss. At the end of the movie she discovers that "he likes John Gilbert too." Oh, well. The plight of the big-city girl was as difficult then as it is now.

Cole dealt with homosexuality in more ambiguous ways such as in this verse from "You've Got That Thing":

"I have often wondered, dear,
Why gentlemen all seem to fall on their knees
The moment you appear?"

Cole occasionally would use a more direct reference to homosexuality. For *Red Hot and Blue* he wrote a song, " "A Little Skipper from Heaven Above," which could easily have been called "A Little Nipper" (a nipper was a cabin boy who provided special services to the skipper during those long voyages of yore). It was sung by Jimmy Durante in drag. It was very pointed and the reason it wasn't more shocking was because the Great Schnozzola tempered it by singing it in his gravel voice and Popeye manner. It has lines like these:

"Years ago I discovers my brother was a nance.
So I gives him my petticoats and puts on his pants
Then I finds me a sailor who's looking for romance."

The point of the song is that the skipper gets pregnant and reveals to his/her crew that he/she's about to have a little skipper from above.

But finding songs with gay references is much more difficult in Porter's lyrics than in Coward's. Porter threw in pointed gay references, such as Georgie Raft's bull being gay, in "Farming" or a song that is not famous since no music survives to accompany the lyrics for "That Little Old Bar in the Ritz.'" It was based on Cole's very real experience of sitting in that famous bar in Paris every afternoon and having cocktails. He also wrote another one for *Hitchy-Koo of 1919,* called "My Cozy Little Corner in the Ritz," which has these lines:

> I simply adorn a secluded corner
> A cozy corner of the Ritz Hotel.
> When I wander each afternoon for tea
> 'Cause I like to see the kings
> And let the queens see me.

This gay sentiment and thought process of going to a bar to see and be seen could only have been written by a gay man who understands the psychology of cruising covertly— the "is he or isn't he?" syndrome. The Ritz Bar in Paris was noted as a place to make contacts in those days, as was the bar in The Four Seasons (New York City) at cocktail hour during the late 1960s, before the Stonewall Riots ended the need for discretion.

When Cole Porter worked gay references into his lyrics he did not destroy the songs for his straight audiences. In fact in the style of the day the gay references were such that only the *cognoscenti* would understand them. To reinforce the gigolo theme in the Cafe Society of that time in Paris he also noted "If you'd like to see the fellow/That your favorite prima donna/Cashes checks on/Go to the Ritz."

He was absolutely fascinated by gigolos and wrote two songs specifically about that social dating custom and one about "the extra man," who society ladies only remember when they need a fourteenth at a table or when some real man can't show. In all these songs the implication is that these men are weak, undersexed, somewhat "lavender" in their nature and slaves to drugs ("I'm a flower that blooms in the winter/Sinking deeper and deeper in snow").

What is remarkable about Porter's lyrics is that he is best at expressing heterosexual sentiments in his songs, probably because he was married and because he had a strong erotic attraction for heterosexual males, and almost no interest at all in the usual avenues of gay interaction. It could almost be said that Porter was straight in almost every aspect of his life except for his physical sexual preference. He was fond of his wife—and close to her on a mental level—but only experienced adolescent or fantasized emotions for men. His burst of infatuation for Boris Kochno was just that, a fascination that burned bright, flared up, and burned out.

In all his songs is found the sentiment that men need women, but who can really understand that fairer sex? The kinds of griping men might make among themselves about how women interfere with men's interests comes up, but always to make a comic point. Nowhere in Porter's songs do you find the kind of negation of heterosexuality that you do in Noel Coward's work. Cole likes heterosexual relationships; marriage is sometimes an interference to having fun—as it actually was at times for him—but the songs express the sentiment that such things can be worked out with a little ingenuity.

Among his unpublished songs is one called "It Was Great Fun the First Time," which details how people have a one-night stand and then keep trying to engineer that initial magic, but boredom sets in. In fact many of his early songs contain plaintive wails about trying to avoid boredom through sex. This is consistent with Cole's statement that his life was an odyssey to avoid boredom. The constant longing to have outlandish sexual escapades with different mysterious strangers is certainly a part of his odyssey.

Perhaps no songwriter produced so many lyrics that used the mystery of night as a glamourous seduction in itself. His song "All Through the Night" poignantly evokes the kind of fevered physical yearning that torments a lover all day until night when her (or his) forbidden lover comes in the secrecy of night to make love. The singer does not live all day, but is on tenterhooks until the shadows fall and the lovemaking can begin again. There is no mistake that this song is an erotic one, a yearning one, and a beguiling one.

Other songs carry out the theme as well, especially "Night and Day." In all of these songs Porter repeats the sentiment of being obsessed with one person as an erotic love object. Noel Coward, on the other hand, seldom used this as a theme. Cole gloried in the splendor of the night; the blackened skies lent a dream quality to his erotic passion, whether he was out cruising the streets in his car or indoors at the high-toned whorehouse run by Clint Moore in Harlem. Cole understood the importance of the proper setting and atmosphere for any occasion, and he carried out this sense of ambience in his song lyrics.

Even though Cole doesn't describe anything, those listening to his songs can build a mental picture of a setting perfect for a particular romantic mood.

Naturally Cole and Noel had to be careful when they worked gay references into their work. Noel learned his lesson the hard way—with the total rejection of *Semi-monde* (not even in print at this time). Cole was content to sing his parodies of his and others' songs at private parties and occasionally sneak a gay reference into his lyrics.

Among their friends, however, there was a different standard. Playwright Leonard Spigelglass has said, "Don't forget homosexuality in that period [the 1930s] had two levels. One, it was held in major contempt, and the other was among Larry Hart and his kind [Cole Porter and Noel Coward] and it was the most exclusive club in New York.

"That's terribly important to realize, that it was a club into which you couldn't get. I mean, no ordinary certified public accountant could get into the Cole Porter-Larry Hart-George Cukor world. That was their world. That was Somerset Maugham. That was Noel Coward. That was it."

VIII

"When Other Friendships Have Been Forgot"

PROFESSIONAL FRIENDSHIPS AMONG CREATIVE PEOPLE are very important as exchanges of talent, as well as an impetus to continue to create. Just as nurturing a child helps the talented tot grow into a productive, creative person, so the continued exchange of ideas and energy among one's colleagues keeps the edge of one's talent honed. An appreciative audience is the final accolade; people of unusual creativity must have the stimulation of others on his or her level to keep from drying up. Even someone like Georgia O'Keeffe, who retired to New Mexico, retained a constant dialogue and remained in touch with what was happening in the art world in New York and Paris.

Noel and Cole's circle of special friends was as important to them as any other element of their lives, creatively speaking.

THERE IS A GROUP of actors who have the aura of being "Cowardesque," although they were all major stars in their own right and made their reputations in theatre as legends before becoming actors in Noel's plays. These include Gertrude Lawrence, Alfred Lunt and Lynn Fontanne, and Beatrice Lillie (Lady Peel). Coward made a famous remark about her saying it was the first time he'd ever seen a Lady Peel, meaning see a noblewoman strip.

The reason they are seen as Cowardesque is because all were so brilliant on stage, and when off stage were famous for the kind of sparkling and outrageous remarks and high jinks that characterized the tone of Noel's plays. They were highly placed, talented people who indulged in the kind of elegant offbeat behavior that makes his plays so wonderfully improbable. Life to the privileged people of their time could be a joke. They had few legal restrictions placed on them; if they stepped over, their fame and status protected them from prosecution. Their money and lifestyles enabled them to have the leisure to be silly, and the same expectations did not apply to them as it did to nontheatrical folk.

Sometimes, however, being too closely associated with Coward had its drawbacks. The Lunts, for example, were often hindered in their career choices. Years later Alfred Lunt wondered why Elia Kazan hadn't offered the Lunts the parts of Willy Loman and his wife in Arthur Miller's *Death of a Salesman*. The reason was that it was assumed they were interested only in doing plays by Coward, S.N. Behrman, and Terence Rattigan. The Lunts did plays by other writers but were caught in a genre.

It shows how completely, even in theatre, the Lunts were allied with the Coward legend. Their story is the story of American theatre during the first half of the twentieth century; detailing it, or their full relationship with Coward, would require writing another book.

BEATRICE LILLIE, ALSO KNOWN AS LADY PEEL, was not just madcap—she was truly mad. Her last years were spent under professional care. One of the toasts of New York for decades, Beatrice was a favorite guest not only at parties but on early TV talk shows. One night on Jack Paar's show she insisted on singing a lovely little ditty she had introduced many years before in London. It was called "There Are Fairies in the Bottom of Our Garden." Paar made some nonverbal reactions, trying to get some laughs, but she swatted him and sang the lovely double entendre. She worked several times with Noel in New York productions of his shows and made them into amazing successes on the strength of her tremendous energy. The first was the New York production of *London Calling* in 1924, then she sang two of Noel's songs in *The Little Review*, and played in the Noel Coward production *Set to Music* in New York in 1938. Her greatest Coward role, however, was as Madame Arcati in the musical version of *Blithe Spirit*, called *High Spirits* in the 1960s.

Whether Noel actually liked "Beatie" is unclear. He said, "If I loathed her with every quivering fibre of my being, which at certain dress rehearsals I have done, I still have to admit that a visit with Bea Lillie is one of the most enchanting things that could happen to anyone."

He found her rehearsal style deadly. She sludged depressingly through rehearsals (eight weeks for a musical), then suddenly on opening night she'd take the lid off, give bloom to her rose, and treat audiences to brilliant performances every night of the run. She needed the audience response.

For Noel, who gnawed through his fingernails if he thought a rehearsal showed no signs of life, this was torture. Bea Lillie had a hard time memorizing her lines. Noel wrote very precise dialogue and the lines had to be exact, he thought, to work.

"Day after day I have sat quietly with my nails dug into the palms of my hands while Miss Lillie stumbles, flounders, forgets, remembers, drives the company mad, and is as much like Madame Arcati as I am like Queen Victoria. Then she goes on opening night and is brilliant and becomes the darling of the critics."

Despite *High Spirits* running for a long time and making a lot of money Noel still never included Bea in his close circle of friends. Part of that was that she worked mostly in New York. He admired her, but from afar. Nonetheless the public views her as a Cowardesque actress, and indeed her performances made that last show the hit it was. When it opened in London with British stage star Cicely Courteneige it didn't work.

BEA LILLIE INTRODUCED one of Coward's most memorable songs in *Set to Music*. He'd written it in the mid-'30s

spoofing the parties of his and Cole Porter's Cafe Society
chum Elsa Maxwell. "I Went to a Marvelous Party" tells us
that "Elyse made an entrance with Mae . . . yes!" and that
"Maurice made a couple of passes at Gus." Lillie's delivery
of the song was superb. Coward himself was the only other
performer who could match her.

Bea said that she was "Living in error/With Maude at Cap
Ferrat/Which couldn't be right" and "Everyone's here and
frightfully gay/Nobody cares what people say," and then
mused, "People's behavior/Away from Belgravia/Would
make you aghast."

Bea also sang, "And young Bobbie Carr/Did a stunt at the
bar/With a lot of extraordinary men," and that "The Riviera
is really much queerer/Than Rome at its height."

The song reveals Noel's true feelings and ambivalence
about the wondrous and shocking worlds he sometimes
inhabited.

Noel, of course, had other non-Cowardesque friends in
show biz. He was close to Katherine (Kit) Cornell and her
husband Guthrie McClintic. He was chummy with Ivor
Novello and Bobby Andrews. Andrews had been a boy actor
in London who grew up with Noel. They had had a brief
fling, but when Noel ran into Andrews in Manchester during World War I, Bobby had settled in with Ivor Novello for
what would eventually become a lifelong relationship, until
Novello died in 1951.

Ivor, famous as a matinee idol and songwriter ("Keep the
Home Fires Burning"), was already a star when he and Noel
met, and Noel envied what the matinee idol had already
achieved. Ivor was no snob and readily accepted the young,
obviously ambitious Noel into his social circle. Later a
young actor named Arthur MacRae, who would appear in
Cavalcade and the 1931 revival of *The Young Idea*, joined
their circle. Ivor Novello would never achieve the international celebrity of Noel Coward but in England he was a
true matinee idol of both stage and screen.

By 1936 Noel had made his first stab at film stardom.
Some say he only did it because he needed money. His

debut was in *The Scoundrel*, a rather good though unsympathetic part. Noel wasn't to make another film for years, but *The Scoundrel* had one great effect. It brought Noel together with the legendary Marlene Dietrich.

The relationship between Marlene and Noel has been described as *amities amoureuses*, which means loving friends ... less than lovers, more than friends. It was used often by Marlene herself to describe some of her other platonic male relationships.

Marlene was the ultimate unreal woman, the kind of legendary female star who appeals immensely to homosexual men due to her style and strength of character, as well as sexually to heterosexual men.

Marlene was one of Noel's "noncoterie" friends whose influence on his career was minimal from an artistic point of view but whose friendship as a mutual star and fan was of immense importance to him. He always said it was important to act like a star if you were one and Marlene did just that, even when she was box office poison during the 1930s.

It was Marlene who courted Noel at the beginning. She'd seen his film and telephoned him to tell him how much she'd enjoyed his performance. It was a mutual admiration society from that point on.

Despite her astonishing series of male lovers the tag of lesbian, which had attached itself to Marlene early during her career in Hollywood, remains even now. Noel used to kid her about "her girls." Her affected mannish style of dress and her inscrutable beauty made her seem aloof to men. Her natural ease in touching other women (and men, for that matter) made her seem lesbian according to the strictured American standards of behavior.

Marlene, through purveying eroticism, nudity, and back room activities, still came off as somehow androgynous.

Still all of her comfortable relationships were with men and women who weren't of the standard American stripe: Ernest Hemingway, who also ran into questions about which sex he really liked; Noel, who was certainly not your regulation football coach; Marlene's mother, who taught her to wear those suits and ties.

It is a credit to Noel that he saw her talent before it was recognized, for she really did not become a legend until very late in life. During the 1960s, when it seemed her career had burned out, she began appearing in Las Vegas wearing see-through diaphanous dresses. Only then did the aging movie queen became a star of legendary status. Then there was the Blackglama mink ad, showing her wearing a mink and nothing else. ("What becomes a legend most?") That clinched it.

NOEL'S FAMOUS FRIENDSHIPS with the Lunts, Kit and Guthrie, Gertie Lawrence, Marlene, and Bea Lillie, had another by-product: they clouded the public perception of Noel's sexuality. Gertie and Marlene's amorous affairs were widely known and he ran with them. The theatrical connection with two of the theatre's most devoted married couples, the Lunts and the McClintics, gave another side of Noel to focus on.

Even his friendship with Bea Lillie helped maintain the Coward myth of eternal bachelor. Beatie was like Noel himself: to all outward appearances she was asexual, but actually Beatie was married and had a son, who was tragically killed during World War II. Like Coward and the others she flaunted all conventions and was above the current strictures of morality because she seemed to be completely asexual. She could take her breast out in public and walk down an aisle like that—she actually did this—and no one would view it as a sexual act, but instead see it as another example of Beatie's outrageous madcap humor.

Noel, by association with these people, was viewed as neither straight nor queer—bizarre, different, and unique, decidedly, even someone who was one of a mold—but sexuality wasn't attached to his public image.

An analysis of Noel's other famous friends reveals, though, how strongly sex was at work in his own mind.

Although Laurence Olivier is by no means considered a Cowardesque actor he owes much of his later theatre craftsmanship to Noel. His relationship with Coward is worth analyzing because Coward had a definite crush on the young Olivier, as he would have on other handsome young actors playing in supporting roles to him through the years. Olivier, when cast in *Private Lives*, was somewhat unsure of his own sexuality anyway. Noel was the legendary star and Larry had a way to go before he could be sure of hanging on to a part after being cast in it. Noel's pattern then, as with so many stars, was to make himself available to the actor in question and if they responded positively, fine; if not they'd get on with the business of acting together.

Olivier had a good track record when he was cast in the supporting male role in *Private Lives* but had often been fired from roles because he had little self-control on stage. He admitted he would lapse into giggles. This not-uncommon phenomenon in theatre is a real bugaboo with actors; witness the hundreds of TV outtakes showing actors breaking as they flub lines or can't control their own reactions to funny ones. Olivier had a real problem and Noel sat him down, almost with a hickory stick, to make him lose it. In this case he did a great service to the now-great actor. He was extremely aware of Olivier's sexual confusion and passivity, and attracted by it. Noel could always pick out a man's latent homosexuality, even when the man himself was unsure of it.

Noel was not a great deal older than Olivier but he became a father figure and theatre mentor to him. Many people do not know how large a debt Larry owed Noel for his acting greatness. Olivier was considered a master craftsman, working out techniques to achieve his characterizations. When he did his famous *Othello* in the mid-1960s he darkened his skin and used modern African male characteristics to make the role, even padding his backside for a high-rise seat effect. But Noel had established modern acting patterns and these were the basis of Olivier's craft.

Noel fell in love with Larry briefly. Whether they made

love is not clear, although Olivier did have gay affairs, especially a long and heavy one with Danny Kaye. His sexual
confusion forced him to make marriage vows with certain
kinds of women. His first wife, whom he married during
the production of *Private Lives*, was a woman with lesbian
tendencies, who was not interested in intimacy with a man.
They married each other for the facade. Olivier's marriage
to the exquisitely beautiful Vivien Leigh was a stormy one,
and certainly included sex, but mostly because Vivien's passion for him was so intense that she was the aggressor.
Otherwise they did not get along and Larry subconsciously
helped sabotage her career because he was jealous of her
own tremendous acting talent. He encouraged her to take
lesser roles; let her throw off her Hollywood contract with
David O. Selznick after she played Scarlett O'Hara so she
could follow him around on his acting jobs; and he treated
her like an annoyance. Larry needed to feel totally wanted,
possessed by adulating fans. Vivien was one; Noel was, for
a time, another.

Olivier had an unpleasant overweening arrogance about
his talent. Among English actors there is a sword that belonged to Edmund Kean, the great early nineteenth-century
actor. It had been passed along to whomever each current
possessor deemed most worthy of it as the next greatest
living actor. When Sir John Gielgud passed it on to Laurence
Olivier, someone asked him who he thought would get it
next. Olivier answered, "Nobody."

Fate, however, cannot be waylaid. Vivien's role as Scarlett
ensured her immortality, possibly the only actress who can
be sure of reaching each new generation in her greatest role.

Olivier died a great actor, considered by many to be perhaps the greatest. Of all the great actors who owe a debt of
gratitude to Noel Coward, and they are many, Olivier is the
greatest. This brings us to a reverse point. Just as Noel
would not have had the entrée during his tender years into
certain segments of society if he had not been gay, so now
in his prime he was able to return the favor. If Olivier had
not been gay, would Noel have taken the trouble to work

out his giggling quirk, or would he have just found someone else to play the role? It can be said that since he formed a powerful attraction for the handsome actor he was willing to go to great efforts to make sure he kept him close at hand as long as possible. Noel was not noted for his patience where his plays were concerned; the fact that he realized that Olivier was a "church member" made him willing to give him the benefit of extra patience.

Coward helped Olivier's career along in other ways. Noel had seen Mordaunt Shairp's daring play *The Green Bay Tree*, in London. He urged the young, dynamic producer Jed Harris to stage it in New York in 1933 and give Larry the lead. The play concerns a young rake who has a much older, gay foster father, who corrupts him even further. The famous stage actor James Dale re-created his London role but was vocal about Olivier not being as good as Hugh Williams had been in London. This part, along with the fact that Olivier had debuted in a homosexual role in *The Rats of Norway*, was married to a lesbian, and was a protégé of Noel's seemed to point to the certainty of his homosexuality.

Olivier, according to his biographers, engaged in a few homosexual liaisons but remained essentially straight and devoted to his last wife, Joan Plowright. Coward's friendship with Sir Laurence remained steadfast for decades.

Noel also had a long-standing friendship with the very gay and beloved Broadway and Hollywood star Clifton Webb. Webb, like Noel, was able to project a masculine image, playing strong father figures and business magnates on the screen. He was enormously convincing in offbeat effete roles as well, never compromising his box office aura. As John Gielgud once said, "I'm an actor; of course I can play a heterosexual."

And there were other gay friends, not actors and not in theatre, with whom The Master had close friendships.

Edward Molyneux, whose name sounds French but who was English, was a friend of Noel's from his early days. Noel made the same kind of prophetic promise to him that he made to Gertie and the Lunts: when he became a success Molyneux would design the costumes for his plays. He did just that, in fact. Molyneux was an enormously successful women's designer who became wealthy from his work. His name is so hard to pronounce that he himself wasn't sure of it; he said it was "Molynoos" or "Molynooks." He was also a close friend of the Cole Porters. When Noel had his first nervous breakdown he had it at Molyneux's villa in France.

Molyneux's wealth and reputation in Paris—a liberal city prior to the war—was a great boon for Noel, who was always cash-shy. When the Nazis invaded Paris, Molyneux simply went to London, eating his losses for the duration, and made another wartime fortune; later he returned and recouped what the Nazis had spoiled.

His designs are evident in photos taken through the years, the elegance of each succeeding generation of glamour developing with the plays. Although Gladys Calthrop designed sets and costumes as well, Noel kept his promise to Molyneux, as he did to all his early friends. In *Shadows of Evening*, the character George refers to the fact that his wife is wearing a Molyneux evening dress.

Not all his famous friends were in show business, nor were they all gay. Noel was close to Diana Cooper, who was once an actress, and her husband, diplomat Duff Cooper. He was also friends with Anthony Eden. Lord Mountbatten, who died during the 1980s and was Prince Charles's favorite uncle, and his wife Edwina, were very appreciative friends of Noel's. Although their long friendship was based on mutual enthusiastic admiration, it had its ups and downs, since Mountbatten was related to the royal family, and Noel had dared to satirize him.

Nonetheless, they were guests often at Goldenhurst, as comfortable there as at home, and when Noel made the movie *In Which We Serve* he played a character based on Mountbatten and his heroism. Mountbatten was enormously proud of the movie, viewing it dozens of times and reviling those critics who reviled Noel for daring to portray

Mountbatten. It was entirely due to the energies of Lord Mountbatten that Noel was at last placed on the New Year's List and given the title Sir Noel Coward. Mountbatten made it his grail to obtain this honor for Noel and he did not give up until he saw it happen.

Mountbatten's loyalty to Noel was noteworthy since it ran him into much personal criticism during the war years. It is due to that friendship that Lord Max Beaverbrook turned against Mountbatten and vilified him in his newspapers, although the exact reasons for the newsman's enmity are wrapped in mystery. It must have been that Beaverbrook and Sir Winston Churchill disliked Coward because he had so much clout with the upper classes, was a commoner, and was gay. These sins against England have throughout that country's history worked against anyone who bore them. Noel himself believed that he was a victim of anti-gay discrimination and he had no way of fighting it. He was fortunate to have had a friend like Mountbatten to help him triumph after his enemies were dead.

However, friendship did not stop the creative Noel from using his friends and acquaintances in his work. He'd already satirized the Sitwells in the 1920s, and used Laurette Taylor and her household in *Hay Fever*. When he satirized the Mountbattens in a one-act play, *Tonight at 8:30*, they were not amused. Lord Mountbatten wrote, "I remember in 1936 Noel sent me six free tickets for the Phoenix Theatre, so my wife, Edwina, and I went with a party. It wasn't until we got to the second play, *Hands Across the Sea*, that we knew why we'd been sent the tickets. It was a barefaced parody of our lives, with Gertie Lawrence playing Lady Maureen Gilpin and Noel Coward playing me. Absolutely outrageous, and certainly not worth six free tickets!"

Through the years Noel's celebrity combined with his sexual preference led to his meeting other celebrities of the same bent.

Lawrence of Arabia, also known as T.E. Lawrence and later as Aircraftsman Shaw, was an early friend of Noel's. This was surprising because Noel described him as having not a grain of humor. They met during production of *Private Lives*, when Lord Lloyd brought the almost mythical Lawrence to a rehearsal. The cast included Gertie Lawrence, Larry Olivier, and Adrianne Allen, and of course Noel, who also was directing. The news of T.E. Lawrence's imminent arrival caused a thrill among the cast, who decided to downplay it out of propriety. Lawrence at the time was going by the Aircraftsman Shaw name, a low-level rank in the Royal Air Force, which he chose to avoid publicity.

He was enchanted by Noel and during a luncheon at an obscure restaurant, chosen so "Shaw" could dine without being recognized, he could not take his eyes off Coward. No doubt the artistic adulation that developed in the famous adventurer was flattering to Noel, but it was even more obvious that he was bored by the heaviness of Lawrence's personality.

For those who don't know the famous story depicted in CinemaScope and starring Peter O'Toole, Lawrence of Arabia was a major factor in the subjugation of the Arabs by the English. The famous tale of his repeated rape by an Arab military leader during his capture has both fascinated and been denied by readers of his story ever since. Lawrence was a shy, small-built man of no commanding presence who, nonetheless, was able to turn his fascination for the exotic men of Arabia into a trust that enabled him to spy on them. The fact that he also had a sexual adulation for them helped as well, as the Arabs were notorious for finding different ways to seduce and sodomize the young, blond officers of the English military.

Lawrence in his book insists that he put up with torture rather than willingly have sex with the Arab officer who lusted after him, and the officer was forced to order two of his own men to march off to his bed to ease the ache in his groin. Lawrence was blond and young and exactly what one imagines an Arab would see as magnificently beautiful. Lawrence's tale of defending his virtue through torture does not ring true. There are those who say he was never raped at all, and others who say he was covering the truth of being a willing victim, and still others who assert the situation never occurred. Why Lawrence felt it necessary to tell the tale at all, unless of course he had a compulsion to make up a theatrical drama in which he was involved, was a key to his passive and fanciful repressed personality.

Lawrence was fascinated, like a moth to a flame, by theatricality and dramatic situations. This was why he had such a fascination for Noel, one of the reigning dramatic figures of his day. Lawrence would have known Noel was gay and the combination of homosexuality with spectacular stage achievement led Lawrence to an idolatrous admiration for Noel's talent. He thought Noel was an absolute genius. Being at a rehearsal of *Private Lives*, one of Noel's most sexually violent plays would have thrilled the mild-mannered Lawrence.

Lawrence was a writer as well, and Noel professed to admire his work, which Lawrence would send him before publication to get Noel's opinion. No matter how much Noel approved of it (and Noel was a very bad judge of talent) Lawrence would compare himself unfavorably to Noel's light, brilliant verbal swordplay. The friendship lasted until Lawrence's death, but Noel became bored with him long before that. The two of them never had a physical intimacy; Noel doesn't even mention him in his biographies, a dead giveaway that they never bedded down together.

After the premiere of the movie of Lawrence's life in 1962 Noel approached the very handsome star Peter O'Toole and said, "If Lawrence had looked like you there would have been more than twelve Turks lined up for the buggering session."

Still Coward was enormously flattered to have the strange and intriguing hero professing such idolatry over him and his work, and even after he had lost all interest in the man, maintained a pretense of friendship for him.

One man whom Noel was almost forced to socialize with was Edward VIII, the Duke of Windsor, who gave up his throne for the woman he loved. The Duke and Noel detested each other, but because of their skewed social posi-

tions were forced to be civil to each other. Like most loyal
Britons, Noel had little sympathy for Wallis Simpson, the
Duke's wife, but later, thrown together as they were in the
fishbowl of Cafe Society, the three became lukewarm
chums, after a fashion; they tolerated each other.

Noel was still close friends with Edward's brother George,
the Duke of Kent and his wife, Marina. Edward and Wallis
may have suspected that something was still going on between Noel and the Prince, who were lovers, or may have
just resented the fact that Noel was received at the Palace
and they were not. As mere fellow night clubbers they had
to accept Noel's presence, whereas if Edward were still King
he could have barred him.

Coward himself explained Edward's animosity to him in
this way:

"He pretends not to hate me, but he does, and it's because
I'm queer and he's queer, but unlike him I don't pretend
not to be."

COLE PORTER DIDN'T NEED FRIENDS to help with the deception
that he was straight. He had Linda for that. He did need
friends as inspiration though and he was friendly with the
other famous and successful composers of his day, who did
a great deal to keep him stimulated creatively. There was
a friendly competition between Cole and others, including
admirer Irving Berlin. Richard Rodgers was somewhat awed
by him, and Lorenz (Larry) Hart was of course part of the
upper and inner gay rich social set, while Jerome Kern, who
was a success earlier than Cole, respected his work. Cole
was proud of the fact that he wrote both words and music,
and he often made disparaging remarks about how it took
two grown men to write one little song.

But his intimate friends were less famous to the general
public and except for Elsa Maxwell were not usually associated in the public eye as being "Porter people." His main-
stay was Howard Sturges and through the 1930s Cole
remained close with Monty Woolley, who wasn't known

yet to the public, and about whose career Cole was known to worry. Woolley was a fascinating citizen of the world and deserves his own biography.

When we see this famous actor in roles such as *The Man Who Came to Dinner*, with his distinguished beard and fine figure of sartorial elegance, it's hard to picture him cruising the streets of New York picking up sailors with Cole Porter. One sees him at the head of the boardroom table, sitting in an opera box with an elegant wife, or in an admiral's uniform decorated with honors, at dinner with the president— or even *being* the president. But no. He and Cole were what gay men call "fuck buddies." They shared a common interest—common pickups—and went out together scouring the gutters for them.

They were best friends in the usual sense of the word as well. They had great admiration for each other, and Cole was constantly playing silly pranks on his dear friend. Once he befriended a circus bearded lady, dressed her up, with a veil over her face, and escorted her to a party Woolley was giving. He had her remove the veil and introduced her to everyone as Woolley's mother. Woolley was famous for his beard. Cole mentions it in his song "Farming":

> Monty Woolley, so I've feared
> Has boll weevils in his beard.

Woolley himself once valued his famous whiskers at $8,000 after Paramount Pictures asked him to shave them off for a movie role. He asked for $2,000 down and $500 a week for the three months it would take to grow it back. Paramount declined, and Monty had a good story for the press.

His given name was Edgar Montillion Woolley, a clue as to why he went with the nickname. His father owned the Marie Antoinette hotel on Broadway and while at Yale Monty and his friends, including Cole, would hole up there for weeks at a time, draining room service until P'pa would get wind of it and kick them out. Monty stayed on at Yale to get his master's degree, cementing his friendship with Porter, since both continued to work on the collegiate shows as alumni, which served as Cole's formal theatrical training. Monty taught there and his students included Jock Whitney and Jack Wilson (Noel's first lover).

After leaving Yale Monty directed *Fifty Million Frenchmen*, one of Cole's early successes (254 performances) in New York, produced by Ray Goetz; *The New Yorkers*, and later *Jubilee*, the show written with Moss Hart, which lost money. But his most successful Cole Porter work was singing "Miss Otis Regrets" at parties around the time that it was written. It became a serious matter to Woolley, this social claim to fame, and shows how his mind worked: social notoriety meant more to him than a career. It was this aspect of Monty that bothered Cole, who had a strong sense of making a serious contribution to the world.

On the international scene Monty Woolley stood equal with Elsa Maxwell, the Cole Porters, and Noel Coward as a social lion. His greatest role was as Sheridan Whiteside in Kaufman and Hart's *The Man Who Came To Dinner*. He starred in it on Broadway and in the Warner Brothers movie in which Bette Davis insisted on playing the supporting role of his secretary.

There is no way of estimating Woolley's influence on Cole's success. To have an erudite buddy of the same erotic stripe as himself, with an equally facile wit and mastery of the quick rejoinder, honed Cole's cleverness. That odd combination of high class and low interests shows up constantly in Cole's lyrics. They both loved sophistication, having been raised with equal access to family money. Both were spoiled rich kids, both intelligent, and both interested in the theatre and ribaldry. They were constantly baiting each other with jokes and pranks, which kept their wits razor sharp.

Although Cole's pranks sometimes went a touch too far in public not to ruffle his actor's dignity, Cole was never contrite, and so Monty always had to let his ire pass. Cole credits Monty with giving him the idea for one of his best and most enduring songs. They were sailing with Linda into Rio de Janeiro past the spectacular Sugar Loaf, which was a famous sight in those days of ocean liner travel.

"It's delightful," Linda exclaimed.

"It's delicious," Cole added.

"It's de-lovely," Monty mocked dryly.

Cole's nimble brain went on with all the "de-" words and in the 1950s a car company added another when DeSoto (now out of production) used it for their advertisements.

It's a stereotype that gay men belt out show tunes at home and at parties but many gay men actually do as Cole Porter and Noel Coward did. If there was a piano in the room and a group of people (groups of one person were okay) they would play and sing their own songs. Sometimes, given the right circumstances, Cole would make up songs as he went along. Because of the bitchy inferences in a lot of their songs it is no wonder that they were being sung and appreciated at parties everywhere in those times.

Each had written a song that had become a standard "must do" at parties of their generation. Noel's was "Mad Dogs and Englishmen," a parody of the British maintaining their Britishness even when they looked like damn fools doing it. Cole's contribution was "Miss Otis Regrets," a song that has a similar satiric intent on the subject of form over good sense among society matrons. Miss Otis has shot her lover out of jealousy and is about to be strung up on a tree by a lynch mob. Her last words are for a friend who's expecting her for lunch: "Miss Otis regrets she's unable to lunch today." Monty usually draped a towel over his arm, since the song was written to be sung by a butler to his employer.

Monty accompanied Cole on many of his journeys, having an adequate income of his own and a successful career as an actor and director. Once the pair went on a drinking tour of Germany starting with the light beers and working up on through the very heavy ones. The binge lasted several weeks and both needed to diet off the excess girth caused by the Teutonic odyssey, but they deemed it a scientific project well worth the sacrifice. This kind of thing was very much a part of the high life during the 1920s when stars were like children—having *no* social conscience—with enormous amounts of money to throw away on indulging the silliest whims as serious projects.

Once Harpo Marx and a friend were in Hollywood when they decided to play a prank on Alexander Woolcott, who was on Long Island. They hopped a plane, flew cross country, hired a car, and drove to Woolcott's country place, where they found him playing croquet with a woman. They stripped naked, and ran out of the bushes whooping and buzzing the players. Woolcott frowned and said, "Just ignore them, dear, and play on through." The pranksters, disappointed at the failure of their prank, retraced their trek back to Hollywood and sat around the pool again trying to engineer a better scheme.

Practical jokes, scavenger hunts, and drinking orgies were all part of the carefree world in which Cole thrived. There was no one to tell them "no." If you were rich and famous you were also expected to be a snob and indulge yourself in whatever pleasure you chose. Monty Woolley was certainly one of the supreme practitioners of such antics, despite keeping up a facade of urbane respectability.

Monty liked to tell a story about cruising with Cole in New York. They spotted a sailor and invited him into the car. The boy was brash enough to ask, "What are you guys, cocksuckers?" Monty shot back: "Now that the preliminaries are over, why don't you get in and we can discuss the details." Monty and Cole were seldom unsuccessful at what they called their "fucking parties."

Truman Capote was fond of telling another story about Cole paying for sex. According to Capote, Cole invited a handsome wine steward, well known in New York's Cafe Society, up to his Waldorf digs. When Cole kissed the man, he said, "That'll cost you $500, Mr. Porter." When Cole squeezed his leg, the man said, "That'll cost you $1000." Capote claims Cole then unzipped the man, hauled it out, shook it, and asked, 'What'll be the full price on the use of that?' When the man asked for $2,000, Cole write him a check, said, "Miss Otis regrets she's unable to lunch today. Now, get out."

Capote's story seems apocryphal. Porter certainly might say the lines, but to pay $2,000 for the satisfaction seems unlikely. Still, it was inevitable that stories such as these would circulate in the Manhattan gay set.

New York gays also attribute this quip to Cole: "People say I'm a practicing homosexual. I think I'm perfect."

Noel Coward's sexual exploits during this time were no different, except for the style of men he made his plays for. As Bricktop and others who knew all three in this period say, "Noel was always on the make." His cruising was more refined than Cole's and Monty's. His conquests were usually of the casting couch variety, or people in Cafe Society who were good looking. He met countless willing partners on the trips he took—alone—constantly and he was well known to be partial to men in uniform. Often he traveled on British naval ships. Like most creative people, straight or gay, Noel and Cole were both highly sexed, but like most successful people they were also highly motivated to work.

Both had enormous amounts of creative energy to channel into their work. Cole worked every day for six hours at his songs, undisturbed. When Noel was writing, he would get up, have breakfast, work from 8:30 to 12:00, break for lunch for an hour, then return to the typewriter until 4:00. Their childhood focus and encouragement made this kind of schedule possible. It is especially noteworthy in Cole because he was a heavy drinker and a maestro pleasure seeker. Nobody had more temptations not to work than Cole. He lived his life in pleasure spas and palaces, surrounded by people who made their living at parties. To find that he could draw on an almost monkish self-discipline for work is boggling.

Cole also had the financial wherewithal not to work at all. How he managed through years of failure to bull through until he achieved success is more remarkable than someone driven by poverty. He didn't have a long string of successes until he was well into his forties, and even then he experienced runs of flops on Broadway. How he managed to stay afloat emotionally is anyone's guess.

Noel had more to sustain him. And his chronic lack of funds was impetus enough to keep him working. How ironic to find that the successes of two of the most brilliant sophisticates this century produced is really a story of determination, sex, and guts.

IX

"Where Is the Life That Late I Led?"

SOMETHING CLICKS IN GAY MEN AND WOMEN in or approaching their forties. Perhaps just as part of the usual midlife crisis everyone goes through, when they say "the hell with it . . . I am who I am," gay people especially tend to let their hair down a bit, enough at least to accept themselves as gay people of validity.

For Cole Porter ceasing to take great pains to conceal his true sexuality occurred with his new love, not a person, but a town with a special lifestyle. His new affair was a dream, another fantasy, the wonderland of Hollywood in the 1930s. What made him loosen up here was first the deceptive insularity of Los Angeles. After living in the very high-profile cities of Europe and New York, the low-lying, automobile enclosed people of Hollywood seemed almost unreal. Incredibly beautiful young people all ready to screw anything that might unlock a studio career were everywhere. His agreement with Linda not to embarrass her seemed not to apply here—he thought he was shielded from the press, and in a way he was right. But at that time the hedonism of Hollywood, the pleasure-based culture made him stop caring so much about being found out. Everything that Linda had to offer him he'd gotten used to. And there were all these hunks smiling and bright, their shiny butts twinking at him, the new golden boy at MGM.

Noel Coward refused to have much to do with the American film colony, except for selling rights here and there to a few of his works. He was wooed continually by film moguls eager to acquire his name and services. He wrote to his mother when he was on his way to one of his rest and recuperation trips in Asia, that he was stopping in Hollywood. He had been offered the use of movie studio limou-

147

sines and accommodations. "I know they're trying to seduce me to work for them," he wrote. "The cars I'll use but I'll not sign any contracts."

Not so Cole Porter. Louis B. Mayer beckoned and Cole answered willingly. He went to Hollywood and while there he "went Hollywood." He loved the whole hedonistic way of life. He loved the luxuries, the houses, the swimming pools, the constant chitchat about movies, and especially he loved the availability of the handsome young males who swarmed all over the place ready to do anything with any-one who might, just might, help them get a foothold in the movies.

COLE'S OFFICIAL MOVIE DEBUT was RKO's *The Gay Divorcee*, based on his 1932 stage musical *The Gay Divorce*. The play had starred Fred Astaire and Clare Luce. The film teamed Astaire with Ginger Rogers. Only one of Cole's songs, "Night and Day," was included in the film. (Another com-poser, Con Conrad, won the Oscar for his song from the film, "The Continental.") Still, it was ultimately "Night and Day" that became the classic.

> Like the beat-beat-beat of the tom-tom
> When the jungle shadows fall
> Like the tick-tick-tock of the stately clock
> As it stands against the wall
> Like the drip-drip-drip of the raindrops
> When the summer show'r is through
> A voice within me keeps repeating
> You-you-you.

Repeating one-syllable words brings an immediacy and intensity to the song. The sense is instantly one of near-insane obsession; you know you're about to hear about someone who not only can't get someone out of his/her mind but is almost on the verge of wishing the torment would be through.

The song was designed as a dance as well. Fred Astaire

uses it to seduce Ginger Rogers, and the music and beat are tremendously seductive. The song was written for the limited and weak voice of Astaire, so many men imagine that they would be able to actually sing it as romantically to a lover as it is meant to be. It is such a powerful song that it doesn't lose its impact because of a mediocre voice. It also is the kind of song that needs no additional emotional embellishment, no acting, to make it work. Simply performing the song as written completes the task.

BUT IT WAS NOT JUST THE SUCCESS of "Night and Day" that made Cole so desirable to the film world. He had finally scored big on Broadway.

The Depression had caught up with many theatre producers, including Vinton Freedley, who had fled the country and his creditors. He went to Cole with an idea for a musical to star Ethel Merman. Cole's name was now so strong that Freedley was able to get backing for *Anything Goes* simply by promising that Cole would do the songs. *Anything Goes* was a smash, including the title song, which certainly typified Cole's attitude about lyrics. It included "Blow, Gabriel, Blow," "I Get a Kick Out of You," and "You're the Top." Howard Lindsay and Russel Crouse did the book, and their long career together included the book for *The Sound of Music*.

Cole and Linda were now Broadway celebrities being written up in all the papers and magazines. Their lifestyle and adventures had great appeal to a nation that had just come through the starkness of the Depression. America was avid for glamour and stories about wealthy indolence and silly sophisticates at play, as if wanting to wipe out any reminder of the poverty that had recently gripped the nation and the world.

Cole's songs were just the ticket for curing the blues at the height of the Depression. "You're the Top" and "Anything Goes" joined "Let's Do It" as Cole's most famous and daring songs.

A Cole Porter song brought to the masses a tune they

could dance to, and words that conjured up fun, style, romance, beguilement, and always sexual delight. If you were to pick the one Cole Porter song that best typified his work it would probably be "Let's Do It." Reprinting all sixty-seven of the verses Cole wrote, as well as the other verses that people contributed to this unique work is excessive. The whole song hangs on that simple frame of mostly one-syllable words.

Why does it have such wide appeal, and why does it never get old? Why does it constantly delight and refresh the sensibilities even after repeated playings? The theme is universal: everyone wants to do it. He proves that by listing the whole anthropological zoo of humans, birds, animals, and insects. In Boston, he notes, "even beans do it." What do they do? They fall in love. Now if he had said anything else the whole song would have collapsed. The unspoken titillation is what gives it the spark that makes everyone wait, even after sixty years, for that unspoken act to be mentioned, and it never will be. Always the trick of saying "Let's fall in love," surprises and delights. The song is as addictive as that unspoken urge that we all look to satisfy. And it can be sung without censure because it lifts the whole thing into the area of genteel acceptance.

Cole loved writing songs that were like taffy strings, songs that could be added to ad infinitum. Cole's '30s hit "You're the Top" is full of topical social and geographical references:

> You're the top!
> You're the Mahatma Gandhi.
> You're the top!
> You're Napoleon brandy.
> You're the purple light of a summer night in Spain,
> You're the National Gall'ry,
> You're Garbo's sal'ry,
> You're cellophane.

In each refrain the lover sings something like, "I'm a worthless check, a total wreck, a flop/But if, Baby, I'm the

bottom, you're the top!" Cole's mixing of the highest pleasures with the lowest most delightful things like cellophane
and turkey dinners, gave the song tremendously wide appeal, as well as showing the diversity of items in the world
that caught his fancy.

Throughout his career Porter would write saltier lyrics to
his songs, which he'd sing at parties. Most of the lyrics were
never written down—few even survive. One of the classics,
however, was the party version of "You're the Top."

> You're the top!
> You're Miss Pinkham's tonic.
> You're the top!
> You're a high colonic.
> You're the burning heat of a bridal suite in use,
> You're the breasts of Venus,
> You're King Kong's penis,
> You're self-abuse.

Of course there were several versions. One says,

> You're the tits on Venus
> You're King Kong's penis.

These parody lyrics abound. The point was any clever
college kid could add more. In fact, Porter's songs have
unique characteristics that made them so universally attractive that they continue to sound fresh today. One never gets
tired of singing or hearing a Cole Porter song.

First they have the distinction of having music and lyrics
that can be enjoyed separately. The music of "Let's Do It" can
be played as a strict instrumental despite the addictive quality of the words. By the same token just reading the lyrics
without hearing the music you can get the meter and timing,
plus all the uplifting comedy in the repetitive rhymes.

Secondly Cole knew how to take very simple words and
make them seem like the richest soup of style and sophistication, pregnant with innuendo and emotional fullness.
Like "When They Begin the Beguine" . . . what could be
simpler than that? Suddenly a simple sentence is turned

into a force that promises mystery, apprehension, raw sexual tension, fear of suffering a broken heart, because you'll be pulled into that erotic miasma as soon as the song begins.

Songs such as "Get Out of Town" and "Make It Another Old-Fashioned Please" are about the bitterness of impossibility when you're in love with the wrong person. This is a quandary always at hand for a famous gay person, unable to know whether the lover is sincere or just using you. The theme of drowning one's sorrow—or boredom—in alcohol or drugs repeats itself often in Porter's lyrics. The tenor of his early love songs is always about the unpossessable love object, the wall that separates lovers who are no good for each other. There is always pessimism about love being able to work out, as well as an underlying feeling that maybe it's better if it doesn't; getting to know the lover as a person might lead to boredom in the light of day. Porter's lovers are happier in the night, wrapped in mystery and free of any other part of the personality except the sweet erotic/romantic part.

Thirdly, Cole's songs always promise something and then keep the promise alive. It is like prolonging an erotic level, that period of time just before orgasm. He builds a beat and a rhythm, whether the song is about love or not. In all his songs, or all his best ones, he writes more and more stanzas based on the refrain as if he could go on forever finding variations on the theme. This is part of his own hedonism. He adored pleasure and continued to move from one delight to the other before each preceding one had time to fade. He wasn't running from something, but pursuing excitement and stimulation. If he didn't find it he created it at his piano.

Cole had a tremendous genius for presenting the most complex emotions, happy or sad, through the simplest phrasings. The elegant simplicity of Cole's songs goes right to the heart and soul of the human experience. Nothing is explained, it is just stated. If it's a need, it is a naked need, free of adjectives and descriptions. He uses the strongest sentence construction, simple noun, verb, direct object. Cole's adjectives never get flowery; he always assumes you will know what words like love, ennui, torment, rapture, and mystery mean to you. The kinds of adjectives he does apply so sparingly are "wonderful," "fabulous" and "lovely," all subjective descriptions. He lets listeners conjure up their own personal meaning in his songs. He says, "fabulous face" but you fill in the blank according to the fabulous face you're envisioning.

For this reason his songs can be used by everyone as a personal sentiment. The emotions he writes about are universal. We all feel love, get horny, like to make a snide remark behind someone's back, torture ourselves when we can't get a lover; his songs are like beautiful blank cards that let you fill in your own personal message.

COLE'S SONGS HAD EVERYONE in America singing and dancing to his tunes. Hollywood wanted him. When Fox Films called, Cole obligingly stayed home at the Waldorf and wrote some forgettable songs for a movie that never got produced. But when MGM beckoned Cole to Tinseltown his movie career truly began. Before he could make the trek westward, though, he had a Broadway commitment. Cole was to write a musical with George Kaufman's new partner, Moss Hart.

Cole and Hart, the rags-to-riches playwright, embarked on a world cruise to write *Jubilee* and enjoy life in the bargain. Linda, twenty-nine pieces of luggage, and a small piano joined them on the cruise. So did Howard Sturges and his friend Bill Powell—described in future missives from the ship *Franconia* as a travel writer. So did Monty Woolley, who, as always, had plenty of money and free time. The group became known as "Miss Linda and her gentlemen," and they were an odd group—a rather matronly woman and five seemingly silly men. The *boys* were convinced that Moss Hart was gay too—he just didn't know it yet, or wouldn't come out.

Because Hart was so at ease with gay men, they figured he too was gay but he wasn't. The reality is that it is usually men who are unsure or protective of their own masculinity who are unable to cope with gay friendships. Hart was comfortable with himself and with others, gay and straight.

Somehow Cole and Moss were able to get some work done. They produced *Jubilee*, which had a few good songs, including "Begin the Beguine." The show was not ultimately a success, but the trip established a mutual admiration between Hart and Cole that lasted for years. Growing up in grinding poverty gave Moss Hart a deep admiration for the kind of fabulous wealth and lifestyle of the Cole Porters.

Like "Night and Day," Cole's classic "Begin the Beguine" languished without note. Then Artie Shaw made his famous recording of it. Anyone interested in Cole's music should obtain this still available rendition. It must be heard, not described, because the experience is unlike any other. All the magic of Cole's music is wrapped up in this rendition.

After *Jubilee* opened on Broadway Linda and Cole left for Hollywood and more of the good life. His first film would be an Eleanor Powell vehicle, *Born to Dance*. Cole composed two of his most famous standards for it, "Easy to Love," and "I've Got You Under My Skin." During the filming of this highly durable movie Louis B. Mayer fell in love with Cole's talent and offered him the sum of $100,000 to write the score for *Rosalie*, which was to star Powell and Nelson Eddy. By that time Cole was in love too—with Hollywood—and despite Linda's strong objections, he signed up and prepared to ensconce himself in the film colony.

Linda hated Hollywood, except for social evenings with the Astaires, Howard Sturges, and Elsa Maxwell. The town was considered a joke by most sophisticated New Yorkers, such as Dorothy Parker, Lillian Hellman, Dashiell Hammett, S.J. Perelman, and Robert Benchley, all of whom ceaselessly satirized it and simultaneously wrote for its movies. Although the money was always a draw for Cole—he always liked the feeling of being freely offered large sums of cash—there were other factors that attracted him even more strongly. Cole loved adulation and appreciation of his work. Louis Mayer was as generous in that regard as he was with the money; by extension every "yes"-man at MGM was parroting the mogul's praise.

Mayer thought Porter was a songwriting god and said so. Despite the crudeness of the man and his underlings, Cole had no problem tolerating and enjoying Mayer's company. Cole also liked to indulge his homosexual nature openly. Mayer, whose most favored and most highly paid director was George Cukor, Hollywood's reigning "queen," seemed to have no problem with anyone's homosexuality. Mayer had asked Cukor once directly if he were "queer." Cukor admitted he was, and nothing more was said about it. He remained at the top at MGM. If you were riding high in Hollywood, your sexual escapades escaped notoriety. Top money, outrageous adulation, and free love—it was all Cole ever hoped for, and the weather was always warm enough for nude bathing.

Cole liked the sunshine, the healthy focus, and the fantasy structure of Hollywood. The once great silent star, now a character actor, Richard Barthlemess, had a grand estate with extra buildings and a swimming pool, secluded nicely for those open-air orgies impossible in New York, Paris, or even Venice. Cole rented the place. Already a health nut, Cole began taking daily skincare precautions, high colonics, vitamins, suntans, and such. Hollywood was the mecca for this kind of sybaritic, youth-extending, body beautiful movement. Also, in those days Los Angeles was an absolutely beautiful place. The skies were smog-free, blue and brilliant all the time. Gentle hills rolled along dotted by the fantastic shapes of villas, castles, and mansions erected by the magnificently rich stars who lived in a world of splendor and bizarre hedonism. It was like another planet where dreams and fantasies were the normal way of life. Cole was never bored here.

Linda was. For the first time she saw herself as a fifth wheel in Cole's life. He had everything he wanted: bevies of beautiful men as plentiful as the oranges on the trees. Besides giving them big money, Mayer had the habit of rushing his high-priced talent out to Hollywood and letting them sit around their pools waiting until an actual film production got under way. Then he'd pay them extra. Cole had little to do except have fun.

Linda was dismayed by the focus of the town; it was all movie talk. Cole found that after he'd been there a week, he wanted to talk about nothing else. Linda instituted their "separate nations" arrangement, since the climate affected her weak respiratory system adversely. She went off to take a cure and Cole went out to drink by the pool. With all that available beefcake Linda was only in the way.

In no time at all Cole was challenging George Cukor's position as top gay dog of the film colony. These two rich men conducted open house every Sunday. These were lavish all-day, all-gay affairs, primarily intended to bring new sex partners to the hosts. Certain heterosexual "sympathizers" whose discretion was assured also were invited. The pools and grounds and certain areas of the house were draped with semi-nude and totally nude bodies, superb and taut, since the owners of them were either already stars or wanted to be. It became a sort of gay political thing to be invited to one or the other. Embarrassments arose if you were invited to both, in which case you'd try for brunch at one and dinner at the other. It was easy to fall out of favor with either Cole or George, since each had stringent requirements about what constituted polite behavior based on their own temperaments. A sudden flash of anger over a seemingly innocuous remark could get even an exceptionally pretty boy banished from the castle.

The guests' offerings of a more intimate nature could be brought to one or the other, much like a concubine could be presented to the king of Siam as a gift. For Cukor, who could not cruise openly because of his position at MGM, this was his only means of getting laid. Cole, without the restraining hand of his wife, began to risk censure by flaunting his bevies of gay men publicly. He would conduct parties of gay people to clubs and restaurants around town. Despite the fact that neither Louella nor Hedda would expose their darling Coley, not all of Hollywood would approve of his escapades. Cole loved to do things lavishly. This sort of thing was what got him kicked out of Venice in the 1920s.

Cole had written a song called "Why Shouldn't I?" which expressed his own attitude about what he thought he should do.

> Ev'y star out in Hollywood
> Seems to give it a try
> So why shouldn't I?

His poolside escapades were becoming a scandal in a town that thrived on scandal. Linda gave him an ultimatum: give it up or she would leave. They had a marriage agreement and he was breaking it. He let her leave.

Cole's greatest assets socially and professionally were his unusual politeness, calmness, and consideration. But he also had a caustic tongue, which was considered a necessary part of the equipment of a celebrated sophisticate. He managed to offset the abrasiveness of his acid wit by his superb poise and kindness.

This personal quality, which showed through his work, the gently kidding barbs of shocking innuendo, even personal slurs, kept any of his negative shadings in a happy light. Whatever he did or said could be taken lightly, because everyone realized that Cole only wanted life to be a fun-filled fantasy. He imparted this desire to everyone through his personality and his songs.

However, Cole had not been in Hollywood for very long before he took on an "I'm a star" attitude. He began to act like one, and when he had returned to New York to do *Red, Hot and Blue*, he was as pigheaded and full of himself as any other boor.

It was something of a surprise when he motored leisurely from Hollywood to New York, arriving *late!* and delaying rehearsals of the show. This musical starred Ethel Merman and Jimmy Durante and pre-legend Bob Hope, so it was difficult to have yet another star-ridden ego on hand.

Red, Hot and Blue did not run long despite its high-powered collection of talent, but it established Merman and Cole as a mutual admiration society, and introduced "It's De-lovely." Cole began his pattern of doing a show almost every year, but from now on his critics began to irritate him. The main complaint was that his songs were not up to Porter's standards. He blew up and asked in frustration what his standards were since they'd panned his early shows so badly.

A Broadway flop is a much more serious blow to the reputation than a Hollywood downer. On Broadway you are only as good as your last review. Film producers took a much more businesslike, long-term assessment—or at least that was the situation prevailing when Cole was working there.

In Hollywood they would give you at least three flops in a row before beginning the push, and even then you could still get a renewal after making one big hit again, but there are reasons for this.

First of all, you can be well at work on a new movie project by the time you find out that your last picture flopped, and a movie can recoup its losses over the years. On Broadway you have no cushion of time; if the audience isn't buying tickets the whole deal goes up in smoke in a week. And with a Broadway musical if a show is a flop the blame is laid right at the songwriter's door. In a movie it can be blamed on the star's inability to bring in audiences, the director, the timing of the release date, the political climate. Music is not the whole picture in a Hollywood musical.

Cole's delicate sensibilities never did match up easily to the sidewalk pressures of working on a Broadway show. Because his movies were big moneymakers and critical successes, whereas surprisingly few of his early Broadway shows were well received on either level, he naturally chose to return to the West Coast.

They loved Cole Porter songs in Hollywood, and he knew

that Hollywood knew what the public wanted, perhaps more accurately than anyone else. If they liked him he must be good. His particular songs lent themselves so well to the versatility of movies in being able to evoke a dream-like romantic mood. What did he care if the producers were men whose manners were crude, their tactics based on assassination and their goals superficial? They liked his music and they presented it in films that everyone else liked as well. No matter how rich or successful Cole became, he could still be depressed or even angry when one of his songs was not well received or was unfairly criticized.

Cole never had a bad experience with Hollywood. Someone there always gave him what he wanted without an argument. The few times he did run into an obstacle it turned out to be for his own good. For example, Louis Mayer kept rejecting version after version of the song "Rosalie," which Cole wrote for the film of the same name. Finally Cole, frustrated by what he considered movie obtuseness, holed up and wrote a satirical version, which Mayer loved. Cole found that the studio head knew his stuff; Irving Berlin later confided to Cole that it was the best of the reincarnations.

In Hollywood and in New York Cole continued to be a leading gay host with the most. He stopped worrying about the visibility of his image. At this point his disregard of their marriage agreement caused Linda to leave him. Even then he did not curtail his activities. He just stepped them up, since he no longer had her reining hand.

It is a testament to his charm that in later years none of the vicious gossip queens, Louella nor Hedda, went after him in their columns. Cole always evoked the mother in women of power and they just adored him. His charm was so great that he got away with it all—the nude male hopefuls in his swimming pool, the Sunday open houses vying in brilliance with those of George Cukor, the forays into Hollywood restaurants and nightclubs with his flock of rare birds. He got away with it. It may also be that homosexual carryings on, especially by a songwriter and not an actor, was not printable in columns that after all went directly into the hands of teenagers and families. Writing about heterosexual dalliances might evoke a certain thrill, but writing about homosexuals, for heaven's sake, might be too prurient for those times.

People in the know on both coasts, whether straight or gay, wanted to be included in the Cole Porter lifestyle. Leonard Spigelglass said, "I remember those houses, with butlers and the carrying on . . . you were a king! That was it! In spite of the attitude towards homosexuality in those days. On the one hand, if you said, 'They're homosexual,' 'Oh, my, isn't that terrible!' was the reaction. On the other hand, if you said, 'My God the other night I was at dinner with Cole Porter,' the immediate reaction was 'Jesus Christ, what did he have on? What did he say? Were you at the party? Were you at one of those Sunday brunches?' So you had this awful ambivalence."

Ambivalent or not, the parties continued. Cole was still paying for sex, perhaps not in the direct way he used to at Clint Moore's whorehouse, but with trinkets of silver and gold, with automobiles for needy would-be stars.

Cole's running obsession with sex for hire was most clearly put to music in two of his best and most beloved standards, "Love for Sale," and "My Heart Belongs to Daddy." The first one is sung by a taxi dancer, which was a popular way in those days for men to have some intimate, furtive contact with a girl for ten cents a dance. Men who could not afford prostitutes would buy some tickets to dance, pawing and rubbing up against the girl on the dance floor until he'd have his orgasm in his pants. The plaintive wail of the song shows that Cole understood the bleak despair of these women, who had no other way to make a living, but it did not soften the sexual impact such a situation had on his libido.

"My Heart Belongs to Daddy" is much more lighthearted, and more autobiographical, and shows pointedly how happily Cole identified with a girl being kept in extremely expensive sexual bondage to an older man. He seemed to think that the situation was okay as long as the price was right. Throughout the song—which made Mary Martin a star—the girl sings about the luxury in which she lives, and how loyal she is to her sugar daddy, no matter how attractive the alternatives are.

The song is also a double entendre of the first order. Cole loved writing lyrics that could be taken in several ways. For example:

> If I invite a boy some night
> To dine on my fine finnan haddie,
> I just adore his asking for more
> But my heart belongs to Daddy.

Finnan haddie is a seafood dish that was popular during the 1930s. The clear implication is that she invites a boy to dinner at her place, nothing else. But if one chooses to interpret it another way: men often compare the smell of a vagina to fish, so she is inviting him to eat at the "Y."

Cole, himself, was never actually satisfied by any sexual act. He had the kind of obsessive searching for sex with man after man that characterizes a certain segment of the gay population and gives it its stereotype. Having had one man, he lost interest and had to have another. It was as if he was on some impossible quest to eventually "have" every single man on the planet ... or have a good time trying. (This was distinctly different from the calmer approach of Noel Coward. He was attracted to particular people, not a two-dimensional type. When he saw someone he liked he'd go after him. But if he didn't see anyone he liked he didn't try to make a conquest for its own sake.)

THE 1930s, BEFORE HIS ACCIDENT, were Cole's "salad" years, professionally and personally. It was then that he had the most fun on both levels. Monty Woolley was often with him and Sturge and their carousing became legendary. Bricktop captured Woolley's persona: "With his personality and his connections from Yale and all, Monty didn't have to put much energy into being a success on the stage. He just put it into being charming."

Cole did not miss Linda at first. Brooke Astor once said: "Cole and Linda, you know, were not a terribly devoted couple for a long time. Her age, you know. He admired her. She gave him something he had not had up to that time. All those parties in Venice and all that sort of thing. Cole adored that type of life, he loved all the excitement and the fun of it. She liked it too, but I really think that Linda enjoyed being in the background."

Linda had gone back to Paris in 1937. Cole stayed in Hollywood to finish up some work. Then he and Howard Sturges and Hollywood friend Ed Tauch, an architect, were planning a walking tour of the Dolomites and a trip to Scandinavia. Cole stopped in Paris, but Linda was not going to reconcile. It appeared that the break was permanent, after all.

Cole's depressions were widely known. He'd suffered from them sporadically in the 1920s and would retreat into them deeply during the 1950s, but there is some evidence that through his depressions Cole was occasionally reminded of his good fortune. He was able to relate it in his lyrics. In 1936 he knocked out two songs, "Rap Tap on Wood" and "Ridin' High," which showed that at some level he was satisfied with his life. The first had lyrics such as,

"When ev'ry meal you take
Is made of milk and honey,
When every stock you stake
Is making mints of money,
Careful, Sonny,
Rap tap on wood."

Cole must have had thoughts of how fleeting his fame might be—and his good fortune.

Later that same year he banged out "How'm I ridin'? I'm ridin' high," with lyrics such as "I'm doin' fine/My life's divine/I'm livin' in the sun."

Cole's songs often listed famous people in the lyrics. Although people today may have forgotten Missus Harrison Williams, Mrs. Simpson and Eleanor Jarrett, or Simone

Simon, the meat and emotion of the song still makes it a universal favorite. We are in the dumps until love rescues us and now "blow horns, beat gongs, our love will never die . . . How'm I ridin'? I'm ridin' high."

Cole returned to New York in the fall of 1937 and Linda remained in Paris. Cole was working on his new Broadway musical but still had time for socializing. The story of "the accident" has been told scores of times. At a weekend party in Long Island he went horseback riding with friends. He chose a spirited mount. The horse fell over on one of Cole's legs, tried to get up only to roll over and crush Cole's other leg. Cole went into shock and was unconscious for two days. Kate and Linda were both notified and jointly made the decision not to have Cole's legs amputated. Both knew how vain he was about his appearance and that being an amputee would surely end his life.

In retrospect it appears that they made the right decision, although Cole would endure decades of pain and dozens of operations to save his legs. What everyone agrees on is that the accident saved the marriage of the Cole Porters. Linda, who'd recently threatened divorce, now rushed to his side and they resumed their marriage of convenience and mutual respect, but on a closer and more loving basis than before.

The whole incident had overtones of déjà vu as Linda had left her first husband, Edward Thomas, and returned to *him* after he'd broken both his legs in an auto accident. Perhaps Cole subconsciously was looking for an accident knowing Linda's penchant for rushing to the bedsides of her loved ones whenever illness or disaster struck. She'd done it for Sturges during his drinking binges, and now she stayed true to form and rushed to be with Cole. She never left him again until she died. As always he gave her a purpose for her life, and his gratitude showed her how much he actually did love her.

RELATIONSHIPS EITHER STRENGTHEN during a crisis or they break. In 1937 while the Porters renewed their commitment to each other Noel Coward's long-term relationship with

Jack Wilson was floundering. Noel published his first autobiography, *Present Indicative,* in 1937. It covered the first
thirty years of his life and ended with the enormous success
of *Cavalcade* in 1930. Jack was mentioned in the book as
Noel's close friend and business manager, but by 1937 there
had been several signs of change.

Jack and Noel's co-producing Noel's work (with the Lunts
joining them on certain projects) had been hit and miss. *Design for Living* was followed by *Operette* and was a disappointment for both critics and fans. Again, almost by accident,
Gertie stepped in to save Noel while he was purporting to
save her. She was in deep financial trouble and needed money.
She owed a lot of back taxes to the United States Internal
Revenue Service and was bankrupt. She urged Noel to write
another show for them to star in. He wrote several.

The result was his artistic tour de force, *Tonight at 8:30,*
a series of ten short plays, written by Coward and performed
by him and Gertrude Lawrence over several evenings in various combinations. (This included the play that offended
the Mountbattens so badly.)

With her first advance, naturally Gertie rented Moyneux's
villa in Antibes to rehearse in and hosted many famous
guests. When Noel and Jack Wilson came to stay and rehearse she turned out her own twelve-year-old daughter to
make room for them—not an unusual decision for an actress whose real family is the theatre.

The new show was a wonderful success and some of the
plays were filmed on their own separately. They represent
an artistic fulfillment for The Master and stand as excellent
and solid pieces of satisfying theatre.

The Astonished Heart is a powerful short play, combining a plot(!), something that Noel didn't usually bother
with, strong serious drama, and a depiction of the darker
side of sexual obsession from a realistic and frightening
point of view. A psychiatrist is drawn into a dalliance
that turns into a torturous and dangerous erotic liaison
that takes him over and leads to his destruction. The plot
is so removed from the superficial image Coward usually

affected in his public facade and in his plays that one wonders where it came from. Its theme was that sexual rejection is the same as being dead, and being loved romantically is being alive.

In one line the protagonist asks his lover how it felt to be female and desired completely. This one line wraps up the whole homosexual dilemma, the desire to know how it feels to have a man desire you completely, to be possessed and wanted beyond anything else. How does it feel?

To experience the fullness of being totally desired as the object of male sexuality goes beyond the physical act, although the physical act is part of it. This scene also reveals Noel's awareness that heterosexual men can be so obsessed by women that they want to experience, to *know* what a woman feels during the sex act, to be the recipient of biological aggression. Noel knew heterosexual men who dressed as women at times, and others who sought to be sexually used anally by other men to more fully understand female sexuality.

Noel makes it clear that the play is not about love, but about erotic compulsion—that the man is driven to want to *be* her, because he can't ever become intimate enough on the physical level. It is astonishing that Coward, the ultimate master of light emotion and mirth, should have given birth to this dark drama. (Years later Noel played the lead in the film version.)

It's almost a relief to know that *Tonight at 8:30* also contains *Ways and Means*, an extremely funny farce about a society couple who has a gambling problem and is always broke. Another play in the series *Still Life* was later filmed as the successful *Brief Encounter*.

Tonight at 8:30 was Gertie and Noel's last success performing together (although she did a revival of the show years later with Graham Payn playing Noel's roles in New York). Gertie's love affairs were as legendary as her acting brilliance. By this time her affair with Douglas Fairbanks, Jr., was over. He went on to date Marlene Dietrich. He tells this story:

"Marlene and I went backstage to congratulate them

(Noel and Gertie). The rumors about Marlene and me had begun to circulate just enough for Gertie to put on a bravura performance of exaggerated charm and bitchy cracks that made Noel dissolve into fits of laughter. I stood there with a silly smile on my face, unable to think of anything to say that would deflect the wit bursting like shrapnel all around me."

Noel was indeed as quick with a bitchy remark as Gertie. In fact he could be very difficult to deal with, especially during this period of intense success, because he really believed he knew it all and could not abide other people exhibiting independent observations about his work . . . especially if they happened to be accurate. He was noted for abusing his household people shamelessly whenever he was in a mood. They said they knew it was "just him" and had no problem accepting and/or ignoring these bursts of bile.

Cole Lesley, Coward's longtime companion/valet/secretary, was constantly under fire from Noel. Lesley told several stories of being cuttingly attacked by his employer in front of famous guests. These outbursts would come out of nowhere incited by a simple casual observation. Noel had the usual Britisher's prejudice that servants were supposed to be dumb. He displayed immense scorn when Lesley exhibited any sign of human intelligence.

Lesley had entered The Master's little circle in 1936 as a young man. He admitted in his biography of Noel that he had no talent for theatre but still wanted to be a part of it. He decided that becoming Noel's Man Friday would serve his needs, and thought himself fortunate when fate wafted him into that position. At first he found Lorn and Noel distant and formal, not at all what he expected. Later he discovered they'd had a run of "bummers," who did not work out after "the family" lavished familiarity and liberality on them. Noel and Lorn decided not to make that mistake again until the new person proved his loyalty and competenc. Cole Lesley did and remained with Noel until The Master died.

It doesn't seem likely at all that Noel and the young Lesley were physically intimate. Lesley was not attractive or famous, and he was a servant. Yet through the years Noel adopted him as family and treated him as more of a brother than he did his own. Lesley took on his duties with great skill and intelligence, although Noel never credited him with being as intelligent as he was. Because Lesley wasn't a performer or writer or creative the way Coward's superbly talented friends were, he was shunted off to one side. Given the caliber of people Noel knew—the *crème de la crème*—it is forgivable that he missed accurately assessing Lesley's true talents. If nothing else Lesley wrote an exceptional biography of The Master, filled with careful indexing and scrupulous devotion to facts, that's also fun to read.

Although Lesley was treated as a servant by all of Noel's English guests at Goldenhurst, he was often treated as a friend by the American stars who lodged there. Noel was fond of Cole and protected him; shouted at him and berated him; and at times transported him around like another appendage. And it is obvious he loved him.

If Lesley had a life apart from Noel's it does not show up in his biography of his employer. Through the ensuing years his close relationships were with Noel's close friends. Noel's overbearing ego gave him the gall to change Lesley's name without even asking if he wanted to. His original name was Leonard Cole but Noel said he loathed and hated Leonard, meaning he wouldn't have a name like that around the house. Cole was permitted to use his last name as his first name, although he personally loved his original moniker. He later was affectionately called "Coley," which led to some confusion in their social circles. (Cole Porter was also sometimes called "Coley." Lesley ascribed this confusion with names as the reason he and Porter didn't like each other much.)

The work of being secretary, butler, bath attendant, and confidant was constant. It was a matter of pride between them, according to "Coley," that the amount of his salary was never discussed. This could mean that it wasn't much, considering the hours and services rendered. But Lesley chose to attach his life to Noel's and he loved it. In later years Noel was seldom seen without his little coterie of Bobby, Binky, and "Coley," enabling him to give full vent to his gay bitchy nature, the one that had to be contained and camouflaged when in public with King George and Queen Elizabeth, or Sir Anthony, or later visiting the president and Eleanor Roosevelt and making them laugh with the kind of wit no straight man ever set forth.

Noel managed to walk that tightrope between outrageously gay remarks and cultivated dry wit. When he was being gay, the remarks could be scathing, even vicious. Lesley received many of these attacks himself when Noel's hairtrigger temper would break loose. It didn't take much. An honest, innocuous appraisal about Noel's work or appearance that was not totally complimentary could unleash a fury of insults. Noel would call him a stupid, moronic idiot in a full tyrannical onslaught of rage, and Lesley would always take it without reply. Sometimes days later an apology, not anywhere near as potent as the tirade, would be given, either grudgingly or magnanimously; still Lesley never took it personally. He assigned it to the artistic temperament. Certainly it took the demeanor of an English butler to withstand such nonsense, since many times the rages occurred in public, usually when Noel was insecure about himself or a work of his that was about to be presented.

With Lesley and Lornie to look after his needs and *Tonight at 8:30* an enormous hit in London and on Broadway, Noel attempted another operetta, a la *Bitter Sweet*, but *Operette* was not a hit. Neither was his autobiography, *Present Indicative*. In its way the book was very truthful for those days. Those who could read between the lines saw that Noel had laid out his gay relationships without baldly stating them. Jack Wilson, Jeffrey Amherst, that Coldstream Guard . . . but he of course interlaced them with mentions of his extreme closeness with Gladys, Lorn, Esme Wynne, and Gertie Lawrence. The book comes across as a sandwich filled with slices of life, the dressing and *garni* serving to mask the fact that there is some baloney in with the turkey breast.

He laid out his ambitiousness, his habit of getting to know people so he could add them to the list of people "who I know and who know me." Perhaps that is the reason why it was received so coolly. If one can't read between the lines it reads like a pleasant recount of a life that most people then were already familiar with from newspaper stories.

In the book Noel leaves the reader with the impression that Jack Wilson is a dear friend, still a member of his little family and a business partner. That was still the case when the book was finished in 1930. When the book came out several years later, their relationship had become strained. Jack had married a woman, Natasha Paley, a Russian princess no less, daughter of Grand Duke Paul. She was divorced from dress designer Lucian Lelong. She also was reportedly a lesbian and her marriage to a well-known (in theatre and social circles) gay man seemed to confirm this. They were obviously, all said, using each other as covers, although why Wilson needed one after being Noel's lover for so long is unclear.

Natasha was a close friend to Linda and Cole as well. Noel snidely called the marriage "Jack's twenty-first fine, careless rapture of youth." Obviously Noel wasn't as unaware of Jack's other twenty raptures as people might have thought.

Noel and Jack had been lovers in name only for many years. Noel attended the wedding at Jack's house in Fairfield, Connecticut. At the reception he and the Baron Nicolas de Gunzburg, bored of the whole middle-class affair, made up a filthy song in French, which they sung continuously at the reception. Most of the guests were Jack's family, so the French allusions were understood only by the bride herself. It basically described the practicalities of using petroleum jelly to make one's little machinery slippery for the wedding night, the inference being that there might be a

heated discussion about which member of the happy couple
would be on the receiving end.

For Noel to give in to such jealous bitchery and embarrass
the woman who had basically stolen his lover shows that
he felt spurned. Nonetheless Natasha was too lovely a person not to be liked. Because Jack and he were still "family"
and business partners, Noel sought to continue the warmth
and closeness of the relationship by becoming friends with
her. As time went on and Jack's drinking and ugliness grew,
Natasha turned more and more to Noel for solace.

Noel and Natasha had more in common than their fond-
ness for Jack. Natasha was now living in the safety of the
United States but she was essentially French. And she,
Noel, and all other Europeans were more keenly aware of
world events than the majority of Americans. Swords were
being rattled on the Continent even though the "war to end
all wars" had only ended twenty years earlier.

Cole and Linda sold their house in Paris and made
America their permanent residence after Cole's accident.
The storm clouds of war over Europe were ending the
worlds that Cole Porter and Noel Coward had created and
lived in.

X

"In Which We Serve"

BEING A STAR, a public personage, and an intimate of the royals it was now incumbent on Noel Coward to set an example for patriotism and wartime ardor. In his position and at his age he could easily have found ways to pay lip service while staying home and sipping champagne. He was in his forties, past the draftable age for the military so he was able to more comfortably offer his services based on his true talents. There is no doubt that his fervor was genuine, as was his mature appreciation for England; he was vocal in his condemnation of Hitler and the need to give the madman no inch or quarter.

Noel was also disgusted and said so at every opportunity when Neville Chamberlin had appeased Hitler. He said it was necessary to fight a bully on his own terms, not to try to appease him. So vocal and disgusted was he that he delightedly found himself on Hitler's hit list, that huge group of elite foes who were marked for extermination as soon as the Reich prevailed. Marlene was placed on it too after she refused Hitler's invitation to return to Germany and make movies for the Nazis.

Whatever isolationism kept Americans from recognizing Hitler for the beast he was no one in England could afford to be fooled. As early as 1937 Noel Coward engaged a singer named Fritzi Massary to play the lead in *Operette*. Besides the fact that he wanted her it was imperative that she get out of Germany as Hitler already had started rounding up Jews. Because of Noel she was able to get out of Germany and then escape to be with her daughter in America when the show closed.

There was an antagonism between Churchill and Coward when war was declared. Noel offered his services for England—a sort of "do with me what you will" offering. Churchill told him his best contribution was to go out and sing "Mad Dogs and Englishmen." Noel was stung by the rebuff although he did eventually go around entertaining the troops mostly at his own expense during the war. The polite conflict between them probably arose because Churchill was a heterosexual and a self-reverent egotist, who expended great wartime energy to make sure he continued to be supplied with the silk undershorts he favored.

He was a larger-than-life figure who affected a studied image and was famous for his spontaneous wit—all traits he shared with Noel. There are scads of similarities between them and it makes sense that each may have felt that this island, this England, wasn't big enough for the both of them.

Still war was war and if Noel was a shirker during the first one (and he had admitted that in his autobiography a few years earlier), he was determined to make this one his personal vendetta against the Third Reich. Each man saw himself as not just English, but as England. This kind of grandiose self-aggrandisement was very much a part of being famous during those years, and was expected and accepted. De Gaulle was France; Hitler was Germany; Stalin was Russia, and FDR was the United States. Looking at famous people then there was a distinct purposeful attempt to make signature images. Roosevelt had his cigarette holder, high jaw, and upper-class accent, which he emphasized. Churchill was never seen without the cigar stuck in his bulldog face and a "V for victory" hand gesture.

During the war especially these strong emphatic images were important for people to use as rallying points. Everyone was scared, the world stood in real danger of falling into a dark night of tyranny. And for most of the war Hitler did a very good job of making it appear that he would win. When a star like Noel Coward offered his contacts and his life to help his country in any way possible the sentiment was genuine. To have the prime minister make a dry remark was a slap in the face.

Hitler had taken over much of Europe by 1940 and still

many were not taking the war seriously. People remembered the First World War and assumed it was just more of the same tiresome noise from the Teutonic Tribes. It was called the Phoney War in England. Noel's first job for his country was to go to Paris and open an office to serve as a liaison with the French Information Bureau. He brought Cole Lesley along and they stayed at the Ritz, where other famous folk were planning to stay during their own occupation of France. Lady Mendl was there, determined to make this "a gay war." Lesley describes Coco Chanel's entrance into an air raid shelter followed at a respectful distance by her maid carrying a gas mask. The atmosphere was distinctly upper.

The Ritz proved too expensive so Noel and Coley rented an apartment on the Place Vendôme. Their first contribution to the war effort was to go out and shop. Lesley describes it like this:

"Noel tackled his first decorating job without anyone's advice, ordering natural wood furniture throughout, with uphostery in the same blue as the curtain, in tweed. A few scarlet cushions here and there and *voilà!*—how chic it looked."

Until the fall of France Paris was perhaps even more of a vibrant place to be than usual. Parties, good food, plenty of gaiety and special excitement. There were spies everywhere, and Noel's being invited to every occasion put him in a special position to carry information back and forth. Rumors were widespread, some true and most not; but the general tenor was that of a huge busy party of intrigue and camaraderie. And Paris was the most beautiful city to host such a gala.

Soon the lack of any real business began to wear on Noel and his natural boredom began to assert itself. He had set his taste for war; for once he was serious and all he was having were meetings and parties. Then Providence stepped in to protect him again. Just when the war heated up as the Nazis invaded Norway and Denmark, Sir Campbell Stuart, whom he reported to, asked Noel to sail for America in April.

Noel wanted to stay and face the action in Europe but Campbell insisted that Noel go to America, and use his clout and social contacts to find out if the United States was leaning toward coming into the war. Noel sailed for the States just before the Germans entered Paris. Cole Lesley stayed almost too late and barely got out of Paris with the thousands of other refugees from the city. The war became ugly.

Around this time Noel dropped—perhaps for good—his view of life as a gay romp. If during World War I he was a selfish bore, he almost tore himself apart trying to find some way to serve his country now. When Cole Lesley decided to enlist instead of taking a job as Noel's wartime assistant in an official capacity, Noel gave his worried blessing. This was an enormous sacrifice for him, to let go of the person who took care of every aspect of his life from making his bed to putting up with his temperamental abuse to planning his parties to cosseting his mum. Noel assured him Goldenhurst was always his home and wished Cole well.

The British press attacked Noel's journey to America as being anti-productive. When he visited President and Mrs. Roosevelt, on their invitation, he was slapped hard by the London newspapers, dominated by Lord Beaverbrook. The attitude seems to have been, that while his fellow countrymen were putting up with bombs and privations, he was safely across the ocean, making merry with the upper crust. Every time he tried sincerely to "get a job" and use his influence to make a strong contribution, something thwarted him. He was as frustrated trying to get into this war as he had been trying to stay out of the first one.

One press slap went like this:

". . . the despatch of Mr. Noel Coward as special emissary to the States can do nothing but harm. In any event, Mr. Coward is not the man for the job. His flippant England—cocktails, countesses, caviar—has gone."

This much was true; the war had ended the world that produced Noel Coward and Cole Porter, and that they had been so much a part of shaping.

The constant biting in the press made it unfeasible for the government to continue trying to use Coward's services in any official capacity. Noel blamed Beaverbrook and Winston Churchill. As it turned out Churchill's flip advice had been correct. Noel's real job as an entertainer was to do shows and keep up the morale of the country.

He made an excellent artistic contribution during these years with his film *In Which We Serve*. He wrote and directed it and played the lead. It is a classic, still aired on TV today. Many of his plays are dated but this movie touches an emotional chord and should be viewed as an example of The Master's best offering. It's a solid piece of work and his acting style is compelling. On the set he was a merciless taskmaster.

Noel Coward was often callous in dealing with those he was most close to emotionally. There can be no doubt that the two women he was devoted to other than his mother were Lorn and Gladys. Gladys Calthrop was always an important element to his success and an anchor in his life. Yet even she was not spared his egotism when her problems came in the way of his desires. Yet, in typical Coward style, he could be very open and honest about his selfishness.

Gladys had been divorced for years, even before Noel had met her in the early 1920s, and she had a son, Hugo, to whom she was devoted. Like almost all young men in 1939 he'd joined the military, and was serving in the British navy. In 1942 Coward and Gladys were working on the film *In Which We Serve*. One day during the filming Gladys interrupted Noel.

"Could I have a word with you, Noel?"

"Yes, of course, what is it?"

"It's about Hugo. I've just heard. He's been killed."

"Well, there's nothing you can do about it, is there, dear?"

Coward later explained his reasons for his curt reply.

"I knew that if I sympathized with her for one moment she would have broken up, which she finally did, but not until months later after we'd completed the film."

And he softened his statement, as all good queens would: "I admired her tremendously."

His admiration at that moment was not much in evidence, but the picture was not delayed. It shows how completely engrossed he was in his own egotism. In every case, he came first.

The caustic Coward wit was evident when he told Michael Rennie after his stint in the film, "Michael, dear, you must be the Dean of Juveniles." Rennie knew Coward thought him too old for the part he played. Always one to temper his criticism with charm Coward added, "You'll be a great star."

"Why?" Rennie asked.

"Because you've personal charm. So have I. But I have talent too. I am very clever indeed. I have this God-given talent, but I don't abuse my talent ever. I work hard at it."

Kenneth Tynan once said that Coward had ". . . two weapons, wit and sentimentality . . . inside him, a poet and a philosopher are shrieking to be kept in. On a few occasions when they have escaped (parts of *In Which We Serve*, parts of *This Happy Breed*) they have died horribly within minutes."

Still Coward's sentimentality in these two World War II pieces did work beautifully and they were just what the world and especially England needed in 1942. The remarkable thing about Noel's portrayal of an English officer in the film was his restrained and convincingly masculine depiction. He was such a nervous and effete gay man in person, yet on film, like Clifton Webb, he was as stalwart, straight, and strong as Gregory Peck.

JUST BEFORE THE WAR Noel had written two plays, *This Happy Breed* and *Present Laughter*, an autobiographical farce. *This Happy Breed* is a plotless soap opera, and at the end it turns into a soapbox for the main character, Frank, to stand on when he makes a long, windy patriotic speech about having to fight for freedom and rails against people who put down

England, which despite some minor mistakes is pretty much all right to Frank's way of thinking. He also scorns people who "get soft and afraid" to fight for their country, people who talk about peace and goodwill and ideals but don't believe in them *enough to fight for them*. (This from the same person who fretted because World War I delayed his plans for a theatre career by several months.)

But this was World War II and Noel was now a national figure (as well as being too old to enlist). Movies and plays during that war were full of those speeches, delivered in monotones and run-on sentences, affirming that no one was going to break this nation of ours, certainly not some rotten little madman who can't understand that decency doesn't mean weakness and that free people won't ever bow under the yoke of a slave master, et cetera. It was all true, as it turned out, but it was odd to hear it coming from Noel Coward.

As for the play, it spans the history of a middle-class English family from 1919 to 1939, and hasn't the slightest gossamer strand of a plot anywhere in the whole three-act voyage. It is soap opera from start to finish, a slice of life, with very little action, a good deal of the kind of family bickering that typified the Coward household, the kind of petrified low-key drama that makes television viewing a dull headache from noon to four P.M. The play could not have been produced if television had been around then. In those days movies and plays served the same purpose; today we would wonder who could sit through an evening of this kind of tripe.

Present Laughter is most interesting in that it is a totally autobiographical comedy, with the main character of Garry Essendine being Noel himself, and other characters being stage versions of Lorn Lorraine, Cole Lesley, Joyce Carey (who played her own role), Binkie Beaumont, Jeffrey Amherst, and others less easily identifiable. In the play the antagonistic female character Joanna, who is a composite of the unpleasant traits of Jack Wilson, symbolizes the negative effect that his lover had overall on Noel's friends and career.

Reading *Present Laughter* is like eating a box of Godiva chocolates all by yourself. At first it's a thrilling and delightful experience, but eventually you get used to the richness and wish there were more of the whiskey creams and less of the cocoa-covered ones. Coward wrote the play to give himself a really knockout role, and one can see and hear him doing it so brilliantly. He reaffirms his position as legend and star here, as this is one of his characters that shows up so often in his plays—the legendary star who, no matter how tiresome his actions, inspires undying loyalty and love among his colleagues.

Since Noel really was like that he succeeds best at writing those roles about and for himself. What is most amazing about this play is that one never tires of the scenes or the dialogue despite Coward's adamant refusal to create a plot. The play is a *tour de force*, perhaps meant to reassure Noel in the face of so much criticism that a play about nothing but himself could be a hit. The fact that he succeeded so well validates his genius. One must never forget that Coward was a star because he never did.

Garry Essendine delivers a speech to his friends in *Present Laughter*, in which Noel seems to be cataloging his own attitudes toward sex. He says to Morris that he ". . . happens to like taking your paltry attachments seriously. You like suffering and plunging into orgies of jealousy and torturing yourself and everyone else."

The second comment he makes toward Henry. His . . . "technique is a little different; he plumps for the domestic blend."

Thirdly, he says of Joanna, she's ". . . different again. She devotes a great deal of time to sex, but not for any of the intrinsic pleasure of it, merely as a means to an end. She's a collector, a go-getter, an attractive, unscrupulous pirate."

Finally, the playwright says of himself, "You believe in your lachrymose amorous hangovers, whereas I at least have the grace to take mine lightly. You wallow and I laugh because I believe now and I always have believed that there's far too much nonsense talked about sex.

"To me the whole business is vastly overrated. I enjoy it for what it's worth and fully intend to go on doing so for as long as anybody is interested, and when that time comes that they're not, I shall be perfectly content to settle down with an apple and a good book!"

But Noel was not quite ready to carry that out fully. Yes he did like his apple and good books, but he wasn't content to just give up. Not even long after anyone was interested in his aging charms.

Blithe Spirit also was produced during the war. Joyce Carey costarred in this play with Noel, and it was she who helped, in a sense, get it written. She was writing a play about Keats at the time, and she and Noel went off together to rest up and write. She worked upstairs, he worked down. He finished his play in a few weeks, and Joyce provided the title, taken from the Keats poem:

Hail to thee, blithe spirit, bird thou never wert.

He dedicated the play to her. Noel wrote the play several years after the other two, but the event of wartime delayed the production of *Laughter* and *This Happy Breed* until things settled down enough to figure how to present a play with bombs dropping on the theatres of London. Coward noted that after his concentrated period of writing on *Blithe Spirit*, he looked it over. He was "willing to rewrite and revise it if necessary," but found it wasn't needed. How right he is was evident in the enormous success of the show, and its freshness even today. It ran longer than any other English play until Agatha Christie's *The Mousetrap*. Whether or not *Charley's Aunt*, which was written in less than a week, has had more actual productions worldwide is not known; but on the West End, Coward's play had a record run.

NOEL HAD MADE MANY SACRIFICES for England during the war. One major contribution was his farm, Goldenhurst. Early on it had been taken over by the army for billeting, because of its location near the sea. He had to make do in a spare room at his bombed out Gerald Road flat, until he was given affordable terms to live at the Savoy. "Affordable" was the key. At the start of the war he was short of money as usual. To make things worse he still had enormous taxes to pay. Then he found himself caught in a court mess caused by Jack Wilson's muddling of his affairs. If he wanted to expiate his guilt about the seven-shilling pension he'd received during the first war, he certainly was paying out in spades now.

Fortunately for his battered ego, the plays, films, and four songs he wrote during wartime were well received. King George VI, Queen Elizabeth, and the two little princesses came to visit him on the set of the movie. As always the royal family retained their high regard for his efforts and their personal liking for him.

During the war he had tried entertaining Australian troops, who had no real idea who he was. This was his first taste of "cabaret style" performing and the lads from Down Under couldn't have disliked him more. The vital young soldiers wanted to see movie starlets in slinky dresses, not a middle-aged man with a clipped accent singing patter songs about some world they didn't know about. He braved it through despite their vocal disenchantment. The Australians weren't as delicate as the British. One newspaper interviewer asked him bluntly if he was a queer.

As if to finish off the bitter cup he had to swallow during these years, Noel's mother added her small but toxic pill to the drink. He had sent her to New York to be safe from the *blitzkrieg*, and installed her in his small apartment in the luxurious address of Fifty-third Street between First Avenue and the East River. His friends Alexander Woolcott, who wasn't known for fits of charity, John LaTouche, the playwright, and others great and small, escorted Violet everywhere in wartime Gotham, using up their ration books on her. She was almost in her eighties, but when she wanted to be she was as delightful and barb-witted as her son. Her sister Vida was living with her, but Violet began to pick on her, alternating abuse with ignoring her and leaving her home alone while she went to opening nights with Noel's friends. Then she'd gloat about it. Violet was not pleasant.

When Vida had enough she risked the dangerous Atlantic waters to go home, leaving Violet to her fun. But part of Violet's fun was in having an audience—another trait she shared with Noel. Soon Noel was receiving lonely complaining letters, accusing him of purposely sending her to the States to get rid of her, then ignoring her. Unfortunately she was stuck there; you didn't just get up and go where you wanted in wartime. Everything was based on an "if." If someone more important than you didn't need your seat, then your ticket would be honored; but you wouldn't know for sure until you were actually on the way. Then you wouldn't know if you'd get home safely or be torpedoed by a German submarine.

Noel tried. Four times Violet packed her bags and went to the dock only to be told there was no space for her. She had to spend a wretched year of loneliness in Noel's apartment, pining for the family she adored and abused mercilessly, until she finally got back home to see them.

During the war the Duke of Kent, the King's brother, was killed in an airplane crash. Noel took the death of his friend and ex-lover very hard. He moaned about the asses he knew who were still alive, including the Duke of Windsor, while his sweet young prince had been taken. Coward cried openly at the funeral and wrote that after all the royals had left the scene, "we all went up, one by one . . . and secretly said goodbye to him." Noel would remain close friends with Princess Marina and her children.

The war years further distanced Noel from Jack Wilson, who was enjoying a successful career as a producer/director on Broadway. Noel had discovered—painfully—that Jack was not the scrupulous detail-minded manager he had hoped. Noel was served with papers and could easily have gone to jail because Jack messed up his finances so badly. There was a law in England that if an English subject made money in another country he wasn't allowed to spend it there and was required to report it. Jack had deposited the money into an American account and was spending it. He probably wasn't aware of the law, or if he was didn't credit it with having teeth. When it bit during World War II, the publicity made Noel look like a wartime slacker trying to cheat the government in its hour of need.

He was only saved from a prison sentence and an enormous fine because he was able to show he had never intended to break the law. Noel was lucky. The prosecutor during the trial claimed that Noel should be fined 61,000 pounds—about $300,000 in those days. His barrister Geoffrey Roberts made a brilliant defense and the fine was reduced to only 200 pounds for one charge, and 1,600 for the second.

For years Noel had been ignoring his financial relationship with Jack. There had been indications all along that Coward was too bored to address the situation. At one point in the 1930s Jack had had a partnership agreement drawn up that gave him half of Noel's earning in return for his services.

Later Noel wanted to cancel the agreement, calling it "iniquitous." Jack sent back word that he was too hurt and angry over Noel's attitude and refused to cancel.

It can be fairly ascertained that Jack was getting more mileage out of Noel's money than Noel was. Further Jack appears to have been as lazy about the bookkeeping as any other artistic type. Even if Noel would have been interested in sitting down and scanning the books he had no skills in money management. One is left wondering if it was the emotional emptiness or the monetary betrayal that really bothered Noel. He later wrote a poem about being no good at love. One of the lines reads, "Suspicion tears at my sleepless mind."

The wartime prosecution was the first serious blow. It began to clear Noel's head. He had to free himself of his ex-lover/manager. The scandal had also denied him the one thing he prized—a knighthood. Many, including the royal family, felt it was time to reward and recognize Noel's contribution to the war effort, as well as his artistic contribution. But the British found he presented something of a problem. The bad publicity surrounding this sensitive subject of wartime taxes was not going to make a knighthood appropriate. Noel was also flamboyant, not necessarily a raging queen, but unorthodox in all aspects of his life.

Now he ran up against the wall of propriety. King George VI wanted to have him knighted. It was considered a *fait accompli*. Then it all fell apart. The reason cited was the publicity over the American monies. The British press made it a scandal, made it appear that Noel was purposely cheating the government. It was a devastating rejection for Noel, who had been the target of abuse in the British press for years.

Suddenly he could do nothing right. To be passed over for knighthood when the King himself had expressed a definite wish to honor him (it had gone so far that Noel had even written to the King saying he would be honored to accept!) sat like a lead weight on his soul. He blamed Lord Beaverbrook and Winston Churchill for sabotaging it. He even made a personal investigation into the matter. He raged and spat and hissed, but he never really settled the matter in his heart. And it was all Jack's fault. Noel blamed himself and Jack but the damage was done and it would be decades before he finally became Sir Noel Coward.

Meanwhile he once again had commercial success to soothe his wounded ego. With *In Which We Serve* on screen, and *Blithe Spirit* on stage, Noel's future seemed as bright as his past. Ironically even though his creativity would be spurred on by renewed love and lust his output would never be of the same caliber.

XI

"Why Must the Show Go On?"

THE DRIVE TO REMAIN ON TOP—in any profession but especially in the entertainment business—has a great deal to do
with ego and power. It also has a great deal to do with
sex—getting sex, that is. Men and women who are rich and
powerful can always buy sexual interludes, but it's so much
nicer to have them come your way with the conviction that
the nubile young woman or the hunky young stud *really*
wants to get it on with *you*. Financial rewards can always
be reaped in other ways: expensive jewelry, a new car, a
part in a musical.

Noel and Cole were no different. As they entered their
forties and fifties, respectively, it was important for them
to remain not just rich, but famous and sexually desirable.

While Noel had had hectic war years in England and around
the globe, Cole had spent the war in Hollywood and New
York, far removed from any real dangers or inconvenience.

After Cole's accident his life was modified somewhat by
the operations, the pain, and especially the painkillers he
had to take in enormous amounts. A new man entered his
life. Ray (R.C.) Kelly was hired as a male nurse/companion.
Cole was still able to travel. He took trips with his valet,
Paul Sylvain, and Ray, but Cole's interest in work did not
abate. If anything it increased. He wrote show after show:

You'll Never Know, which had the hit song "At Long
Last Love."

Leave It to Me, which had the songs "Most Gentlemen
Don't Like Love," "My Heart Belongs to Daddy," and "Get
Out of Town."

Then back to Hollywood for *Broadway Melody* ("I Concentrate On You"); then Broadway again, for *DuBarry Was
a Lady, Panama Hattie, Let's Face It.*

Each show was less of a hit than the previous one, but Hollywood still wanted Cole and Cole was still addicted to the film capital, especially since it was filled with uniformed youths serving their country's call. Now that Paris was occupied and world travel was limited Cole spent more time on the West Coast.

He and Linda had made a new pact; when Cole went to stay in Hollywood now, it was mostly for the sun and work, both of which were therapeutic to his crippled legs. One era of partying had ended, and another had begun with the town filled with servicemen. Cole still had sex and parties, but his days of running around town flaming with contingents of gay birds squawking, was ended. His parties and sex were conducted in the privacy of the house. The result was that both Cole and Linda got what they wanted; he got Hollywood, the studs, and their marriage intact; she got Cole, peace and quiet, and the resumption of the public elegant facade of their previous life together.

At this point Linda had been relegated to surrogate mother. Cole respected her and was grateful to both her and his mother, Kate, for their support during the accident and recovery, but the Porter marriage was now really a facade. They had never been sexual but in the past Linda had served as an important emotional/social part of Cole's life. This was no longer true. Linda was now too old and tired to accompany Cole on his trips, or even to opening nights and parties. She had once served as an attraction for people Cole had wanted most to meet. He had used her not for attracting sex as some gay men use their wives or women friends, but for social reasons. Now, in short, she was just too old for all that.

Another gay man in this position—or even a heterosexual—might have just divorced his older wife, but Cole Porter was too well bred. Besides he was genuinely fond of Linda and saw no need for divorce—just a reorienting of their positions and their schedules.

She now truly moved to the position of second mother; she was loved, trusted, and cared about (as was Kate) but not allowed to interfere with his daily life. She still arranged to give him the glittering cigarette cases on his opening nights, which had become their private legend, but she was no longer a part of the opening nights or productions. She was often in Arizona for her health, but she desperately wanted to play some active part in Cole's life. She insisted, now that their home in Paris was sold, that they should have a country home outside of Manhattan. It was necessary for her to have a salon, and for him to have a retreat. Cole had no desire to live anywhere but in a sophisticated city where the action was, so he was not enthusiastic when she found Buxton Hill in the Berkshires.

He knew they'd spend little actual time there together since her health would certainly deter them from the winters in Massachusetts, but she insisted they buy it. He couldn't stop her of course. When she announced that they would build a separate house for him to work in, his own "warren" so to speak, he acquiesced in her desire to buy Buxton Hill.

Boredom was more anathema to him than pain. When he broke his legs and was suffering pain that would have put most of his big, muscular sex partners away, he found in his pain a source of creativity, of focus; in any event it killed his boredom. He even named his legs "Josephine" and "Geraldine" (names that later were adopted by Billy Wilder as the drag names for Tony Curtis and Jack Lemmon in the movie *Some Like It Hot*). And he would take the "girls" back to Hollywood as often as possible.

Cole was aware of the crassness of Tinseltown as well as the dream quality that he loved. In one of his "list" songs, "A Picture of Me Without You," he pictures "love in Hollywood without divorce." He spotlighted Hollywood several more times either with sincerity or parody. He wrote a song called "There's a Hollywood That's Good" for his 1950s show *Silk Stockings*, but it wasn't used. Many of his songs had little references to L.B. Mayer. Some were digs ("I've never been defined by refined L.B. Mayer") to the mere use of the name ("Not stars like L.B. Mayer's are we"). But Cole had fun incorporating famous names from every walk of life into his songs to get a topical laugh, from FDR to Lily Pons's throat.

An unused song of his, written for *Let's Face It*, was called "A Humble Hollywood Executive," and he makes a mocking admiration for the qualities of this type.

> A helpful Hollywood executive
> At Bar X
> Taught me for several weeks consecutive
> About sex.

This verse is repeated for each different executive, using the casting couch to conduct lessons in "studio politics."

One of Cole's old Hollywood songs was revived during World War II. "Don't Fence Me In," sung by Roy Rogers in *Hollywood Canteen*, became a roaring success. It was later recorded by Bing Crosby and the Andrews Sisters. Cole was often embarrassed by the song because it was one of the very few that he hadn't written the lyrics to. They were based on a poem by a real cowboy, Bob Fletcher. Porter, when he was working for Fox in 1935, had bought the poem and all rights for $250.

There were a few weeks of unflattering publicity about Cole stealing someone else's lyrics, but the Hollywood press boys soon put an end to that. If they could handle his escapades with servicemen, they certainly could plaster over some long-ago incident involving a cowboy's one-time bout with verse. Besides Cole was "in the hospital," which was the only reason Fletcher hadn't received his promised credit when the song was recorded. In addition Cole signed over a part of the song's royalties to him, not legally necessary since he'd bought it outright.

There is no doubt that Cole was eminently suited to the kind of money and adulation and lifestyle he enjoyed in Hollywood. Some of his very best work was done for the movies, and it brought him to an audience of young people who responded strongly to his work all his life. People who never went to Broadway shows, or even knew what they were all about, went to the movies to snuggle with a date, or just because they liked movies. And Cole was writing for some of the biggest moneymakers for three decades. Perhaps more than anything it was his film work that established his position as the preeminent American romantic songwriter.

In addition to the casting couch, part of Cole's happiness with the movies was the film version of his life, which starred, at his request, Cary Grant. This smash hit, which had as much to do with Porter's real life as with yours or mine, was a fantasy that pleased him greatly. What short, bug-eyed cruiserweight would not want Cary Grant to portray him on the screen? This was one love affair in Cole's life that never saw a cloudy moment. It also was something new to be shared with Linda, who chose Alexis Smith to portray her.

A clever wag has called *Night and Day* "one of the outstanding science-fiction films of the age." Films of the 1940s never dealt with homosexuality, of course, but the fictions concocted in this film to mask Cole's sexual preference and give the story some plot were preposterous. The studio stressed that these films were authentic in the minutest detail, such as costumes and backgrounds (but curiously in Hollywood, never hairstyles or makeup). In Cole's case he had even, according to Warner Brothers' publishing, submitted his own personal scrapbooks for research. On most biographical films the studios had to console themselves with children or wives or distant relatives of the celebrated subjects for factual accuracy. But this film had the man himself supposedly overseeing the proceedings, so surely it must all be true.

Film biographies always have more impact than written ones. For one thing millions more people will be exposed to a biopic; for another the celebrated figure will be portrayed by another celebrated, and usually handsomer, figure. Bette Davis was Queen Elizabeth I; Henry Fonda was Abraham Lincoln; and Spencer Tracy was Father Flanagan.

Irving Berlin, who had done a sort of semi-autobiography,

This Is the Army, for Warner Brothers suggested to the studio that they do Cole's life. He admired Porter tremendously, not just for his talent but especially his courage to come back after the terrible accident that took out his legs. But what about the fact that Cole was a homosexual—how could that be handled on film? The answer: he was married and had been for decades. It's quite possible that if Cole Porter hadn't had a wife the studio would not have considered the film bio.

Hollywood had straightened out other famous lesbians and gay men before. With Cole's famous wife this would be an easy task, especially since she'd been such a beauty.

In the script other elements of fact disappeared as well. Linda's first marriage evaporated. She was no longer eight to fourteen years older than her husband, although the age spread between the stars Grant and Alexis Smith was noticeable. The film highlighted the "triumph of the hick from Indiana" aspect of his life, as a sympathetic ploy for the middle America audiences. They surrounded Cole with chorus girls, implying (for the husbands in the audience) that he was tempted to cheat on his beautiful wife, and to really mask the truth that he'd rather cheat with the stagehands. They made Cole's friend Monty Woolley, who played himself, of course, a "skirt chaser" instead of a "fly swatter."

The studio decided to make Monty's character one of Cole's professors, not a classmate, and they hired him as a technical adviser. His main duty seemed to be to point out there were too many boys wearing sweaters with the letter "Y" on them.

The script was laughable. Cole in the trenches of World War I composing "Begin the Beguine"; Linda as a Red Cross nurse's aide; Cole composing "Night and Day" during the war when these songs weren't written until fifteen years or more later. When they melded Cole's inspiration with his heterosexual romance, everyone bought it.

The accident and Cole's rising above it was the main part of the script. Screenwriter Jack Moffit complained to Hal Wallis, "Instead of dramatizing Cole Porter songs, which all

Americans know and love, Mr. Schwartz (the producer) has dramatized the man Cole Porter, whom few people know and most people would dislike."

Wallis and the studio didn't care. They knew they'd have a big biographic hit and they were right. The film was a smash. Porter and his wealth and lifestyle were downplayed. His mental depression before Linda and his physical ordeal of pain after the accident were highlighted. Even today when people think of Cole Porter, they visualize Cary Grant. *Night and Day* became one of Hollywood's memorable films, melding subject with star for a combined classic image of untruth.

NOEL COWARD TOO HAD ENJOYED the benefits of stardom and power. He'd had his pick of willing servicemen during the war, many hoping later to be remembered and cast in a new West End musical. One young boy had, we're led to believe, waited fourteen years for The Master to notice him—again!

Graham Payn was born in 1918 in South Africa, and his theatre career showed early similarities to that of the young Noel. When Graham was thirteen he first appeared on stage at the London Palladium in a Christmas production of *Peter Pan*. When he auditioned for Coward in 1931 for *Words and Music* Noel was so taken with the boy he gave him two small parts in the revue. The story is that it was not until years later when Graham was an adult that he and Noel met again and became lovers. Only Payn knows when he and Noel first had sex together but one thing is certain: by 1945 Noel was so smitten with the twenty-seven-year-old actor that he was writing special songs for him and announcing he would star in Noel's first postwar revue, *Sigh No More*.

In 1945 in the aftermath of the war itself and Noel's own personal battles for victory on other fronts, including the mess produced for him by Wilson, he saw in the young actor some sort of respite, like the sun shining again after so many years of clouds and storm. Noel also was forty-five, a watershed year for a man. He was middle-aged. He was a legend. In gay terms he was over the hill. He could no longer dash about the clubs of London doing silly things and picking up members of the Palace Guard. He was intimate friends with the King and Queen.

Graham's biggest assets were his personality and good looks. Good looks of course are common commodities in the theatre, and his were not spectacular, as had been Wilson's, but he was no dog either. And Noel liked him. Cole Lesley liked him, Lorn liked him, everyone who met him liked him.

Jack Wilson hated his guts.

Around Good Friday, 1945, Graham Payn had his first lecture about his career from Noel. He was firmly advised to set higher standards for himself. It was clear that Graham had cut through Noel's wavering resolve to be more self-protective in affairs of the heart; Graham moved into the inner circle. Noel had written a song, "Matelot," especially to show off Graham's voice to its best advantage. Hearing about this put Jack Wilson on the offense. He invited Cole Lesley to lunch at the Carlton and cross-examined him. He demanded that Lesley admit he hated Graham's guts the moment he walked in the door.

Lesley described Graham as enthusiastic, kind, *honest*, generous in spirit and with money, and being loving as well as lovable. Wilson remained Payn's enemy, but his influence over Noel had waned and The Master remained staunchly committed to Graham for the rest of his life.

Payn was handsome, not as striking as Wilson had been, but was one hell of a lot nicer. His basic sweet nature made him a pleasant addition to company, but unfortunately one doesn't achieve stardom in the theatre by being nice. Noel soon made it his grail to help Graham achieve stardom, writing roles for the singer/dancer/actor that were plums. Nothing worked. To become a star requires an intense inner desire, which Payn did not possess.

Graham was one of those actors who has talent but no fire. It seems almost that the attraction of an acting career for him was the off times as well as the on stage times. He had no push. His parents had some money and his mother had been a stage mom of the type who does it all, while the child is more a tagalong. So with Noel he was content to let Noel do the work while Graham waited to go on stage. There's not an actor in the world who wouldn't want that kind of opportunity and at the same time knows that it's the kiss of death. If you don't make it on your own in show business, nobody credits you with having any talent. It's a stigma.

Their early relationship demonstrates Noel "in love." He began "throwing the house out the window" for his lover, trying to give him the world as a gift. Since Graham was not a user in the sense that Wilson was, Noel, who had a typical gay man's need to *do* something once he was attached to a lover, began using himself for the passive, nice Graham.

Although enormously likable Payn was not overly intelligent. He began an innocent baiting of Noel in the mistaken assumption that The Master wanted give-and-take teasing. In reality Noel wanted obedience, an audience, and a general appreciation for his own witticisms. Lorn and Coley gently warned Graham away from this tack, much like a mother doe nudges her fawn away from danger. They used lines from a poem, "Little Lad Beware," and the name stuck. From that point on Noel called Graham, "Little Lad."

Noel was very good at friendships, at family relationships, at being himself in his coterie of professional and personal dealings. But when he fell in love and took a lover, he didn't know what to do. There was this *person* sitting there, and Noel was suddenly the primary person in his life. What in bloody hell should he do now? Perform a scene from *Private Lives*?

He decided to reshape the lovable lump of clay that was Graham Payn, help him, do something with him. He had to be nice to him—at least during the honeymoon period. Noel, whose bitch temper and tyrannical rantings were commonplace, suddenly had to be sweet so as not to spoil those all-important early days of the relationship.

So he went to work. He wrote roles with Graham in mind but Noel only knew one kind of role. He'd been writing for himself all his life. Somewhere in his mind it became the standard, not the vehicle. Casting Graham, who was as opposite a personality as you could find, in the kinds of roles Noel played so brilliantly himself, showed that he was trying to remake Graham into a little Noel.

Many people couldn't understand that although Noel had a new lover Jack Wilson was still an important part of his life. Coward's relationships with both Wilson and Payn show a pattern that persists among gay people, men and women, and their ex-lovers. Unless there is an out-and-out brawl, complete with broken dishes and blackened eyes, often, even when the sexual part of the relationship ends, the "family" part persists. If that word, family, seems an odd one it really is what happens in gay life. Once the love relationship is declared there are a variety of factors that keep it going even after it is obviously no longer a full "marriage." Gratitude is often a major factor leading to lifelong loyalty. In Noel's case he would always remember that the young and spectacular Jack Wilson chased him down and tenaciously held on to all aspects of their relationship even after he'd married Natasha Paley. They had been lovers and Noel could not forget the sweetness of those early days.

Neither Wilson nor Payn would have sought Noel out if he hadn't been the famous person he was. But he was famous and that was an inseparable part of him. To hypothesize what would have been if he hadn't been famous is ridiculous. Wilson's affection had been genuine because Noel was what he wanted: a successful theatrical star who was willing to let Jack take control of his life. If Noel hadn't been those things, Jack wouldn't have wanted him, and would have gone on to some other person who would fit his needs.

Graham Payn's mild manner made him more the kind of controllable lover Noel needed later in life. Payn was in love with the theatre and Noel was among its brightest stars. Why shouldn't he love Noel? Again when the physical intimacy and the romance ended, Graham stayed on until Noel's death. We know that the "lover" part of this relationship ended and that Graham became "family" because Noel was back out there looking for sex and even love within a short time.

Very often ex-lovers in a gay relationship will continue being friends and will extend the family warmth to new lovers. Noel extended deep friendship to Jack's wife and remained steadfast and genuine in his affections for her. Noel had implanted this pattern in *Design for Living*. We find three characters who put aside conventional hatreds and decide to be a three-way marriage instead. In real gay life this situation exists very often, especially when one man marries a woman. The three continue on their "modern" merry way.

Gay people, who often get no real warmth from the "straight" world, are noted for going to great lengths to give solace and support to each other. It is easier to continue the warmth and intimacy of a former lover than to face the chilling shutout of evicting them emotionally. The memory lingers and is a source of safety and comfort, even if the relationship was difficult. For Noel, whose pattern was to make many of these "nests" of support among his friends, it follows that he would not want to give the smallest part of that emotional familiarity once it was established. It is the reason he could be friends with the wives of ex-lovers and sex partners, going on to be godfather to their children in some cases. He needed this special intimacy much more than the simple act of sex. In fact the one area of failure in which he could truthfully take a cavalier attitude was in the area of sexual encounters. He might make a concerted effort to bed down an object of his lust, but if he struck out he was able to chalk it up as an incomplete pass, rather than rage and bite at his entrails over it. It was emotional and artistic rejection that he couldn't abide. For that reason he could not bring himself to cut out someone he once loved because he identified so strongly with the pain involved. He would rather put up with Jack's misuse of his money and Graham's lackadaisical approach to his career than push them out of his affections.

Sigh No More did not make a star of Graham Payn. Some thought the song "Matelot" had homosexual overtones (how could it not?) with lyrics such as

> Though you find womankind
> to be frail, one love cannot fail. . . .
> > and
> Jean Louis Dominic right or wrong
> ever pursued a new love. . . .

However, the song could still be safely sung as if the "true love" were his mother, not another man. Graham's sailor character of "Matelot" fame seemed to be Noel's way of dressing him up in a sailor costume that he himself had always found attractive. It was warmly received when presented, but Graham did not have the drive nor the reach to build it into a path to stardom.

Cole Lesley tells us that Noel never really learned that times were changing. Without someone like Cochran to guide him Noel soon lost touch with what people wanted to see. During the war *Oklahoma!* had opened and immediately reshaped the look of musicals from the loose and sexy revues that were hit-and-miss to being a cogent integration of plot and song to move a story line. Personalities were still important, but a show could now make a star, rather than vice versa. Noel was still mired in the idea that a "Noel Coward Show" was what people wanted, even though people kept telling him that it wasn't so anymore.

His past success had become a trap for him. Never a craftsman, his plays had to come out of him in a complete flow. Just as he would be irritated by the mundanities of life, he could not stomach sitting down and rewriting or reworking a scene or song. It had to be born from him as a baby, fully formed. His entire career was done by "flourish." He waved his elegant hand and *voilà*! It was consummated. Such an imperial attitude led to constant battles in theatre, the most famous being with Mary Martin in *Pacific 1860*.

He had written the show with her in mind for the lead, a puzzling choice since she was so wrong for the part that even she knew it. Nonetheless she idolized Coward and wanted desperately to work with him, so she allowed Noel to convince her and her manager/husband, Richard Halliday, that she could play the role. Mary's usual experience was that all new plays go through rewrites to make them harmonize with the actors. She had a rude awakening. Noel had no intention of rewriting. He handed the cast the script, demanded they be "letter perfect" in two weeks' time, and became an unapproachable tyrant.

Mary's voice was wrong for the operatic role and her Texas drawl didn't work as well as the clipped English favored by Noel's prose and verse. The fallout came over bows, however. Before signing onto Noel's theatrical ship, Mary and her husband had specifically designated that none of her costumes would have bows on them. Mary hated them and felt they worked against her. If this quirk seems silly one must remember that actors need to feel presentable on stage if they are to function. If they feel ridiculous their performances suffer.

Gladys Calthrop, who had designed all costumes for Noel's plays since the Year Zero, showed up with gowns and hats loaded with bows. It looked as if a migration of butterflies had worked their way into Gladys's studio to light on Mary's clothes. The spit hit the fan. Noel had never passed on Mary's stipulation to Gladys. To Mary it must have looked like a purposeful slap in the face. He defended Gladys's designs and demanded that Mary wear them. The crowning insult was a huge picture hat—also with bows—that caused the break in their relationship. Mary Martin had small features; on a stage under a huge showy hat she would appear to have no face.

The battle was on. Mary and her husband stopped talking to Noel and his coterie, which included her leading man, Graham Payn.

The strangest part of this fiasco is that Noel didn't like bows himself and considered them to be in poor taste. His insistence on supporting Gladys's designs sprang from some kind of nasty streak in his personality that made him demand that people obey him blindly when working on his plays, even if it spelled disaster, loss of friendship, and made a lifelong enemy.

Noel's ego made him see his plays not as total productions but as settings for his clever verbal wit. He saw the actors as mouthpieces to convey his words, and insisted that they memorize and deliver the lines exactly as written. This demand was not always well received by actors, such as Mary Martin, who knew from experience that not all written lines play well when spoken. Also most actors know that their interpretation had enormous merit on the stage and that there are times when a line isn't going to play no matter how many inflections it's given. Noel didn't want to hear about it—ever. He had a temper that could send him into a towering rage if an actor left out, added, or misplaced a single word he'd written. Part of this came from his nervousness, his compulsion to have everything his own way. He saw interpretation of his lines as a sort of rejection.

The knowledge that he could command and get what he wanted even when it led to disaster for his plays—as it did in *Pacific 1860*—seemed to have been more important than success. He had no sense of proportion.

Pacific 1860 was a failure not only for Noel but also for Graham. It had been a disaster from the moment rehearsals started. It didn't help anyone's career that Noel and Mary had become nonspeaking enemies. Graham was caught in the crossfire. Naturally he had to be loyal to Noel, but how could he convincingly make love on stage to Mary if he had to cut her dead every time he saw her off stage? Some of Noel's friends were brave enough to suggest that Graham's failures might not be all his own fault. Perhaps Noel's obsessiveness was partially to blame.

One of Noel's closest friends was the writer Clemence Dane (Winifred Ashton). Gladys Calthrop and Ashton were also close friends. Noel had known Winnie since 1930 but their real closeness began during the Second World War.

She was a sculptor and painter as well as a successful play-wright and author; her 1917 novel *Regiment of Women* was about lesbianism in an all-girls school. She'd also written *Bill of Divorcement*.

Noel and others used Ashton's house and studio as a gathering spot for London's creative set. Noel would often go there to meet pals like the Lunts and Kit Cornell, who appeared in Winnie's plays. In a sense Winnie was Noel's female counterpart; her creative energy was boundless. She both sculpted Noel and painted his portrait (both works are in Britain's National Portrait Gallery).

He enjoyed her bawdiness and outrageousness (and modeled Madame Arcati after her), but Noel could not have Madame Arcati say the outrageous sexual double entendres for which Winnie was famous. As in all of Noel's really close friendships, there were periods of fierce antagonism in this one.

One of Winnie's other dear friends was Richard "Dick" Addinsell, the composer. He wrote the Warsaw Concerto. Noel commissioned him to write the film score for *Blithe Spirit* and Addinsell wrote music for *Sigh No More*, as well. When Coward cut Addinsell's music a feud erupted between Noel and Winnie.

Noel could not abide rejection and when, during the production of *Pacific 1860*, Winnie became cool to him, Noel in his own words, "found myself paying Winnie compliments I did not mean. Insincerity quivered in the air. The warm magic that we knew in the war was gone. It is her fault. She has made a change, without reason but with a female prejudice. It is a pity."

Gladys Calthrop intervened, and Winnie and Noel tried to patch things up by airing their grievances. "She told me that for the last three years I had been becoming so unbearably arrogant that it's grotesque; that everyone is laughing at me; that I am surrounded by 'yes'-men; that the reason *Pacific 1860* is so bad is that I have no longer any touch or contact with people and events on account of my overweening conceit; that I have ruined Graham and made him give a preposterous performance; that I have encased Mary Martin in a straightjacket of my own dictatorialness [sic] thereby crushing her personality; that I am disloyal and behaved badly over *Sigh No More* (cutting Dick's music)."

Coward said he wasn't upset with Ashton, but the next day when it had all sunk in he was very upset. He concluded that most of what she said was "balls." He was not arrogant, not surrounded by 'yes'-men, and she just wanted to kick him when he was down. But perhaps Noel should have taken at least some of Winifred Ashton's diatribe to heart. During this postwar period his work was definitely second rate. Like most friendships of long standing, however, good advice or insight is sacrificed to keep the emotional ties. They made it up and "got back to the relationship we used to know."

ALTHOUGH HE SUPPOSEDLY SETTLED INTO A RELATIONSHIP with Graham Payn, Noel still had his dalliances, especially of the casting couch variety. He was producing *Peace in Our Time*, his postwar drama about what might have happened in England had the Nazis won the war. He'd seen the young and strikingly handsome actor Kenneth More in a London production of a poorly attended but critically lauded play, *Power Without Glory*. Springtime was prematurely warm, and the uncomfortable heat coupled with the floundering play no doubt had Kenneth's spirits low.

When Noel called the day turned brighter. Coward invited the young actor to the Haymarket, saying he "had something that will interest you." More arrived and was shown to Noel's dressing room, where Noel was cleaning up after his performance in *Present Laughter*. Coward opened the door, in his silk dressing gown, patches of makeup still on his face, and offered tea to More. While the two ate, Noel briefed Kenneth on his new play. Noel was interested in having More play the role of George Borne, head of the British resistance. Noel gave a copy of the script to Kenneth and said they'd be in touch.

After reading the play More went to Noel's luxurious—
and well-known to the gay population of London—residence
on Gerald Road. Coward was again in his famous gown, the
lights were down, and the fire stoked. After dinner, Coward
took a seat at the piano and played his own songs, while
Kenneth sat enjoying the evening with the great star. The
obviousness of what was coming began to grow ominously
in the room.

Coward wrapped up his music, stood, and sauntered
pointedly toward the nervous More. Kenneth stood and
blurted, "Oh, Mr. Coward, I could never have an affair with
you, because . . . because . . . you remind me of my father!"

Noel, unruffled as always, looked at the frightened actor,
then said, "Hallo, son!"

With Coward having that out of the way, Kenneth More
did act in Coward's play and the two remained friends for
years. It was all reminiscent of Noel's days with Olivier in
the early, '30s. (Of course there were others in that decade
too; Louis Hayward went yachting with Noel in the
Mediterranean.)

Possibly because, for a basically homely man, he had had
such unusual success in the sexual and romantic arena with
both men and women, Noel was able to cope easily with
those kinds of rather amusing rejections that come when a
gay male passes forty-five. He never refrained from making
the pass when he ran into someone he liked but was well
able to joke about those that ran away.

Peace in Our Time, with Kenneth More in the lead, was
a dreadful flop. After World War II one of Noel's contemporary drama critics, Beverly Baxter, who was also a Conservative member of Parliament, asked Coward if he thought
he'd survived the war. Noel was outraged. He never forgot
the remark. Through the years Noel would write in his diaries that he was still being published, produced, revived. He
was still performing. "Yes, Mr. Baxter, I've survived the
war." Even in 1964, Coward listed his current projects and
sarcastically pondered, "I wonder if the *late* Beverly Baxter
is at last convinced that I've survived the war."

But the presumptuous Mr. Baxter had made a good point. After World War II Noel Coward never really regained the position he'd held in British theatrical circles. True, his reputation was so strong that it would metamorphose into legend, but the glory days of being in the vanguard were "past perfect."

Noel's career was finding its twilight, just as Cole Porter's was. The times had changed drastically in theatre and Noel's themes just didn't cut it anymore. And he was going to great lengths to tailor roles and songs for Payn, but he was dressing for a lesser talent. Where his major successes had been tailored for gigantic talents such as the Lunts, Gertie Lawrence, and himself, he now was trying to make starring vehicles for a minor player. Perhaps because other giants such as Olivier and John Gielgud had started out in secondary and understudy roles in his plays, he thought that anyone could be turned into a star given the right role. This proved not to be the case with the sweet-natured young man who was now primary in his affections. One wonders what kind of stretch Noel would have had to make to write plays if someone of the caliber of Olivier was his lover instead. Would we have now a later series of brilliant dramas bearing his name?

Probably not. Part of the problem was that after Wilson and the war Noel wanted what most middle-aged men want after a lifetime of hard work and success: he wanted to rest on his laurels. Such was not to be the case, of course. He was coming face to face with his own greatest challenge when he found himself insolvent, with no audience, and the tax man inhaling everything he did earn.

Noel's friend Gertie Lawrence was also in financial trouble, and her agent suggested Noel revive *Tonight at 8:30* in America. Noel certainly had no intention of working that hard on stage again, but it seemed to be a great opportunity for Graham. He'd be launched in America, starring opposite Gertrude Lawrence and proving to all (including Noel) that a new Noel Coward had been discovered.

Jack Wilson, who by now had made a mighty reputation

for himself as a director and producer on Broadway, was supposed to direct. Jack had gone on to heavier drinking bouts, a thing Noel could not abide.

There were a series of emotional crises between the two ex-lovers that must have affected the production. Naturally Graham Payn was the target of Jack's jealousy; Natasha, who had grown closer to Noel as her husband had grown more hostile, tried to help, and Gertie went out of her way to show her own friendship and grace by being an emotional rock to Noel and Graham. It couldn't have been easy for any actress to prepare a demanding performance such as this and still maintain enough emotional composure to support a friend, but she put her own sensitive needs on the back burner to support the production. Finally Noel fired Jack and took over the direction himself.

He had said of Lawrence, "It was fun to work with an old pro like Gertie again. Her talent is equally kaleidoscopic to her personality." Her loyalty and strength during this time proved how right he was to choose her as a friend. On stage, he said, she can play a scene one night with perfect subtlety and restraint; and the next with such obviousness and overemphasis that your senses reel. He felt she would have been the greatest actress in the world except for her lack of critical faculty. She had a tendency to overact in certain situations, a factor attributed to her lack of self-confidence in the demanding roles she nonetheless did so well.

Noel also admired her ability to have successful affairs and admirers. Gertie and Marlene once had a one-upmanship banter on a cross-country train jaunt with Noel and Katharine Hepburn about who had received the largest gift from an admirer. Gertie won since she had received a yacht. This kind of high-stakes glamour was what Noel felt a star should epitomize.

Graham was taken ill in San Francisco, and Noel played opposite Gertie for several performances, the very last time they'd occupy a stage together. But reviving *Tonight at 8:30* in America with Payn playing his old role made it clear that Noel was working against himself for the benefit of a lover—albeit a worthwhile and devoted lover. The critics made mincemeat out of Graham's performance. Whether or not they were fair had little to do with it; the plays had been enthusiastically received out of New York, but in America there is a big distinction between audiences west of the Hudson and those attending Broadway performances.

The production was a flop, which Noel finally admitted. Again he was tired of striving and getting cut down by the press. And friends note that during this period he was becoming cantankerous. One reason was his increased drinking.

By the late 1940s Noel's drinking was taking its toll. Coward naturally was surrounded by adoring sycophants (with the possible exception of Lorn or Gladys) who'd never interrupt a story or dare question him. His country house in Dover was filled on the weekends with the likes of Joyce Carey and Graham Payn and their friends.

One weekend Gertie Lawrence was also in attendance. While Noel was telling a long anecdote, Gertie stopped him. "You've already told us that." Only an old friend like Gertie would have dared point out his repetition. Coward was "shaken dreadfully," according to Cole Lesley. "He was angry with himself for having lost control."

He tried to laugh off the incident by quipping, "one martini too many. I must watch it." But all there knew The Master was terribly upset with himself. For years he'd watched Jack Wilson gradually turn into a blubbering, often incoherent alcoholic. Noel was determined not to suffer the same fate.

He did, in fact, moderate his drinking somewhat, but did not stop altogether. In his later years the drinking and the onset of hardening of the arteries, attributed to his heavy smoking, made it difficult for Coward to memorize his lines, and ended his career as an actor.

But in the late 1940s he could still perform when he wanted to. Noel even did *Present Laughter* in Paris (*Joyeux*

Chagrin) in French. He amazed even his closest friends with his versatility. It seemed, however, that he preferred writing and trying to launch Graham Payn as the performer of the family. He was beginning to show his age, and he wanted to see a young actor play Noel on stage.

XII

"Another Opening, Another Show"

THROUGHOUT THE LATE 1940s Cole had problems with his legs and his career. He'd written the score for MGM's version of *The Pirate*, but the Judy Garland/Gene Kelly vehicle was a box office disappointment (and mediocre musically). Even Judy complained that Cole's songs were not up to his best standard. The producer agreed. Only five of eight Porter songs submitted were used.

But when Cole returned to New York and skeptically began work on a musical version of Shakespeare's *The Taming of the Shrew* things began to change.

In 1947 as far as Broadway backers were concerned, Cole Porter was washed up. It took a great deal of time persuading people to back *Kiss Me Kate*. It was Jack Wilson who staged this awesome Cole Porter/Sam and Bella Spewack musical, doing more to help Cole's career at that point than Noel's. The Spewacks were among the most successful authors on Broadway. They had also written the book for Cole's 1938 hit *Leave it to Me*.

Kiss Me Kate contained fourteen songs and dances and was called a frame-within-a-frame play, because the main story was narrated by another fictional character. The musical combined Renaissance and modern themes, because it featured a "troupe of strolling players," traveling through Italy performing Shakespeare's play, which made it a complicated and challenging show to direct. Wilson's direction was essential to its becoming a hit.

The fact that by this time Jack's drinking bouts had become expeditionary, and his personality more abrasive, made his success even more noteworthy.

The show's success not only revived Cole's career and his spirits, it set the pattern for a new level of Cole Porter song,

richer in depth and innuendo, more mature in its romantic
and ribald content, and almost fabulously decorative in its
musical range.

Kiss Me Kate provided the venue for Cole's best songs
about the battle of the sexes as well as the battle for sex.
Kate herself sings a song of feminine scorn for the penis-
motivated goals of men:

> Of all the types I've ever met
> Within our demo-crassy
> I hate the most the athlete
> With his manner bold and brassy.
> He may have hair upon his chest
> But, sister, so has Lassie!
> I hate men!

Her suitor Petruchio verifies her scorn by singing,

> Still the damsel I'll make my dame
> In the dark they are all the same,
> I've come to wive it wealthily in Padua.

Now, almost thirty years after his marriage, Cole could
joke blithely about references to his own marital status.
Truthfully he had married money. But in one line Petruchio
sings that he has "oft stuck a pig before," and that, at least,
could not apply to the Porter marriage. Linda was no pig
and Cole had certainly never stuck one.

When Bianca (Lisa Kirk) in *Kiss Me Kate* sang her desire
to marry "Any Tom, Dick, or Harry/Any Tom, Harry, or
Dick, ending with the refrain, "a dick, a dick, dick dick,"
repeated six times, her objective and her urgency were very
evident, but it has never been considered an offensively
dirty song. "Always True to You in My Fashion" was considered the naughty song from the show, again reviving
Cole's fascination for women who sell their charms.

Porter believed in sexual freedom for all. Although he
wrote songs from the male point of view about sexual liber-
tines ("Put a sack over their heads and they're all the same")
he did not forget that women get hot pants as well. In *Kiss*

Me Kate, Bianca sings of her willingness to bed down with one and all for a Paris hat, dinner, diamond clips, or just plain old penis if that's all the poor lad has to offer.

> I could never curl my lip
> To a dazzling diamond clip
> Though the clip meant Let 'er rip!
> I'd not say nay.

Still, the last lines of the wonderful dramatic song "Marry Me" are Cole's most outright dirtiest ever! Even today when listening to Lisa Kirk on the cast album sing

> Any Tom, Dick or Harry,
> Any Tom Harry or Dick
> I need a dick, dick dick

one is struck by the outrageousness.

One need not also point out—although in the interest of accuracy and scientific research, we will—the words "Harry or Dick," when quickly sung, evoke the sound "hairier dick." When Cole started indulging his own erectile imaginings he could become subtly clever and filthy.

The desire for the male organ receives attention often in his songs. An innocent seeming, veiled, but leering reference to a man's endowment is the point of a song, "He Certainly Kills the Women," which was dropped from the 1943 Danny Kaye movie *Let's Face It*. Meant to be sung by a woman, it's about a cheap, badly dressed, stupid, abusive chiseling heel, but in each of the three refrains, Cole writes,

> The clothes he wears when out of doors
> Are ev'rything the well-dressed man abhors,
> Of course I've not seen him in his flannel drawers.

Or, Shall we refer to his physique?

> I hardly call it classic Greek,
> So far I've not caught him in his so-to-speak.

And lastly,

> He's not a champ at water sports

> Yet when he dives, why ev'ry matron snorts
> It must be the color of his nylon shorts,
> 'Cause he certainly kills the women!

Still the difference between the sexes was used as lyrical fodder by the Porter mind. He knew that in general women are more interested in being faithful once the right man was found, whereas he wrote "Most Gentlemen Don't Like Love" (they just like to kick it around). His reason was that "most gentlemen just ain't that profound." One of his unpublished songs is a direct attack: "Ev'ry man Is a Stupid Man," except the one you love. This was written in 1953, after years of suffering. And perhaps he was thinking back over the focus of his sexual interest, perhaps finding solace in the nonsexual choices he'd also made in his life, the ones that had kept him from being a fool for love and instead turned him into a great songwriter.

He wrote another song, which had become a great standard during that time, which shows a deeper sense of values. "It's All Right with Me" is sung by someone who finds a mate who isn't the right mate, but it's all right even if it isn't his/her fantasy.

From Bianca's song, to "I Like Pretty Things" ("as for example, sparkling rings"), to "Love 'Em and Leave 'Em" (a mother's advice to her daughter) Cole always had a high regard for getting what you can while you can. But he also wrote the more serious "When a Woman's in Love."

> They say a woman's love can be bought
> With any vain, tawdry treasure
> . . . I say that when a woman's in love
> From her one love she wanders never.
> I say that when a woman's in love, alackaday,
> She loves forever.

Was he thinking of Linda's faithfulness in this instance? For all her pursuit of expensive things Linda would always immediately put aside her interests when a human need took precedence.

Linda had no illusions about her role in Cole's life; she

knew she had provided him with wifelike emotional comforts, but as mother figure who brought financial security and order to his life. She kept up his spirits. She kept him on schedule. She ensured that his need to work would remain paramount in his focus. Even when she was near death she kept his career and his security in her thoughts. All their friends mention that she was obsessed with saving money in her final years because, "I want to leave Cole an even two million when I go." This woman who'd lived so lavishly now became uncharacteristically frugal. But despite her attempt, when she did die, her estate was just shy of the two million mark; she left him only $1,900,000.

The aging and ill health of Linda and Kate and his own deteriorating health continued to plague Cole. In Buxton Hill and at their Waldorf apartments Linda had to have oxygen tents.

Cole's career had a setback with his new show *Out of This World*. George S. Kaufman said the men instead of the women were scantily clothed, and after all theatre box office always depended on butter and egg men (visiting out of towners), not on female audiences. (Saint Subber, the producer of this show, was also gay.) Many were offended by the emphasis on male bodies. Ironically in London, where Noel's shows were being produced by his pal Hugh (Binkie) Beaumont, the same barbs were being made .. that Binkie and his "ring of homosexuals" had taken over theatre production.

Despite the recent triumph of *Kiss Me Kate*, Cole's depressions now became more severe. A major worry was money, or rather his money running out. During this time income taxes were extremely high and the art of the tax loophole had not come into vogue. Someone of Cole's income would pay out between 80 to 90 percent of it in taxes. For someone who had been raised without income tax, then lived so long in Europe prior to the war, he must have found it a shock to be residing in the United States full time and see his earnings fly past him into the IRS coffers instead of into decorations for his palazzos.

Most of his paranoia came from the painkillers he took, as well as seeing Linda suffering the afflictions of old age. The mortality of the two women who were his source of security, emotionally, was evident on a daily basis, and his own body wasn't acting in a very reassuring manner either. He underwent shock treatments, which was the third-degree treatment for depression at the time. The wonder is that he kept on writing, as if on automatic pilot, as if he didn't really know how *not* to write.

Despite pleas from his friends he would not undergo psychotherapy. Since Cole did not confide in anyone there is no clear evidence that his depression was linked to an unresolved acceptance of his sexuality, or the strain of leading a double life in hiding it from the public. He may have suffered from clinical depression. He may have accepted the theory that creative people are supposed to be neurotic.

Many creative geniuses who suffer from neuroses refuse to seek therapy and many alcoholics and drug users resist giving up their narcotics because they fear that their creative talent will diminish or even end without the personality disorder that makes them the way they are. In their minds they connect the personality flaw with their creative spark.

Somehow, without the aid of therapy, Cole regained himself enough to resume work. But while he was putting together the songs for *Can-Can*, in 1952 his mother had a cerebral hemmorhage. Cole rushed to Peru to be by Violet's side and waited for her death. She was in her nineties, so he was prepared, but it was a blow at a time when he was going through the start of a long tunnel of personal depression that would last throughout the brilliant maturity of his career. Although he was losing his joie de vivre, his work was becoming better and better as he advanced in years.

His celebrity in public was also greater than ever. He had become a living legend. A whole new generation was growing up with an awareness of "Cole Porter songs" as a genre unto themselves.

Both Cole and Linda lost most of their mobility due to their separate problems with their health. Still they gave their lavish dinners at the Waldorf Towers, inviting people such as Pulitzer Prize playwright Robert Sherwood and his wife; CBS Network chairman William Paley, and Charlie Chaplin.

Cole still went to the theatre. He saw his pals the Lunts do his pal Noel Coward's play *Quadrille*, and predicted that despite its bad reviews it would be a great hit. But it wasn't.

Can-Can opened, and was also panned by the critics, but it did become a big hit, his most successful show after *Kiss Me Kate*. Linda had not been able to attend opening night, but she maintained her old tradition of giving him a specially designed cigarette case, as she did to commemorate every opening of his shows.

Cole was in Hollywood when Linda took a turn for the worse. Years of taking experimental medicines for her ill health, coupled with years of smoking had made her emphysema acute and she spent almost every moment gasping for breath. Cole rushed back to New York to be with her. Although she'd spent her life in the public eye, seeming to prefer the background, she now was afraid she would be forgotten. She expressed a wish for some sort of immortality. Cole was touched by this and had a rose developed and named for her after her death. It was an unusually fragranced, deeply blushed tea rose.

He overrode her desire to be buried at Buxton Hill, though, having her remains interred in his own family plot in Indiana, where she was laid to rest next to his own space.

AFTER LINDA'S DEATH IN 1954 Cole began exhibiting some strange expressions of his loss. There was no doubt among those who knew him best that he was devastated by her death. He became obsessively punctual, to such a degree that it caused him to break with many old friends. No one else could conceive of such martinet standards about punctuality, especially in a world where traffic jams reigned supreme, and most people considered it proper to be fashionably late. His punctuality worked in reverse as well. If a departure had been set for 10:45, and everything was ready to go at 10:30, everyone had to sit and wait the fifteen minutes before departing.

Once scheduled to have dinner at a home where he'd never been before, Cole did a "dry run" the afternoon before, going through the steps needed to get there so he'd know exactly how much time he'd need the next evening to get there on the dot. Linda had been strict about being on time, but he turned it into a weird ritual in her memory.

After Linda's death he never again entered the house in Massachusetts that she loved so well and had lavished so much special attention on decorating. He only stayed in the smaller house, called "No Trespassing," which she had set up for his use as a studio. He would not even go into the big house to get something, but would go to the door and have the maid bring it out to him. Once when it was raining he would not even step over the threshold into the entry. Finally he decided to have it torn down, at enormous cost (estimates range from 100,000 to 250,000 in 1950s dollars). He then had the stone and cement studio moved onto the foundation of the main house to take advantage of the spectacular view.

Most of this quirkiness and depression was due to the drugs and medications he was increasingly forced to take, coupled with the fact that he continued to drink heavily and smoke. His sexual escapades did not diminish, and he stopped caring who knew about it, although at the end he expressed a fear that he might be remembered as an "old queen." He continued to pay the beefers to come up to his Waldorf Towers apartment, where more than once he was interrupted as he was performing fellatio between two big legs. He seemed to want now to be embarrassed and degraded to drown his grief and despair.

When Cole was well along in years and unable to walk without aid, one story tells how Jack Cassidy (the musical comedy star and actor, who later married Shirley Jones) sadistically forcing Cole to crawl across the room to get what he wanted.

"You want this?" Cassidy would taunt, exposing himself.

"Yes, yes."

"Then come and get it."

But as Cole crawled closer, Cassidy would move away.

During the war Cole met a young Marine, Robert (Bob) Bray, a former lumberjack from Montana, who was stationed in Los Angeles. He was a big, burly type, heavy in the chest muscles, who wanted to be in the movies after the war. Cole was attracted to him much as he had been to Jack Bouvier at Yale. Bray was for all outward appearances heterosexual. Yet he wasn't turned off by Cole's attentions, and was comfortable in the company of Cole's homosexual friends. For the next ten years their intimate friendship flourished (although Bray ultimately married and fathered six children).

Many who were on the scene say that Bray replaced Ray Kelly in Cole's affections. Kelly was now married himself and Cole later was godfather to his children. Bob Bray, like another Montanan, Frank (later changed to Gary) Cooper, found there were many eager agents and producers in Hollywood to help a straight guy who wasn't averse to letting his pants get unzipped when he'd "had a little too much to drink." In the late 1940s Henry Wilson, the notoriously gay and very successful agent, could often get handsome young men standard contracts at the studios (he handled and renamed people like Rock Hudson, Rory Calhoun, Guy Madison, and later Tab Hunter). So by 1947 Bob Bray was making westerns with Tim Holt at RKO.

His career, however, was second rate, and he remained in "B" pictures for the next few years. But Cole kept a watchful eye on Bray, and in 1949 wrote to his pal Jean Howard— who was married to agent Charles Feldman—imploring her to look after Bray. "He is so alone and lonely." Cole felt it was "important for him to be with a lady instead of a tramp."

Cole and Noel could still retain the attention of younger

hunks like Bray because they could provide the entry to society and the step up the professional ladder (and even emergency cash if need be).

Through the years Cole's lyrics had unmasked his hidden life. As early as 1929 he'd written "Find Me a Primitive Man," revealing, "I can't imagine being sad/With any arrow collar ad./Nor could I take the slightest joy/In waking up a college boy."

Cole knew what he wanted: "I could be the personal slave/Of someone just out of a cave"; he wanted a man who didn't belong to a club but "had a club that belongs to him."

Many of his songs juxtapose the object of love being sung onto a pedestal, while the singer is pictured as a happy slave bowing down before the adored one. Although this poetic imagery was common in his time, coming from the Greek ideal of adoration of perfect beauty high above oneself, as well as the chivalrous ideal of loving pure and chaste from afar (hardly his personal style), something of Cole still shows itself here. He was known to like to grovel during the sex act. Whether he actually liked being degraded because of some inner feeling of low esteem is highly questionable; the kick probably lay more in being a diversion from boredom, being jaded by the regular sex act done so many, many times—usually simple one-sided fellatio in his case that involved him in such scenes. He wasn't masochistic so much as turned on by engaging in outlandish scenes.

Throughout the years Cole's songs showed a definite note of sadomasochism. "Taunt me, and hurt me, deceive me, desert me/I'm yours till I die." As well as, "How can you be jealous/When you know, baby, I'm your slave?" (both from *Kiss Me Kate*).

With "Why Do You Want to Hurt Me So?" from the 1950s show *Out of This World*, he really laid it out: "You used to use your arms to wrap me/But now in the face you slap me" and "You used everywhere to tag me/Now by the hair you grab me," and additional lyrics of being kicked, punched, and whacked. But the song was much too violent for the show and was replaced with a mellower number.

There is no evidence that in his own personal "pay for sex" life Cole ever indulged in actual physical masochism, but there is no doubt that from a psychological point of view he knew he was setting himself up to be used and hurt, and often degraded. Indeed who is the one being degraded when one pays for sex? The payer or the renter? He knew the meaning of and liked "rough trade."

Cole also revealed his own battles with depression. He often used phrases like "depth of inferno" and "the depth of despair" and "down in the depths on the ninetieth floor" in lyrics, as a reaction to sexual deprivation or love gone wrong. The cure is always, of course, s-e-x.

NOEL COWARD, MORE PERSONALLY DISCIPLINED, never allowed himself to fall into the depths of despair. But his high style of living (combined with his tax bite) often left him in the depths of debt. He had his various houses and his considerable staff to support. Up until Graham Payn's entrance in 1945 Cole Lesley had been Noel's replacement for Wilson (not sexually, but Noel needed a close male companion). The need for male companionship (even on a nonsexual level) is just as important to a gay man as to a straight man.

"Coley" did not care what people thought about his relationship with Noel; he always wanted to be a confidant to a great man, which is what he was. He basked in the glory even though he was technically still Noel's valet.

Although Cole Lesley said that he liked Graham and was never threatened by his relationship with Coward, Payn's inclusion into the little group had altered Lesley's position. By the late 1940s Lesley had grown tired of being just a servant/companion. Now he wanted more. Noel understood, or said he did; he later got angry, then relented, then allowed Lesley to help him creatively (but gave him no credit). Noel hated to have the status quo disrupted. It wasn't until 1950 that Cole was officially promoted to secretary and Lorn Lorrain retitled Noel's representative.

Lesley and Graham Payn later collaborated on a musical, which Noel patronizingly tolerated, and which went nowhere. In 1950 Noel tried to launch Graham's career again with a new, different kind of Noel Coward show, a nightclub musical, called *Ace of Clubs*. Once again Payn was playing a sailor. The show introduced new songs: "My Kind of Man," "Something About a Sailor," and "Sail Away." It wasn't a hit. Graham's career was still in neutral. Through Noel's producer, "Binkie" Beaumont, Graham might sing a Coward tune in this or that revue, but a big stage career was never in the cards for him.

Through the years Noel worried that Graham was aging and hadn't established anything for his old age. He worried that Payn was lazy and wasn't striving to get anywhere in his career. What Payn was was an aging juvenile actor of the type whose theatrical life ends around thirty. The most important talent such an actor has to have is youth, and Graham wasn't a kid anymore.

The major factor working against Payn's career was the actor himself. He would take it if a role was available, but he would never go out and fight for a job. He accepted Noel's largesse, enjoyed the ease of being his lover, living in his various domiciles and living the life of a privileged semi-kept man.

It is also possible that theatre people knew all about his "marital" status and would not seek him out knowing that Noel was part of the package. If Graham had been a star before meeting Noel the situation might have been different, but there is a tradition in show business that you have to make it on your own—you don't have a career handed to you. Real talent doesn't have to be sponsored.

When Noel wrote plays for the Lunts and Gertie they succeeded because the public wanted to see them in anything. No one knew that Coward was writing "down" to accommodate Payn's lack of fire; they only knew they were being presented with uninteresting shows with an unspectacular actor.

Cole Porter never allowed himself to get into this predicament. Porter had too cold an eye for talent and in his estimation his songs came before any performer. He would never write down to fit a lesser talent. He might tailor a song for a great talent who had weaknesses, such as when he wrote "Night and Day" to be sung by Fred Astaire. Before Cole would let a star ruin his song, he'd take it back and write something the performer could do well.

Noel's playwriting career bounced back after *Ace of Clubs* with *Relative Values* and the aforementioned *Quadrille* with the Lunts. *After the Ball* (a musical version of Oscar Wilde's *Lady Windemere's Fan*) was a disappointment, but *Nude with Violin* was a success in London, starring his old buddy John Gielgud. Then Noel's career took a different turn. Suddenly he was back to being a performer.

XIII

"Play, Orchestra, Play"

WHEN NOEL DID A COMMERCIAL for the Gillette Razor Company he did so in typical Coward fashion. He was asked to list things that had style. Among the litany, "Gertrude Lawrence, any Cole Porter song, and Marlene's voice . . ." (Marlene actually didn't have much of a singing voice—it was her character that got her through the last two decades of her career.) Noel didn't have much of a singing voice either but it served well enough in reviving his sagging career. He needed the money and like Cole Porter the fame if he wanted to continue bedding down younger men. Although ostensibly in a relationship with Payn, Noel was still on the prowl. He returned to performing to polish his image of stardom, but not on the theatrical stage. He'd been offered a cabaret spot and he decided to take it. He parlayed his success at Cafe de Paris, London's premier nightspot, all the way to Las Vegas, and a new career on American television.

Kenneth Tynan's observation that "the style Noel Coward embodied as a performer and writer alike was the essence of high camp. He was one of the brightest stars in the homosexual constellation that did so much to enliven the theatre between the wars." This was even more applicable to Noel's Vegas performances in the 1950s.

For Noel's opening night at the Wilbur Clark Desert Inn Frank Sinatra had chartered a plane and brought the Rat Pack from Hollywood: Betty and Bogey, Judy, David and Hjordis Niven, and the rest. And there were other big names in the audience as well, including Noel's pals Joseph Cotten and Joan Fontaine. The act was a smash success. Everyone it seems was going to Noel's "marvelous party" in the desert.

Noel Coward's songs must be heard to be appreciated; unlike songs by Cole Porter one cannot "read" the full impact and delight of Coward's versatility without a performance. He understood perhaps better than most playwrights and songwriters how written words should be performed, and he always wrote toward that end. The sentiment was not as important as the dramatic rendition in his songs. Trying to read Noel's lyrics, even the delightfully explicit phrases of "I Went to a Marvelous Party," cheats the reader of the fun.

The best performer of Noel's work was Noel himself. He also was one of the best performers of Cole Porter's lyrics as well, sometimes writing additional verses to Porter's songs. If you just read the words to "Marvelous Party," for example, unless you are in tune to the whole society of people he wrote about, you may wonder why they're so witty. Someone "wearing mosaic stones from St. Peter's in Rome" seems somewhat uninspired. Then you hear the song performed and you want to hear it again and again, and soon you find yourself leaning over a piano in a bar trying to get the pianist to accompany you.

Noel's satiric classic, "Mad Dogs and Englishmen," became a beloved song in his country. He had to sing it repeatedly until he was heartily sick of it. When he realized during the 1950s that he'd have to include it in his Las Vegas act he decided to rattle it off and get it over with so he could do the songs he liked. He sang it so fast that Cole Porter remarked that he'd never heard a song sung all in one breath before.

Noel's capacity to rattle off words faultlessly at great speed was his trademark. He developed this ability during his first visit to New York, when he heard the actors on Broadway delivering their lines at a faster pace than the measured tones of the English stage. He was enchanted by the idea and wrote and performed songs and plays to be delivered at a runaway pace. It was an innovative idea and made his pattery lyrics take on a more delicious attraction, since the listener had to pay strict attention, and become totally absorbed in listening to the actor if he were to catch what was being said.

This use of speed delivery should not be underestimated when evaluating Noel's songs. The atmosphere of his plays is wrapped up in this kind of delivery and interpretation. It gives an immediacy and a brightness to his work. The words may seem empty, even devoid of meaning when read but when performed they take on the characteristics of sophistication, breeziness, and the kind of brittle superficiality that characterized the generation that Coward was part of.

"Mad Dogs" is a strong, pointed slap at English empire building. The tack that if it's English, it must be correct was questioned, but never changed, by the English. Coward did not invent the phrase "Englishmen and mad dogs," which he found when he had research done to see if it was his own original or if he had subconsciously absorbed the phrase in his readings. It turns out that the phrase had been used several times before, but it was Coward who turned it into a semi-national anthem.

> Mad dogs and Englishmen
> Go out in the noonday sun.
> The Japanese don't care to,
> The Chinese wouldn't dare to . . .

Noel was at his best when satirizing his country's blustery poses of Empire and military correctness. "The Stately Homes of England" is a wonderful satire of the lords and ladies moving obliviously through their manors unhampered by reality until the money goes and they must find ways to keep these castles up.

One of his best, however, is the lesser known, "Whatever Became of Him?" also known as the Indian Army Song. Noel included it in his Las Vegas act and it shows perhaps most effectively why they called him The Master, and exactly how a satirical song is to be sung. Noel's manner is breezy but not rushed; precise but blithery for comic effect. He acts out a song more than sings it, and it becomes a richly delicious confection instead of a dated period piece.

In it he not only satirized the tradition-laden emptiness of military personnel who helped govern England's subjected countries, he boldly turns the soldiers into cartoon characters doing outrageous and perverted things out of boredom.

He sings of "young Kelly, who was cashiered/For riding quite nude in a pushcart through Delhi/On the day the new viceroy appeared." Or the one who was a terrible souse, who "took two tarts in the governor's house." Then there was Mills, who "took to pig-sticking in quite the wrong way"; then quickly, "I wonder what happened to him?" And of course no military song by Coward would be complete without a pointed reference such as "young Phipps, who had very large hips."

"Well, it appears a curious doctor in Washington Square/ Gave him hormones to strengthen his hair/and he grew something here, and he grew something there/I wonder what happened to her—*him!*"

The musicality of Noel's songs relies on the lyrical verse. So many of his songs are talked rather than sung, although certainly he wrote many pretty musical melodies to carry the words. Nonetheless it is the word that matters most because Noel used words more than either music or movement to convery all his dramatic messages, musical or not.

Even his tender song "Matelot" is primarily designed to express the words rather than using the music to build an emotional response. Reading the lyrics to this song, a person could almost invent the tune itself while reading and not be too far off the mark.

"Matelot" was written from the point of view of a sailor who, wherever he roams, is always followed by two voices, his mother's and that of his own true love. This probably rang true for Noel because Violet was never far from her son's thoughts, nor removed from his devotion, and Noel's fantasy lover and the hope of meeting him was also constant.

Noel's faithfulness to people he once loved and the bittersweet memory of his affairs were often expressed in his work. In the song "I'll See You Again," he writes:

But what has been can leave me never
Your dear memory
Throughout my life has guided me,
Though my world has gone awry
Though the end is drawing nigh
I shall love you till I die ... goodbye.

Whether this song was written with Jack Wilson in mind, or as a tribute to his mother's undying support is not known. The sentiment is true as far as Noel is concerned. Noel was intensely loyal to the people who loved him and in all his work there is never a betrayal of those people. Even in *Design for Living* the three characters cannot ever stop loving each other no matter how horribly they've treated each other. Love was the motivating factor of Noel's life, and he maintained an eternal loyalty to whomever he had loved, even Jack Wilson. Conversely he could be as cold and callous about anyone he didn't like, placing them in the trash heap of his emotions.

It is interesting to note that in his love songs Coward often wrote from a woman's point of view and many of these songs were sung in his shows by girls portraying prostitutes or pretty little virgins waiting for their lovers to return.

One of the best and most enduring of Coward's songs is "Mad About the Boy," which was supposedly written with Douglas Fairbanks, Jr., in mind. A movie fan is infatuated by a movie star and sings her love song to him, using the phrase "mad about the boy."

In this song the fan watches the star on the silver screen and moons over his classic good looks. Noel was a friend of Fairbanks and probably entertained fantasy designs on the film star, who was known for his ways with women. Fairbanks had affairs with Noel's pals Gertie Lawrence and Marlene Dietrich, and once was wed to Joan Crawford, who got the Crown Prince of Hollywood when she was young. Noel met Douglas and Joan when they were still married while he was playing in *Private Lives* with Gertie. Fairbanks was strictly a ladies' man, but that didn't stop Noel from using his classic profile as the example of perfect male beauty.

Noel's preferred type was the dashingly handsome, slim figured, well-bred man, typified by Jack Wilson, and of course epitomized by Fairbanks. Today the male model would be his preferred look, the polished, perfectly featured, non-mysterious type. Cole Porter's beefy union types held no charm for Noel.

Still there is a telling line in the song that gives away the small amount of danger that enticed him and held him attached to Wilson:

> I'm mad about the boy
> Even though there's something of a cad about the boy.

The caddishness, the promise that one might be betrayed, held a spice, an added attraction that promised to cause pain. Perhaps too, like many homosexuals, Noel was attracted to traits that ultimately would end the affair out of a need to verify that one's desires were wrong in the first place. Whether or not that applied to Noel it is true that despite his two very long-term relationships he never felt that he had been successful in love. It was like an elusive goal that he could not realize despite the fact that the lover was there, right there, and in no danger of going away. The satisfaction of one's desires is always in the mind, and this theme shows itself always in the high floating dreams of love that Coward's characters sing about in all his songs.

For the American debut of "Mad About the Boy," Coward had written a very openly pointed verse for a man to sing, but he was convinced to drop the idea. Even New York City was not ready for *that* in 1938. In his Las Vegas performance Noel never actually sang "Mad About the Boy"—much too revelatory—but the music was used as an introduction instrumental as presumably the audience was mad about the boy Noel.

When entertaining the troops during the war Coward had

learned that they weren't interested in an aging man singing his operetta-style love songs, and so most of his romantic and self-revealing lyrics were dropped from the act. His nightclub audiences were deprived of "I'll Follow My Secret Heart" (till I find love); "You Were There" (I saw you and my heart stopped beating); and other ballads. Noel knew the crowd responded best to his anti-Empire songs, such as "Uncle Harry's Not a Missionary Now." Noel's songs spoofing show business were also very popular. "Don't Put Your Daughter on the Stage, Mrs. Worthington," "Louisa," and "Why Must the Show Go On?" made it seem as though Noel was spoofing himself. The bewilderment about a star wondering why he ever went on stage in the first place was sure-fire material.

Years after being treated so "shabbily" by his countrymen, Noel even wrote about how all Britishers might not be so eager to serve with, "Don't Take Our Charlie for the Army," and some stiff upper lipper (like himself) might prefer warmer climes and friendlier people ("Mrs. Wentworth-Brewster at the bar at the Piccolo Marina discovers life in Capri").

Among Noel's patter songs was "What's Going to Happen to the Tots?" He updated and Americanized the old song, but the theme remained the vanity of modern society, more interested in face-lifts, hormones, injections, pills, pleasures of the flesh, than in future generations. Ironically in deriding those matrons who don't realize "that the pleasures that once were heaven/Look silly at sixty-seven" Noel was satirizing people like himself (he'd had his own nip-and-tuck) and Cole Porter who desperately wanted their youth back.

During the war Noel had asked Cole for permission to write additional lyrics to the by-now classic "Let's Do It." With the Vegas debut and subsequent recordings the American audiences were treated for the first time to Noel's clever additions to the song.

Noel's lyrics weren't necessarily wittier than Cole's, they just incorporated more contemporary references. It was the verse that Coward wrote about Porter that was special. He paid tribute to his old friend noting that while "Irving Berlin/often emphasizes sin"; that Coward wrote that "sex was here to stay," and Richard Rodgers took a romantic view "of that sly biological urge" the verse concludes: "But it really was Cole/Who contrived to make the whole/ Thing merge."

Coward not only wrote his own set of lyrics to "Let's Do It," he also wrote a set to Porter's "Let's Fly Away," a song with a similar kind of verse arrangement. In the first one Noel mentions his friends ("Marlene just might do it"), the Lunts, "nice young men who sell antiques do it," and Liberace. In the second, he mentions "those ubiquitous Gabor girls." Like Cole Noel loved dropping famous names as well.

Through the years the boys had even used each other's names in their work. Cole wrote "What Am I to Do?" for the Beverly Garland character (based on Noel) to sing in Kaufman and Hart's *The Man Who Came to Dinner*. When the song was published he signed it Noel Porter.

Coward spoofed Cole in his 1945 ditty "Nina" (from Argentina) about a Latin beauty who "declined to Begin the Beguine." Nina "Cursed the man who taught her to/she cursed Cole Porter too."

Noel could have no greater fan than his old pal Cole. Porter made it to Vegas, though not for the opening; Tallulah was there that night, Van and Evie Johnson. Coward was duly appreciative.

"The Wednesday night supper show was thrilling . . . it really was sensational. I was so glad because I wanted Cole to see me at my best and he certainly did."

But as the week dragged on the audiences were less enthusiastic, perhaps not so sophisticated or "in" a crowd and Coward was forced to "press on"—he "got them in the end, but it was grueling work."

When the Las Vegas stint was ended Noel and his coterie moved on to Hollywood, where the entertaining was "incessant." Cole threw a small dinner for Noel and the two men had, in Coward's words, "a lovely, rather pissed-up heart-to-hearter." Both of them drank heavily. It was never questioned in their era that one should.

The Bogarts gave a party, then Sinatra threw a bash. But Noel's fondest recollection was a quiet dinner with movie star Tom Tryon. The startlingly handsome young actor (he'd been in *The Cardinal*) was then in his beefcake prime; he too was a heavy drinker and would keep his own homosexuality under wraps for years. Later he gained more fame as a best-selling novelist (*The Other*).

Noel's ability to attract and bed down handsome young men was assured, at least for a few more years, by the enormous resurgence in his career status and power. Television beckoned and Noel responded. He wrote and starred in a successful ninety-minute special (a standard in earlier television) with Mary Martin, old wounds all healed up without even a trace of a white scar.

He played the lead on CBS television in *Blithe Spirit* opposite Lauren Bacall and Claudette Colbert. (That friendship crashed on the rocks when Colbert couldn't remember her lines. Friendship was one thing, but he'd written those lines!)

In Noel's diaries he says, "Clifton [Webb] gave a *gentil* 'company' party to which we all went except Claudette, who lost the way because, she explained to Clifton later, she had mislaid his address. To mislay both Clifton's address and a perfectly good friendship in one evening is quite an achievement."

Bill Paley didn't want Noel to do *Present Laughter* on TV, and he was right of course. Middle America wasn't ready for an effete playwright prancing around in prime time discussing his love life. The sponsor, Ford Motor Company, canceled the third show, saying the ratings weren't high enough. Noel claimed it was because he'd ridiculed the sponsor in interviews. It was all settled and he proceeded with the broadcast of *This Happy Breed*. To publicize it, Noel appeared on Ed Murrow's *Person to Person* and sang on Ed Sullivan's show. Despite his friends and colleagues who told him what a great success he'd been on American "telly" CBS offered no more projects.

HIS NEW POPULARITY also made his private life open to examination in the burgeoning scandal press—the forerunner of today's supermarket tabloids. The 1950s saw *Hush, Private Lives* (ironically), *Rave,* and the most notoriously vicious, inaccurate, and therefore most successful tabloid, *Confidential.* (*Private Lives* really upset Noel.)

One of the primary targets of these scandal sheets was to reveal homosexuals. There was no pretended altruism here; the press wasn't doing it to help a person face his or her own hypocrisy or to nudge societal acceptance of the lifestyle. It was purely wrecking people for money, a trend that has moved into the so-called legitimate press and TV. Liberace was vilified, although the beloved star was hardly hiding anything from anyone. Rock Hudson's career was saved only when his studio sacrificed a lesser box office draw, George Nader, to throw up a smoke screen for Rock. The rags usually went after the easy targets, but they knew the real money wasn't in newsstand sales, but in blackmail. A deal was struck. The studio had the story on Rock squashed, the rags still could come back again and reblackmail them, and Rock quickly married his agent's secretary Phyllis Gates. Later he divorced her and ended up losing money when she threatened blackmail. Rock left his money to George Nader and his lover when he died as sort of a consolation for the loss of his career.

Noel didn't rate a spread in *Confidential.* His popularity was not of the general public type. But *Rave* decided he was famous enough to stir up the old rumors.

Noel wrote, "Success also must be resolutely attacked. In America today there has emerged a squalid rash of weekly periodicals . . . *Private Lives* (this to my personal chagrin). Anyone successful and in the public eye is fair game and libel laws in the USA being curious . . . these magazines are permitted to assert freely that so-and-so is a dope addict, and so-and-so's private life is one long homosexual orgy, etc. . . . There was an article in *Rave* which, complete with photographs, stated that I was the biggest tulip (better than pansy) who had ever been imported into America; that during the war I sang "Mad About the Boy" to an RAF officer and was ducked in a pond by his incensed comrades; that I had set up a young man in Jamaica in a travel agency. . . . It doesn't upset me but it does give me to think. . . . If I had been seen naked in an opium den with several Negroes stripped for action and the story appeared, I should be in exactly the same position I am now . . . I must gird my slandered loins and be prepared for fresh onslaughts."

SCANDAL MAGAZINES OR NOT Noel was sexually active and fully intended to remain so. He thought (and rightly so!) that it was no one's business but his own. He could not have had any doubt that his success in that arena—even at a much younger age—was because he was Noel Coward the star. If he were not famous it is not likely the weedy lad would have had such spectacular success once maturity took the bloom off his extremely young and pudgy face. Still he had what is the prime requisite for sexual success: chutzpah. He went after what he wanted based on his own sexual desires, unhampered by any thoughts about whether or not he fulfilled the other person's sexual fantasies. The most successful lions in this arena, straight or gay, are the ones who go hunting with the confidence that they will get what they want, and certainly Noel approached all his goals with that attitude. He was unhampered by any possibility that someone would say no; he simply would never take no for an answer. This particular success tactic came to him naturally. He knew what he was and didn't consider what anyone else might want. He presented himself as he presented his plays: like it, or else!

Noel approached middle age with the same vigor that he did the early part of his life. He did not see himself as getting old; he had always lived as a star and had the idea that his youthful mind and energy canceled out the lines age had etched in his face. He often wrote that his figure was good; he worked at keeping it and complained bitterly when finding himself in recurring patterns of indulging himself in sweets.

He would later satirize in his plays aging women who went to "Dr. Boromelli," an offstage character who supplied injections of unborn sheep's fetus extract as a rejuvenator for wealthy old women—and men. He himself tried whatever was available in Switzerland at the time. He had reconstructive surgery to remove his middle-aged jowls and, Marlene-like, had some other facial snippets. He made fun of her in public for doing it, but he did it too. He was after all an actor and a public figure and understood how much depended on appearance. That his private hope for gay sexual successes was a factor in motivating him goes without saying. Anyone, straight or gay, who is still seeking new sexual partners hates to look in the mirror and see an old person looking back. Married folk may joke about it, look at their equally upholstered spouses and say, "Come grow old with me, the best is yet to be." But for many the search never really ends, even when one is involved with a lover.

A gay man is more likely to say, "Gay and gray? No way!" In those pre-AIDS days having a lover did not end the prowling for sex. The male desire to continue to make conquests was recognized by both partners in a relationship and accommodated. Gay men realized that racking up scores of "tricks" was not a threat to a relationship, and their own sexual interaction was likely to be shortlived no matter how long they actually stayed together.

In short Noel was still in circulation.

Ambrose de Bek was an executive at CBS in the heyday of live television, the head of set design in the 1950s. He was friends with Babe and Bill Paley and through them met Noel Coward. He was often invited to Coward's Blue Harbor estate in Jamaica, where the Paleys also had an estate. Mr. de Bek was famous in New York for his parties, all-male affairs to which invitations were coveted mostly because all clothes had to be left in the hallway.

Noel joined this crowd enthusiastically, as de Bek demanded secrecy and discretion from his guests. He was not amused by a young actor who came running out of the bedroom screeching, "I've just had sex with Noel Coward!"

"Well, shut up about it!" de Bek ordered.

Ambrose de Bek also knew Cole Porter; they'd met in Hollywood during the war. He recalled that Cole always had a sailor on each arm and "they were always shorter than he."

Cole was more open about being seen with young men in public and Noel more discreet. Coming from the old school de Bek admired Coward's way; he believed that one's life should be kept private.

WHEN COWARD TURNED HIS ATTENTION back to theatre, novels, and short stories, he found no better success than he'd had on television. *South Sea Bubble* had a respectable run but wasn't critically well received. His pals Vivien Leigh and Larry Olivier upset Noel when Vivien pulled out of the production abruptly because she was pregnant. She said days later that she'd actually had a miscarriage. Whether she ever really was with child is doubtable because her mental state was very grave at this time during her stormy relationship with Olivier. The show closed and Noel was angry. He hadn't done a play in New York in years so he decided to perform there in the American premiere of *Nude with Violin*.

All was not well in his private life. His obsession with his physical appearance had caused him to diet, which made him irritable. He saw less of Graham and noted, "I know how much he misses me and it can't be helped." Payn was still trying to get his career off the ground but as usual most of his work was in Coward productions.

Noel's chronic financial worries resurfaced, partly due to his extravagant lifestyle. Noel lived well beyond his means.

In 1955 he had two large residences in England, staffed with servants. He was living on his royalties and fees from his newfound career as a Las Vegas performer and TV personality. He had no capital outside of that, and was paying out between 25,000 and 50,000 pounds a year in English taxes. He decided to become an expatriate and live outside England six months a year to avoid paying these taxes.

This stroke of financial genius (a first for Noel) set a trend among other famous stars who decided they'd like to keep their money rather than fork it over like bales of hay to their governments. Suddenly it seemed more stars were living on the wrong sides of their respective borders for six months a year than were living home full-time. The press had a fun day with Noel, again accusing him of anti-patriotism, but he could hardly care. He was getting old and needed his money to assure his old age.

The fact that so many stars lived outside of their countries for tax reasons was sensible because they traveled so much that they didn't spend much time at home anyway. Noel kept two large estates going and hardly spent more than a few weeks in them a year. It was a madness to have to keep them up.

First he bought a house in Bermuda, and later he purchased land in Jamaica, where he built a house in which he did live much of the time. He also bought a residence in Les Avants, Switzerland. Leaving England cut his expenses dramatically and stabilized him not only financially but professionally as well. Because he couldn't set foot in England for tax reasons, he opened plays in Dublin. He may not have had his homeland, but he had his work and his bevy of friends, which supported him emotionally.

The American production of *Nude with Violin* brought an added attraction; a young actor named William Traylor intrigued Coward.

Writing in his diaries, which he knew would be published posthumously, Coward was very circumspect about his infatuation with Traylor. Although he was quick to reveal his own and other people's bodily functions, surgeries, embarrassing moments, etc., he could not bring himself to honestly discuss his deepest emotional feelings for another human being.

Coward's need to hide his homosexuality, even after death (since no one would read the diaries until then), led him to such silly phrases as "My secret news is that I fear that Old Black Magic has reared itself up again." He did reveal that this was "stimulating, disturbing, enjoyable, depressing, gay, tormenting, delightful, silly . . ." but also called it "sensible" for some unfathomable reason.

Of course his vanity was working overtime. "It may also be that now that I'm slim as a rail again I'm more attractive not only to myself but to others."

Traylor was obviously not as attracted to Noel as Noel was to himself, but although Noel's aggressive behavior toward him may have caused him some distress, the actor was not about to give up his chance to appear on Broadway. Traylor was handsome, about twenty-seven, heterosexual, married, and a Catholic. At first Traylor was obviously flattered by Noel's kindnesses and attention. What young actor wouldn't be? Here was a legendary playwright/star/producer giving him gifts and making him feel special. It was a turn-around, and all actors want that attention. When it became intense and Noel made his intentions known Traylor, for lack of a better term, freaked out. According to Charles Russell, who was then Noel's producer, Traylor couldn't deal with Coward's pursuit and attempted suicide.

Nude with Violin opened in New York in November of 1957. It was a glittering opening night crowd. Cole Porter was there with Moss Hart and Kitty Carlisle. The premiere and the party were wonderful. The play and the reviews were mostly not. Walter Kerr summed it up: "It's delightful to have Noel Coward back in the theatre; it would be even more delightful to have him back in a play." Noel the realist knew it would be a short run, despite the fact that Kerr's vitriol was always expected. Traylor must have had his own inner conflict; he was not attracted to Noel, yet he had a meaty and wonderful showcase role in a major play by a major playwright, who was ready to hand him the world. But Traylor wasn't gay; Traylor's anxiety about his masculinity should have been clear to Coward and he should have backed off.

The next six months were torture for Noel emotionally. He'd wait for Traylor's promised phone calls. He'd agonize over Traylor not showing at a prearranged tryst. His dearest and nearest were aware of his torment and had to deal with his anger and pain. Lorn and Graham were in London, but Cole Lesley was with Coward in New York. Lesley said Coward's greatest asset was his ability to laugh at himself. That deserted him now. He was bereft. He celebrated his fifty-eighth birthday without the usual mirth. Still in his diary he noted his own agony with a certain detachment in the style of a romance novelist.

"My private emotions are going through the usual hoops . . . that I fondly imagined I had discarded years ago . . . I scale the heights and tumble down to the lachrymose ravines. I lie awake arguing with myself, and worst of all pity myself. All the gallant lyrics of all the songs I have ever written rise up and mock me. . . ."

Coward decided to close *Nude with Violin* on Broadway where it was playing to half-empty houses and produce it in California in repertory with *Present Laughter*. He cast Eva Gabor as Joanna and they became fast friends. In later years Gabor would talk about how she "pimped for Noel" during these San Francisco and Los Angeles productions. There was no doubt that all Noel's friends thought the best way to help Noel get over his continuing obsession with Bill Traylor was to persuade him to see more willing young men. (Noel also got his first toupee and thought it made him look twenty years younger, and hopefully more attractive to Traylor and others. He couldn't accept the fact that the actor just wasn't able to reciprocate and it had nothing to do with Coward's looks.)

When the tour ended Coward and Lesley returned to Jamaica and Noel returned to writing. Thoughts of Traylor waned, his wounds slowly healed, and he philosophically accepted the inevitable. Still without naming names or specifying sex, he wrote, "I can remember—I can remember—the months of November and December and the ecstasy and the nightmare. I know I couldn't bear to live it all over again, but I wouldn't be without it."

According to Cole Lesley it was the last time Noel Coward fell in love. Sex for its own sake was another matter. At the height of his obsession with William Traylor Coward had written: "I wish to God I could handle it, but I never have and I know I never will. Let's hope that it will ultimately rejuvenate my aging spirits. Let's hope that at least I get something out of it."

What he got out of it, creatively at least, was a short story. In Coward's *Cheap Excursion* a young actor generates deep passion in an older star. Noel revealed that he knew what his close friends had thought about the Traylor affair. "I don't care how high my position is, or how much I trail my pride in dust. What's position anyway, and what's pride? The hell with them."

And he was honest about the emotions he'd endured during the heartbreaking six months. In the story the star declares, "I'm in love and I'm desperately unhappy. I know there's no reason to be unhappy, no cause for jealousy and that I should be ashamed of myself at my age, or at any age for being so uncontrolled and for allowing this God-damned passion or obsession or whatever it is to conquer me, but there it is. It can't be helped. No more fighting, no more efforts to behave beautifully. I'm going to see him, I'm going now, and if he is unkind or angry and turns away from me, I shall lie down in the gutter and howl."

In the short story the star is the young actor's leading lady, not man. Unfortunately even in his writing it was still necessary to express homosexual emotions through heterosexual means. If Noel wasn't going to reveal himself in his own diary he was certainly not about to do so in print. But the *cognoscenti* knew the star Noel referred to was himself.

William Traylor died in Los Angeles in 1990. The career

he sought never materialized but he'd achieved his fifteen minutes of fame as Noel Coward's last love.

Back in London Graham Payn was still struggling to make a career for himself. Noel's obsession for Traylor must have been very unsettling for him. In many gay relationships (as in some heterosexual ones) physical infidelity is expected, even tolerated. The obsession of the kind Noel ran into, and which he had once written a play about for *Tonight at 8:30*, made it clear that Noel was not only open to sex, but was available, even perhaps covertly fantasizing about, having another emotional attachment that could oust Payn from his circle. The fact that the person was another young actor shook Graham.

At this point Payn, Lesley, and to an extent Lorn were living off the beneficence of The Master. Their future was tied up to his. This gave Graham the leeway to be less urgent about the success or failure of his career. Because Noel was his lover, Graham felt he would always have a role somewhere.

Lorn had been around to remember Jack Wilson and how he took over Noel when he was young. She probably could easily imagine what catastrophe a similar type of person might wreak having influence over Noel at this point in his life. They all must have breathed easier when they saw Noel's acceptance of his state: "After all, I'm middle-aged— well, a little more than middle-aged."

The thought itself, the fantasy, must have remained in Noel's mind nonetheless. His song of the period, "Time and Again," said it all: "Sex and champagne as social institutions/Stampede me and lead me astray."

He freely admitted that although he tried to control his hormones to be "less aggressively male/Time and again I try/Time and again I fail."

He expressed it more bluntly in his lyric, "I'll be damned if I'll sacrifice/Sugar and spice/To be precise/Nothing's as nice/As sex is." He knew he not only couldn't "restrain my lecherous libido" he also knew he had no desire or intention of trying.

The lives of Noel and Cole might be summed up in three words: work, travel, and sex. Both men had championed travel in their lyrics. Noel had said, when life got to be difficult, "Sail away, sail away." After Linda's death Cole still had work. He'd done *Silk Stockings*, a musical based on the Garbo film *Ninotchka*, for Cy Feuer and Ernest Martin, the Broadway producers who'd score such a hit with *Can-Can*. He still had his friends like old pal Howard Sturges and younger ones like Jean Howard. He also still had his amours and his paid-for sexual encounters. It is a testament to Cole Porter that even a decade after his death his biographers never mentioned his "last intimate friend" as Jean Howard described Bob Bray. Bob was handsome, personable, and comfortable in the company of both men and women. There was also a "mystery affair," a student at UCLA during the late 1940s who lived at Cole's Hollywood house with him and was driven by a chauffeur to his classes and cheerleading practice each day. Cole always had someone for sex, even while retaining ongoing relationships with those with whom the sex was over; nonetheless, the friendships remained.

When Jean Howard suggested a trip in the fall of 1954, both Cole and Sturges responded enthusiastically. The trip was planned for the following winter; Cole had to be in New York till then for the opening of *Silk Stockings*.

They were invited by Stavros Niarchos to use one of his yachts to cruise the Greek Isles. It was a party of three, but according to Jean Howard, Bob Bray would join the group from time to time, then fly back to Los Angeles for work. Others would also join them for a few days at a time, or weeks, including Marti Stevens, an actress/singer friend of Jean's and daughter of MGM mogul Nicholas Schenk. Marti was a close pal of Marlene Dietrich's and hence also a friend of Noel's.

It was a glamourous trip punctuated by lunches or dinners with the likes of Audrey Hepburn and Mel Ferrer, Jean Cocteau, Vivien Leigh, Eddie Fisher and Debbie Reynolds, Lady Cooper, José Ferrer and Rosemary Clooney, etc., etc., etc.

Humorously because Jean was usually alone with the men, rumors back in New York began to link her romantically with Cole.

Porter may have liked the idea of a cover, or the idea of replacing Linda's presence with a woman both of them had been close to and loved specially. Jean was bright and beautiful, younger and jovial; they could be new life companions. They'd live apart and accommodate each other's lifestyles. It was a nice thought, which Cole must have considered for a while.

But for much of the trip Cole and Howard were accompanied by handsome men. Sturges's Greek pal Christos Bellos was with them much of the time, and other brawny guides, chauffeurs, and old pals were constantly at their side.

Silk Stockings opened in New York during this months-long trip. Songs from *Can-Can* were already becoming classics and it appeared Cole's career was again in high gear. He still had the cottage in Buxton Hill, after all that expensive redoing; and in New York he'd taken a bigger apartment at the Waldorf Towers and had it decorated by Billy Baldwin. Change, and more change, was Cole's remedy to refocus his environment and forget the past.

In Hollywood Cole still had the house in Brentwood. Feuer and Martin offered him the opportunity to do the musical version of *Little Shop Around the Corner* (Bach and Harnick did it as *She Loves Me*). He instead decided to write songs for MGM's new musical version of *The Philadelphia Story*. It was a wise decision. *High Society* was a tale about the people he knew.

Despite the fact that Cole was at his lowest ebb emotionally when he did the movie, the songs for this film are as strong, brilliant, happy, and ingenious as the ones for *Kiss Me Kate*. They go a step further into adult sophistication with tender love songs replacing the sexually oriented lyrics of *Kiss Me Kate*. "Mind if I Make Love to You?" is a straightforward honest song carrying the economy of verse and rhyme that characterize "Night and Day" and "All of You."

Because the film was about a Philadelphia society wedding, replaced to Newport, Cole was able to give full creative vent to this milieu, although he was somehow kinder than he had been in "Mrs. Lowborough-Goodby."

He revived "Well, Did You Evah?" from *DuBarry Was a Lady*, and made it into a 1950s satire on society parties. It's a rollicking good time, with bawdiness replacing explicit innuendo as Frank Sinatra and Bing Crosby get drunk together.

> FRANK: And have you heard of Mimsey Starr?
> BING: Oh, what now?
> FRANK: She got pinched in the Astor Bar.
> BING: Well, did you evah?
> BOTH: What a swell party this is!

In *High Society* Celeste Holm and Frank Sinatra, playing two scandal sheet reporters, look through the bride's gifts and sing, "Who Wants to Be a Millionaire?" Louis Armstrong plays himself visiting his pal Crosby to bolster him because ex-wife Grace Kelly is marrying a "square." With Armstrong's famous band they do a song called "Now You Has Jazz," which is unlike anything Porter ever attempted before. Even the tender short love song "True Love" is a departure into a new, more conventional tenderness about love without the brittle wit and undercurrent of sexual intent. It sounds like a betrothal, based on a sincere wish for a lifelong commitment.

> I give to you and you give to me
> True love, true love
> So on and on it will always be
> True love, true love.
> For you and I have a guardian angel on High
> With nothing to do
> But to give to you and to give to me
> Love forever true.

Is this the same songster who wrote about the marriage game only five years before? ("Oh, yes, in the day/It's easy to play/But oh, what a bore at night!") This is a new Cole Porter whose genius has finally reached the outer range of genuine warmth, not just cleverness. And it's sung together by the lovers, not back and forth like a duel; this is more like wedding vows.

Frank Sinatra sings "You're Sensational," which is what might be called "High Cole Porter," combining worldly sophistication with the hope of opening up a woman's heart, and not just her legs. A song of seduction to the cool heroine played by Grace Kelly, he sings that he's known a lot of girls and doesn't care that she's called "The fair Miss Frigidaire." She's sensational, that's all. "Making love is quite an art/What you require is the proper squire to fire your heart." Where Cole's early songs have a repeating rhythm of torment because the lover is absent, in this song the lover is present and being drawn gently closer by the repeated and gentler throb of music.

The Jazz Age is over, the new softer approach is here. No longer does Cole write of lovers yearning for the elusive satisfaction; now there is no separation between lovers, just healing and expansion into the deeper, more satisfying emotional areas of love. Where it used to be all passion and eroticism, now it is evenly paced, patient waiting in the sure knowledge that success is at hand.

The same joy of loving had been in *Can-Can* just a few years earlier with "C'est Magnifique." Here the lover may stray but when he returns, c'est magnifique! What a switch from a decade before when he wrote "Ev'ry Time We Say Goodbye (I die a little)." Or his late 1920s song "What Is This Thing Called Love? (I saw you there one wonderful day/You took my heart and threw it away)."

The older Cole was more at peace with love as a reality. He wrote not so much about the heartache and longing, the thrill of rejection and the wonderful pain of rolling about in a burning sea of sexual longing. Now instead of mystery, there is fulfillment. Losing Linda must have awakened him to the fact that after all he had had true love as well as erotic pleasure and the two weren't as woven together as he had thought. The wall that was always there has been taken away; the mystery is gone.

Usually when artists reach this point of resolution their work loses its magic. Not so with Cole; like the fine wines he appreciated so well his work seemed to mellow with age into excellence.

Things seemed to be going well. Then Howard Sturges died suddenly of a heart attack. Cole was shaken. They'd just spent time together in New York. He'd endured his mother's passing, and even Linda's, but Howard was his last living link with the days of being enveloped in his secure, nurturing group of loving "family." He resorted to travel once again in the hope it would ease the pain and help him stop having to face the present. Another trip was planned to Europe and the Middle East.

This time Jean Howard insisted that Marti Stevens join them for the entire itinerary. Bob Bray replaced Howard as Cole's close companion. Again they began in Switzerland, and went on to Rome, Cannes, Athens, and Sicily. And again the glamourous people, Paulette Goddard and Erich Maria Remarque, the Duke and Duchess of Alba visited, and the glamourous spots, Beirut, Damascus, and Istanbul were visited. But Cole was more irritable on this trip, losing patience with Marti because she couldn't or wouldn't keep the precise schedule he had set. All Porter's friends recall that he had become irrational and strange over punctuality—not a minute before or after the appointed minute was acceptable. The tribute to Linda had become a macabre mind-set.

They ended the trip in Greece and Cole and Bray returned to Hollywood, where Cole worked on songs for a new film, *Les Girls*. Later that same year Cole invited Jean Howard to stop by his Waldorf apartment. He told her he was going to Jamaica the next winter and added that he would need a "hostess."

Jean offered, "Okay, here I am."

Cole dropped the bomb. "But I want to make it legal," he said, his tone crystalline.

Jean was a bit puzzled and appropriately laughed out, "Okay, it's legal."

Porter, not wasting time at all, introduced Jean to a tall, handsome man. "Jean, I want you to meet Robert Montgomery, my lawyer."

Jean nervously fabricated an excuse about an appointment, saying flustered good-byes as Cole showed her out. The incident was never discussed, or even mentioned again, between the two. But if it was marriage that was on his mind, Jean was sure of one thing, "I wasn't and never could have been Linda."

Perhaps the gossip column rumors when they were in Europe had given Cole the idea. Maybe he just missed Linda. Whatever the incentive Cole, like Noel, was rejected in his old age when he tried to establish a new relationship. He was now mostly alone. Only his trusted staff was left and his business friends and associates. Bob Bray was on the West Coast most of the time. Cole had become close to a *Look* magazine reporter, George Eels, but there was no close, intimate person from the past.

With his physical pain, the bouts of depression, the years of alcohol and medication taking their toll, the spark left Cole. His two new songs for the film version of *Silk Stockings* were mediocre as were his tunes for the film *Les Girls*. Only one of the songs from the 1951 TV special *Aladdin* is worth mentioning—not because it's a great Cole Porter song but because its lyrics have left all his friends and biographers wondering if it was autobiographical.

The song is called "Wouldn't It Be Fun?" (subtitled "The Emperor's Song").

> Wouldn't it be fun not to be famous
> Wouldn't it be fun not to be rich!
> Wouldn't it be fun not to be known as an important VIP
> Wouldn't it be fun to be nearly anyone
> Except me, mighty me!

Was he bored with being Cole Porter, or was he going through what so many go through—just wishing he were young and healthy and had it to do all over again?

Much was made of this last song but it should be remembered that Porter's boredom with life had been the subject of his songs since the beginning. "Poor Young Millionaire" was written in the late 1920s; he was "tired and bored, bored, bored." "Why Don't We Try Staying Home?," also written in the late 1920s, told of his boredom with Cafe Society (opening plays/closing cabarets). He also wrote other songs about the rich and their empty lives—which he continued to indulge in all his life anyway.

Unlike his famed lyric Cole did once get a kick from champagne and once did get a kick from cocaine. Now he was undoubtedly "out on that quiet spree, fighting vainly the old ennui" and looking for the next "fabulous face" to give him that kick, "though it's clear to me/You obviously don't adore me."

In the '20s and '30s and even through the '40s it hadn't mattered. Through alcohol, drugs, and especially through sex, Cole could always battle the boredom successfully.

After years of operations to save his legs, the doctors told him one would have to be amputated. With Linda's and Sturges's passings and after he'd lost his leg, when he didn't have the physical capacity or emotional support to fight the boredom, he succumbed to it and became a recluse.

Noel knew what Cole feared: lack of physical attractiveness. In May of 1958 Noel visited Cole twice in the hospital as Cole recovered from the amputation of his leg. Coward noted in his diary that, "I think if I had had to endure all those years of agony I would have had the damned thing off at the beginning, but it is a cruel decision to make and involves much sex vanity and many fears of being repellent."

Noel also predicted, ". . . it is now done at last and I am convinced that his whole life will cheer up and his work will profit accordingly." In fact Cole never worked again. He was fitted with an artificial leg in time and kept to a certain schedule, but his professional life was over.

*   *   *

COLE'S LAST INTIMATE RELATIONSHIP, with Bob Bray, ended after the second trip to Europe and the Middle East. Bray's career seemed at last to be gaining steam. He played the bus driver in a Marilyn Monroe movie, *Bus Stop*, and he had the lead as Mike Hammer in *My Gun Is Quick*. He later appeared in *Never So Few* and Rock Hudson's *A Gathering of Eagles*. But other factors led to the dissolution of this once-close friendship. Cole's drinking made him more and more difficult to deal with. Also after the loss of his leg his vanity prohibited him from seeing many old friends, which strained his relationships with the few people he would see.

Bray got the part of the Forest Ranger on the TV series *Lassie*, which he played for five seasons. The rest of his life was spent with his wife and children and out of the orbit of Cole Porter's friends. Bray was not with Cole when he died. Cole was attended by his agents Robert Raison and Stanley Musgrove. He seemed to reject all others. Monty Woolley, shortly before his own death in 1963, tried to see Cole and sent others to see him as well. It's fair to say that even had Bray tried to see Cole he may have been turned away.

Illness beset Cole constantly through the last years of his life. He was racked with pain. At one time his weight dropped to eighty pounds and he became susceptible to infections that most people could easily fight off. Through it all Cole maintained a vanity and a sense of style, utilizing sun lamps to bring up his color, continuing his precise grooming patterns and his sartorial elegance, down to wearing an untrimmed carnation in his lapel. He had to be lifted from one spot to another, a fact that wounded his personal vanity. When friends came to dine they would discreetly look out the window while he was carried to the table.

He became tremendously set in his ways, refusing to accept warnings from his doctors about smoking and drinking. His friends finally convinced him to switch to vodka as a drink so they could secretly reduce it in the tonic mix without his noticing because of its lack of flavor. When his alcohol consumption dropped doctors noted an improvement, but he outfoxed them by switching back to gin, and again his health deteriorated. He did not care anymore. Once a friend walked in unexpectedly and found Cole hammering his fist on the bed and screaming, "Why can't I die? Why can't I die?" until he discovered he was not alone. He quickly regained his sophistication and said, "I'm not being good, am I?"

Cole's death was a bleak one. He went in the hospital for surgery to remove a stone blocking the passage between his bladder and kidneys. He developed pneumonia and never regained consciousness. He died on October 15, 1964.

NOEL RECORDED COLE'S DEATH in his diaries, mourning the passing of "another figure from the merry early years." By now Noel's diary was peppered with notices of deaths of his famous and witty friends and, worse, catalogs of their illnesses. For the most part Noel was spared the indignities of old age and a withering career. He was revived. His old plays were suddenly new hits and he was in demand as a movie star.

The need to stay on top drives homosexuals as well as straight folks. Just being wealthy isn't enough. Fame is the aphrodisiac. Author/composer Ned Rorem proudly listed the four *Time* magazine cover men he'd had sex with, including Noel Coward, whom he met in Paris in 1961. The others were Leonard Bernstein, Tennessee Williams (who hadn't slept with him?), and John Cheever. Is it likely the young and good-looking Rorem would have got in bed with these particular men if they were not famous? Whether straight or gay, male or female, the axiom is as you get old and fat, you must stay famous if you want to get laid. (Mr. Rorem, we hasten to add, is a gentleman; he also listed the famous men he *didn't* have sex with.)

There will always be people who rack up their famous list of partners as Noel Coward used to rack up his list of famous friends—yes, including the ones he'd had sex with—back in the '20s, when he was still star struck.

After Cole's death when the terms of the will were announced many people were shocked to learn that Bob Bray was not mentioned. Porter had left half of all his future royalties to his old friend and employee Ray (R.C.) Kelly and his children. Most of Cole's friends hadn't seen or heard of Kelly in years. Cole also made provisions for other employees and their families, most notably $75,000 for each of the daughters of his longtime trusted valet, Paul Sylvain. Most of his estate went back to his cousins in hometown Peru.

Half of all future royalties (which amounted over the years to millions) seemed a disproportionate amount to leave to Kelly. This generous and unusual bequest fueled speculation that his friendship with Cole was more than Kelly had admitted. Kelly had been there though during Cole's most difficult time, the three or four years after the accident. He'd provided that brotherly, masculine steadiness that most gay men are seeking and he was nonjudgmental about Cole's lifestyle. If Cole could be so devoted to Linda, it makes sense that this other kind of warmth—a real platonic friendship with another man—would mean a great deal to Cole. Because of his sexual interests in such men as Ray Kelly, the first assumption would be sex when Cole was involved; yet he was known hardly ever to make deep friends with his tricks or lovers. Trying to second-guess Cole's intentions in the light of his whole unpredictable life is an exercise in futility. There are things that don't have to be known, and Cole was essentially the most secretive of people.

XIV

"When Soon or Late, You Recognize Your Fate"

IN HIS SONG "Sail Away," Noel Coward expressed his feelings that travel was the only recourse when life became too difficult—especially when dealing with emotional or psychological problems. But the song also included the coded message that when, sooner or later, you accepted your fate "That'll be your great, great day."

After years of compromising and hiding his sexuality, or cloaking it in heterosexual venues, Coward was bubbling to be himself. He wanted to somehow tell the world that being gay was all right.

WHEN JACK WILSON DIED at a fairly early age Noel did not grieve. He felt and expressed only bitterness, stopping just short of saying he was glad the man was gone and he'd never have to bother with him again.

He noted in his journal: "I cannot feel sad that he is dead. He has been less than half alive for the last ten years, a trouble and a bore to himself and everyone else." A sad epitaph for a man who'd been so deeply a part of his life since the beginning of his public career.

Yet his relationship with Jack in the mid '20s had caused him to explore his own sexuality as a possibility for creative material on the stage. He did not do this again until after Jack's death.

PERHAPS THE MOST SIGNIFICANT work of Noel Coward's in relation to his homosexuality and his life is one of his last

246

plays, *A Song at Twilight*. Noel claimed to be inspired to write it after reading a piece about his old friend the actress Constance Collier visiting her old lover the artist/critic/satirist Max Beerbohm when she was in her late seventies and Max in his eighties.

Her visit upset him, and Noel thought this was an amusing idea for a play. He then added the concept of blackmail over old love letters—letters from the old man's *male* lover. The accepted version of this story is that Coward then thought of his old pal Somerset Maugham, since Maugham had written Noel a letter after his lover had died. And so the story continues, with Maugham now in mind as the lead character.

Noel constructed the play about a famed writer who has lived his life hiding his gay persona from his public, marrying a woman, having heterosexual affairs as well as gay ones, never coming to terms with his real emotional bent.

In the play Hugo Latimer, the famous writer, bitterly complains that his ex-lover, Perry Sheldon, was a self-destructive alcoholic. (Gerald Haxton, Maugham's lover, had been; but then so had Noel's ex-lover Jack Wilson.)

When Noel played the part in London he made more attempts to link the character with Maugham. He dressed like Maugham and even spoke like him. The implication at every instance that the story was about the famed novelist/playwright was so strong that Robin Maugham, his nephew, filed a lawsuit against Noel and tried to stop the production of the show. Somerset Maugham ended the controversy by dying shortly before the play was to open; since, as Noel said, one cannot libel the dead, the suit had to be dropped.

But was the Hugo Latimer character really Maugham, or Coward himself? Coward to the end continued to wrap the main character Hugo in a thin veil of Somerset Maugham, putting enough characteristics of that other homosexual English playwright/novelist in the role that everyone decided that it was in fact a tale about his friend. Maugham was irascible, crusty, uptight, and more ancient than empires to the English literary world. Everyone knew what he was and who he was, and how his temper worked.

Noel was hampered by his own homosexuality, not because he was still trying to hide—although that was surely a factor—but because he was not free enough to address it objectively. He must have realized that if he "came out" and wrote about homosexuality from his own point of view, that act would overwhelm an objective assessment of the play itself. The news value of such an admission would eliminate any possible valid critique of the play strictly as a dramatic work. He had to know that his homosexuality was no great secret; but for him to actually say it would suddenly place him in a different category should he simultaneously write a gay play. His ploy of displacing the character onto Somerset Maugham, who was deceased, was a smart move politically; the play was judged for good or ill on its own merits.

It is a loss that this most skilled dramatist of sexual themes should have been denied the opportunity to address this most controversial of lifestyles, especially since he was its quintessential practitioner. Social restrictions and the insistence that anything other than male-female reproductive relationships is an "alternate" lifestyle, made it impossible for Noel to write about his own experience without losing his status as an objective artist. Years later Gore Vidal would be able to avert his own homosexuality and still be taken seriously as a writer of versatility, but by the time it was possible for Noel to do this it was too late for him to start swimming in a different direction. His image was established; he was too old to take on a new persona that would perhaps cause the same kind of sensation that *The Vortex* did in his youth. His emotional structure was too fragile to handle the blunt impact of the press anymore, and his physical health was deteriorating rapidly. Coward was such a prolific artist that we can hardly regret having lost anything from him. He was overly generous in showing us every word he ever wrote and spilling forth rich torrents of spoken and sung verbiage. But this very essence of his creative being was left to atrophy in the dark of his soul.

The play itself would have been dismissed as an emptiness if not for the implication of homosexuality. It lacks the wit, humor, and tension of his early works. Also Coward, never known for his subtlety, is heavy and overly direct in this play. Short as it is (it was produced with two other one-act plays), it drags from lack of action and revelation. Basically Hugo is a great and successful, *rich* writer (Maugham was the first novelist to become a millionaire from his writing), who is married to Hilde, a grimly devoted German woman (whose best friend is a former Hollywood lesbian), and who is always maddeningly one jump ahead of ascertaining his wishes, from what he wants served for dinner with his former actress lover to secretly hiding his gay love letters in a strongbox so he won't be exposed. She is a nightmare of unloving devotion.

Hugo is written in a way that makes one wonder why anyone would be devoted to him for two seconds; he is selfish, insulting, and unloving. We are left to wonder why Carlotta, his female ex-lover, is coming to see him after decades of absence. After coyly wasting the whole first scene drinking, eating, and leering at the cute waiter, she pretends to want permission to publish his love letters to her. Being refused, she drops a bomb just as the curtain falls by saying, by the way, I have those love letters you sent to your lover—Perry.

This gets a rise at last out of the old cuss who spends the next scene begging her to return the letters, not to expose him. In the middle of it all the German woman comes home—*tipsy!*—and says blandly that she's known for years about the gay lover. On top of that she's been corresponding with a Harvard professor who wants to do a biography on Hugo when he dies, addressing his homosexuality! What irony. This is the same professor to whom Carlotta has also been threatening to give the letters.

Hugo is livid (possibly because the turgidity of plot would have offended Noel if anyone else had written it).

The anticlimax comes when Carlotta returns his letters, promises to keep quiet since he never really loved her anyway, and goes off to get her next urgently needed series of fetal sheep injections, which keep here looking a tired fifty years old.

This dreadful play is the closest Noel came to saying, "I am what I am." He makes no strong point that it was vital in his and Maugham's day to keep their gayness secret if they wanted to stay out of jail, nor discusses how difficult it was for someone in their position to maintain sanity, much less a sweet temper, when having to act out affairs and even marriages that went against their deepest feelings. The humor is bitter, not black as in *Design for Living*. It lacks the zest of *Private Lives* and the macabre demonstrations of passion that move his best plays across the stage like prizefights. The bursts of violence and bizarre eroticism, played by elegant sophisticates, is not here.

Noel's tendency to write a first draft and not craft it into a subtle, nuance-filled play works against him here. He wanted to make a point about homosexuality and how having to hide it embitters a person and forces him to reject even the smallest expression of kindness to people who represent his oppressors—which is what happened to Maugham. What is not added was that Maugham channeled his unexpressed tenderness, compassion, and heartbreak into his novels. Noel's own camouflage made him turn out the best and funniest satirical songs and plays in the English language. Yet in *Song at Twilight*, he trivializes Hugo's career as being commercially successful but lacking greatness because he couldn't open up to people.

Noel himself forbade any of his biographers to mention his homosexuality. He touches on his phobic rejection of this part of himself in the play with only one line when Carlotta asks if he considered being called a homosexual an insult. He answers, "Wasn't it intended to be?"

What is most interesting in this play is how it carries through another underlying theme in his plays of a man who is trapped and dominated by the women in his life when he really wants to be free to run off and live on his own terms. In the play there is a waiter, Felix, who is described as "startlingly handsome" and Carlotta and Hugo constantly remark on his physical attributes. With him Hugo is a different person, sweet, and overly considerate and warm—a marked contrast to the bitter bile he heaps on the women in his life. Coward may have written this to show how gay men are like their heterosexual counterparts when faced with a sexually delightful fantasy. Or he may have written to show the character's remorse for his bile.

Maugham's renowned viciousness toward his wife and intimates was attributed to the emotional pain under which he operated. Noel's pressure manifested itself in an inability to cope with contradiction and he released his emotional pain through nervous breakdowns. Cole Porter, however, predated the dictum "Living well is the best revenge." Noel's early plays and songs, under the guise of other themes, worked much better than this attempt to come to terms with his homosexuality on stage. After a lifetime of cloaking it the attempt to open up failed. His "Noel Coward image" would have had to be sacrificed and at that late hour in his career he saw no reason to do it.

Although he had no contempt for the state of homosexuality itself he cringed at being identified with the kind of stereotypical behavior connected with gay men. He did not want to be pigeonholed as a homosexual, but be accepted as a person with a variety of personality traits. Had he labeled himself in the 1960s, when homosexuality was more accepted than at any other time in modern history, he would not have had the options to function in the versatile ways he had done all his life. The new "ID" would have condemned him to endless and boring (to him) discussions about it to the exclusion of everything else.

Noel hated the implication that any of his work could be analyzed based on his personality traits. In *Song at Twilight* he makes that point, ridiculing biographers and literary analysts, just as he vilified newspeople and critics in his early plays. He also makes the startling point in the play that there are no secrets for the famous, despite their formidable pretenses. Carlotta and Hilde both inform Hugo that the rumors and gossip, as well as the indiscreet people of his past, have built a "myth of truth" about his real sexuality. This is the real admission of Noel Coward to be found in this play. He knew his own gay identity was an open secret, just as he himself gossiped about people he knew. No famous person can go to bed with anyone without that person having to tell *someone* and that someone having to tell someone else. Noel knew that. This play is his way of saying he knew we knew.

This play was also Noel's attempt to write a rattling good role for his last performance on stage. He was old and sick, and he knew that he never would write plays or act in them again. The fact that Hugo is nothing like Noel, except for being a legendary writer who had bisexual affairs, is true; but would he have bothered to write such a play had he not been gay himself? His desire to protect his image in the process is nothing new in theatre. All great stars create a facade and eventually "become" their own creation. Marlene did it, as did Cary Grant. It's part of being a star instead of just an actor. Even the "natural" images of Mary Tyler Moore and Debbie Reynolds have little to do with the cool judgment and hard choices they needed to make to achieve superstardom. Noel did the same thing.

The important point is that he addressed the topic at all. The real sadness is that his illness and physical state and encroaching Alzheimer's (in those days it was called "hardening of the arteries") diminished his dramatic powers so that the roles are enfeebled and toned down so he was able to perform them. Lilli Palmer, who played Carlotta, much to Noel's chagrin had to cover for his missed lines and cues throughout the four-month London run of the show. His mind and tongue had lost their fabled precision!

Song at Twilight was presented in London along with two shorter plays in a bill called *Suite in Three Keys* (when it came to New York after Noel's death, only two plays were used and it was titled *Noel Coward in Two Keys*).

In all three of the plays one finds that the speed of pace and quickness of movement so typical of Coward's early work are replaced by dignity and polished grandiosity. Noel was an old actor, and could not play fast-paced athletic and nervous characters anymore.

In this dramatic set the character of Felix, the floor waiter in the hotel where all three plays take place, ties the theme together, but also reflects Noel's viewpoint of sexuality—particularly male sexuality—as a variegated plant. In one play Felix refers to his own homosexuality and the "friend" he goes on ski weekends with; in another he discusses with the American businessman who gives him a large tip his fiancée and his wish to marry her; in the third he is the correct and dense servant to the bitchy American *nouveau riche*. His public image is constantly being revamped for the "public" he must deal with, just as Noel's was. If there is any character in these plays that is identifiably Coward himself, it is Felix. He also represents Noel's desire to remain ever youthful.

The three main characters are all aging and refer to it constantly, and are all taking measures to somehow grasp renewals of youth. Noel also knew that the audience needed a pretty young actor to look at in an evening dominated by three aging actors. Felix provides the erotic prettiness; he is the "piece of candy" to sweeten the dramatic pot. Felix also carries out the theme of Coward's whole career, that of the lower servant classes making fun of the pretenses of the rich, who nonetheless are screwing around like rabbits same as anyone else. Noel was proud of his middle-class roots, and the fact that he rose from them to become the biggest star in England. Unlike Cole Porter, he was not a snob.

In one of the plays, *Come into the Garden, Maude,* he made a final dig at Edward, Duke of Windsor, by having the American wife give a dinner party for a deposed and execrable social sponge who had once occupied some throne. Noel's delight at poking fun at the upper classes is a typically British pastime.

Song at Twilight and the other two plays comprising *A Suite in Three Keys* are not very popular. His "thin, brittle plays," *Private Lives, Hay Fever, Fallen Angels,* and *Blithe Spirit,* are revived almost ad nauseam. But these short, serious plays are all but forgotten. His first play about homosexuality, produced just as the gay liberation movement was about to explode, failed.

Noel always struggled with public acceptance of his sexual preference, convinced, probably justifiably, that if the truth were published his work would no longer be taken seriously. He was also concerned with the creative impetus that his homosexual bent gave him. He couldn't *not* write about it. In addition to *Semi-monde* and *Song at Twilight,* Noel wrote one of his most famous poems, "Not Yet the Dodo," about homosexuality and society's acceptance or rejection of it. In the poem he painted a picture of England's upper middle class, who "despite two wars and the Welfare State/And incomes sadly inadequate," still clung to their lifestyles.

In the poem, General and Lady Bedrington have a trusted maid, a Scotswoman named Maggie MacDonald, who sees them through everything and becomes nanny to their only surviving child, Barry. The Bedringtons are horrified when Barry announces after Oxford that he intends to go on the stage. They weather that blow but can't quite accept his "roommate," Danny Hoag, who designs for *Vogue* and drips with Irish charm. Lady Bedrington's dear friend Eleanor wouldn't interfere if they weren't "such old and valued friends," and insists that ". . . action must be taken, something done/To salvage the reputation of your son." But Lady Bedrington discusses it with Maggie, who philosophizes, "People are made the way they're made/And it isn't anyone's fault."

She concludes, "I don't mind whether he's strange or not/ Or goes to bed with a Hottentot." The Bedringtons, of course, repent at the end of one of those chatty upper-middle-class letters. Lady Bedrington adds a P.S.

"Please give our love to Danny and remember/That we expect you *both* in mid-September."

Clearly Coward was saying that the upper classes were caught in their rigid ideas of respectability and placed that over human values, whereas the British working class accepted people as they were. He wrote this poem in the late 1950s but didn't allow it to be published for a decade.

Around the same time one of his short stories, "Me and the Girls," also explored the theme of homosexuality, concluding that people are "born that way" rather than the then-prevalent attitude that it was caused by parental mismanagement, or simply a matter of choice.

In the story, a dying dancer muses, "You're either born hetero, bi, or homo and whichever way it goes there you are stuck with it." Coward also takes a swipe at the British courts, which were still struggling with repealing laws against homosexuality, noting that it was still a crime and "poor bastards still get hauled off to the clink just for doing what comes naturally, as the song says. Of course this is what upsets some of the old magistrates more than anything, the fact that it *is* [as] natural as any other way of having sex . . ."

After his final stage performance it was evident Noel could no longer do plays because he couldn't remember lines. He could do film jobs, because they were cameo roles, they did retakes, and he didn't have to sustain a running dialogue. He was now being cast based on who he was rather than on his ability as an actor. It was, for example, "Noel Coward as the Witch of Capri," in *Boom*, the film version of Tennessee Williams' *The Milk Train Doesn't Stop Here Anymore*. Before that he had been in *Bunny Lake Is Missing*, and did a cameo in *Our Man in Havana*. He did a bit in *The Italian Job* as well. He spent most of the decade enjoying his homes in Jamaica and Switzerland and enjoying his friends, who visited constantly.

When his little boat was scooted finally into semi-retirement, suddenly he could do no wrong. Slights were rectified by his knighthood; all the critical cattiness of the past years became kudos; he was the adored one, the Grand Master. You'd think he'd never had a flop or an unkind word from the press. Even his expatriate residency was considered okay by the British, who kept calling him back for some honor or revival. It was as if everyone suddenly decided to agree with him on his status as star and genius, and even better to let him know. In his final years his famous cigarette smoking did cause medical problems, and his health was failing; but he'd survived a life spent under the stress of living in the glare of publicity better than most legends his age.

When he finally was raised to the English peerage almost at the end of his life it may have been that he was glad that they'd waited. If he had received it in 1941 when he was "supposed to," it would not have had the special impact that it did at the end, when he really needed it. It was almost as if he'd saved the best for last. He was fortunate too that it was not awarded posthumously; he had the added satisfaction of knowing he had triumphed over his enemies at the end.

Noel also had saved up other, more human aspects of his life for these last days as well. When he died he still had Cole Lesley and Graham Payn attending to him. He did not die alone, and he did not die unhappy or unfulfilled or depressed. Although the death of Lorn Lorrain just a few months before his own caused him enormous grief, because she was the last of those who had been with him since before his fame began, he must have found some deep comfort in knowing that his former lover was still there with him, as well as the enormously faithful Lesley. During the last few years of his life Noel also had a new person on hand to take care of his needs. This was a masseur in Switzerland, Jean-Rene Huber, a giant blond, blue-eyed physical specimen (heterosexual) who was engaged to make up for Noel's inability to take exercise. Despite the fact that sex was out of the question, one wonders at Noel's luck in finding such a fantasy to massage him, drive, cosset, and argue with him for the rest of his life. He was a perfect foil for Noel's outbursts of impatience and bad temper; Coward would call him a "stupid cunt" if he did something clumsy, raising only a laugh from the gigantic masseur. Jean-Rene took care of all of Noel's needs for the rest of his life.

Noel was also blessed in the fact that his close friends Gladys Calthrop and Joyce Carey kept in constant touch with him, so that his final years were spent as closely as possible to the way his life had always been. It is a great comfort to the aged to have everything around them maintained as it always has been, friends, environment, lifestyle. Noel read voraciously—also a blessing since so many lose their eyesight—and even continued to travel. He became a hoary grand old figure in the public eye, and where once his openings had been events of special notice, now his very appearance in public was a newsworthy event. *Cowardy Custard* was a hit in London. Another revue, *Oh, Coward!*, was a smash in New York.

He and Marlene escorted each other to a special performance of the latter in New York, and it was like two grand parade floats moving together, except in this case it seemed they were each holding the other up. The quintessential symbols of eternal youth, glamour, and *chic* were great with age. Noel was fatter, whiter, slow-moving, and his speech had lost its precision. Marlene had her face taped so tightly she could not speak without the tapes pulling her upper and lower lips in opposite directions. All of her youth and beauty was done with braces and struts, so to speak. But still, who could look anywhere else except where they were standing in that glittering crowd?

XV

"From This Moment On ..."

WE ALL ADMIRE THE LEGACY of Cole Porter and Noel Coward—songs and plays that still entertain. Today Porter is revered more than Coward since, as noted, his lyrics strike a universal chord, whereas the world Coward wrote about has all but disappeared.

It should be said that as an artist Coward risked more than Porter—he tried to tackle some important social and psychological issues of his day. Two of his now forgotten songs are telling examples. In 1944 as World War II was winding down and Allied victory was assured, Coward wrote "Don't Let's Be Beastly to the Germans."

Coward was way ahead of his time in spoofing how the Allies would immediately forgive the Germans after the war. "It was just those nasty Nazis who persuaded them to fight." Other lyrics:

> Let's be sweet to them
> and day by day repeat to them
> that 'sterilization' simply isn't done.
> Let's help the dirty swine again
> To ocupy the Rhine again
> But don't let's be beastly to the Hun.

The song was misunderstood at the time—even damned—and seldom performed. It exists today only in collected lyrics of Noel Coward and some scholarly studies of that period.

Another of Coward's songs, "Don't Make Fun of the Fair," from the early '50s, which he rated as one of his best and one of his favorites, also is unrecognized. Perhaps because if one doesn't know postwar conditions in England the song has little contemporary meaning.

He was satirizing the Labor government and the Festival of Britain—a world trade fair meant to help the British economy. The song includes such dark lyrics as:

> Labour leaders lead us all
> Though we know they bleed us all
> If the hands that feed us all
> Should get badly bitten
> Any surgeon without a fee
> Would amputate them and shout with glee,
> Hurray for the festival,
> Make way for the festival,
> Sing Hey for the Festival of Britain!

Those two songs—and works such as "Peace in Our Time" and "In Which We Serve"—illustrate that Coward hoped to reach beyond simply entertaining his audiences. He wanted to make them think.

Porter, on the other hand, was content to thrill his audiences with wonderful melodies and sophisticated lyrics. Some of his phrases, such as "I've got you under my skin"—"Night and day, you are the one"—"You do something to me"—will live as long as people are sexually attracted to one another. Porter's music is easily arranged to appeal to modern tastes and is preformed today by a wide range of people from gay men's choruses to rock and roll groups.

Both men left a body of work to be studied and enjoyed by future generations. Would Cole Porter and Noel Coward have been as prolific if they'd been straight instead of gay? Perhaps. But one cannot discount that part of their motivation to succeed was based on their drive for acceptance in a straight world.

The particular kind of creative work that is so Porter, and so Coward (they have become their own genres), could not have occurred had they not had the insight created by their homosexual nature. They had an extra dimension in wit and lightness, just as Stevie Wonder says that his blindness lets him hear sounds that sighted people don't notice.

No one would claim that Porter's and Coward's homosexuality is solely responsible for their work, but it certainly was a strong factor in their direction and artistic output, just as heterosexuality was in, say, that of Henry Miller, Ernest Hemingway, or Charlie Chaplin.

Some might argue Coward a greater artist than Porter— since Noel wrote plays, short stories, a novel, lyrics, and music—while Cole only wrote words and music. And in a sense Cole had an easier time getting his message across since his songs could be sung by either a man or a woman. Cole could leave the listener of the song to infer its subtext while Noel, in his plays, had to imply the subtext to his audience.

Although Porter didn't have to transfer his emotions from same sex to male/female ones, as Coward did in his plays and stories, Porter was still influenced by his sexuality. He was driven to stretch the limits of his talent and risk being different. He was the first major songwriter to hint at sado-masochism.

If Noel and Cole were openly gay—would their work have been as daring, as witty—or as clever? Probably not. If their sexuality hadn't been repressed it wouldn't have been redirected into their work.

As this book goes to press, a London production of *Design For Living* is exploring the heretofore downplayed physical relationship between the male leads. Reviewers are saying the play is being "outed" and that the production has "an updated dismantling that 'fearlessly' brings out the gay subtext." Isn't it interesting that in 1995 it is still considered "fearless" to accentuate the sexual aspect of a *ménage à trois*? Still, Coward's plays can now be viewed taking into consideration the author's sexuality and his intent. And his early works—which are perceived by many as wooden relics of a bygone era—may have a renewal. Can an all-male—or all-female—cast of *Private Lives* be far in the future?

FOR YEARS PRODUCERS HAVE BEEN trying to present an all-male cast of Edward Albee's 1963 drama *Who's Afraid of Virginia Woolf?*, feeling that play should be viewed from a homosexual point of view. Albee has prohibited it. But Coward is no longer here to object to such an interpretation of his work.

Today, homosexual writers need not make their characters heterosexual in order to get their work produced. The theatre now has Terence McNally, who writes plays with all homosexual characters and has taken the tack that straight people can enjoy the plays and see themselves in the depiction of any emotion—just as gay people have for years seen themselves portrayed in man/woman relationships.

Both Cole Porter and Noel Coward helped pave the way for the works of people like Terence McNally, Tony Kushner, James Kirkland, Gore Vidal, lyricists Bernie Taupin and Howard Ashman, and even Madonna, who in our day have written about their emotions and aren't questioned as to whether their feelings are any more valid than a heterosexual's.

Psychiatrists and sociologists will argue through the next century on the link between sexuality and creativity. Common sense tells us that one's sexual preference and drive must influence one's talent. And that one's genius and one's lust are interconnected.

It's obvious that Cole Porter and Noel Coward have a special place in the history of music and theatre. In the studies on creativity and sexuality that are sure to be conducted in the ensuing years, they'll also have a special place in the history of homosexuality's influence on creativity.

INDEX